CONCURRENT ENTERPRISING:
Toward the Concurrent Enterprise in the Era of the Internet and Electronic Commerce

THE KLUWER INTERNATIONAL SERIES
IN ENGINEERING AND COMPUTER SCIENCE

CONCURRENT ENTERPRISING:
Toward the Concurrent Enterprise in the Era of the Internet and Electronic Commerce

by

Marc Pallot
MP Consultants
and
The European Society for Concurrent Engineering

and

Victor Sandoval
Ecole Centrale Paris

SPRINGER SCIENCE+BUSINESS MEDIA, LLC

Library of Congress Cataloging-in-Publication Data

A C.I.P. Catalogue record for this book is available
from the Library of Congress.

ISBN 978-1-4613-6823-6   ISBN 978-1-4615-4070-0 (eBook)
DOI 10.1007/978-1-4615-4070-0

Printed on acid-free paper.

CONTENTS

PREFACE

Electronic commerce converts the extraordinary benefits of the Internet into new business development opportunities in business-to-business transactions, especially for small and medium-size enterprises (SMEs), in business-to-market relationships, and particularly in government-to-business relationships. Electronic commerce is a powerful driver to create new markets, new applications, new businesses, and new jobs. It has the potential to dramatically change the business environment toward a real global marketplace. Using electronic commerce, small businesses can easily access the global marketplace without the huge investment typically required to set up a distribution chain. Large enterprises or even SMEs can be directly, by electronic means, colocated with their customers and empower consumers with previously unavailable individual impact and commercial choices. Furthermore, even governments could improve their services and offer more efficient support and reactivity to their citizens and enterprises.

Development of electronic commerce requires a review of traditional practices and regulations. Updating or possibly abolishing current policies would leave electronic commerce as a boundaryless global marketplace. Most important, it is necessary to prevent the creation of trade barriers, either technical or nontechnical, since such barriers would inhibit the job-creation and economic growth potential of electronic commerce. Finally, new business models and paradigms should lead the way toward economical growth by enabling development and efficiently applying new technologies. Enterprises will survive only if their adaptability level to fast market changes is well structured. It is well known worldwide that organization adaptability relies on reactivity and flexibility to set up new solutions while this particular capability is dependent of the creativeness and innovation potential.

Today, new products and services are more frequently developed by a consortium of organizations where each organization or individual brings its own expertise and dedicated tasks are performed separately. Actually, most of these business consortia still use traditional working methods. Trading partners, members of consortia, have different cultures and often languages for multinational projects, geographically dispersed sites, and different processes and ways of applying technologies. These rich diversities generate difficulties that considerably increase overhead. Within this context, classical solutions consisting to suppress non-value-added activities or rationalizing the use of means, are quite limited. For example, business process reengineering (BPR) can never solve the problem of organizations having, say, more than 50 percent of the product added value coming from providers. BPR does not consider business processes as evolving, and it does not involve, systematically, external project partners. Furthermore, there are invisible boundaries between trading partners, as often there are between departments of a same organization, that disable fruitful collaboration.

Under these conditions operating concurrently with the market, trading partners and users provide the best opportunity for decreasing global product costs and for shortening time. Then concurrency becomes a key factor for competitiveness because it integrates the new ways of doing business, with working, managing, and learning acting as the key factors in business restructuring.

Concurrency for competitiveness is creating a new process, concurrent enterprising, which is related to the electronic commerce domain addressing business-to-business applications, where the information and communications technology (ICT) provides the opportunity to have faster, earlier, cheaper and more efficient interaction loops between trading partners. Concurrent enterprising is not another Internet issue. Rather it is a business issue linking all partners, know-how for increasing reactivity and flexibility to better serve customer demand, as well as creativity and innovation to maintain competitive advantages.

These improvements should no longer be based on reengineering current business processes only but on introducing new ways of doing business, working, managing, and learning that have a much more significant impact on global performance and address a long-term and strategic framework. Concurrent enterprising is a new approach focusing on the whole value chain and on new ways of interacting within the global marketplace, especially for SMEs having to collaborate within business consortium. The idea is to use the Internet and its related technologies for creating virtual spaces as rooms where people from different disciplines will be able to interact. These virtual spaces are very similar to the virtual salesroom concept emerging within the development of electronic commerce on the Internet.

The main goal of this book is to present the concurrent enterprise business model and concurrent enterprising approach, which is emerging as a crucial challenge for organizations in all geographical locations and economic sectors. To achieve this goal, we study the main aspects of the merging context in which enterprises are doing business. This context is characterized by the fastest-spread information and communication technologies (ICT) that constitute the new infrastructure of the global marketplace. The book discusses a set of most advanced enterprise paradigms created during the 1980s and 1990s, most of them supported by advanced research programs, especially in the worldwide manufacturing industry. The book discusses differences between these enterprise paradigms and presents Internet-related technologies as a main driver toward a new business model. Then this book examines less theoretical questions - among them, how to implement this new business model and how companies can move to the concurrent enterprise paradigm in creating a concurrent business environment. And it introduces a methodology for enterprises willing to maintain or even improve their competitiveness in the global marketplace.

This book has eight chapters. The first two chapters concentrate on the advanced enterprise paradigms, and their advantages and limits for maintaining or improving competitiveness in the global marketplace. Chapter 3 studies, separately, the virtual enterprise and related approaches. Chapter 4 studies another fundamental ingredient of the new business model - concurrent engineering (CE). Chapter 5 summarizes these preceding approaches and establishes a foundation for building a concurrent enterprise. Chapter 6 presents specific business cases illustrating the advantages and limits of virtual enterprise applications and introduces electronic commerce and electronic documents. Chapter 7 presents concurrent enterprise as a new business model, and Chapter 8 synthesizes the concurrent enterprising process.

This book is a reference and a user's guide designed for business managers, IT managers, engineers, researchers, scientists, and other individuals interested in learning how to use a sustainable business model driven by the Internet and electronic commerce.

1 NEW BUSINESS TRENDS

1.1. Introduction

This chapter studies some aspects of the environment in which enterprises are evolving today and will evolve more and more in the near future. First, this environment is characterized by the global market trend. We study the global market trend following its dynamic, customer behavior, strategic alliances, product life cycle, geography, and information and Communications Technology (ICT). The global market is related to new paradigms of productive systems and in particular to the general framework characterized by what we call the transition from the information age to knowledge age. All these elements are linked to the telematics networks, which have a strong impact on business and commerce. Some people also call this period electronic commerce era. In this era, ICT become an essential component of economic and social systems. Thus all countries, organizations, and institutions, without exception, are affected by this development. As we know, ICT is a very wide field, and we propose here to focus on its impact on the creation and recreation of the new paradigm. This is the context in which we propose to develop the Concurrent Enterprise approach.

1.2. The global market approach

It is widely accepted that we currently live in a very competitive economic environment due to a number of factors. All economic sectors, and not only manufacturing, are affected by these factors, which include an increased level of globalization. Most companies are required to redesign their businesses on the strategic, tactical and operational levels in order to remain competitive. Some reasons follow:

- *Dynamic markets:* The nature of the market has changed drastically and will continue to do so. For example, classical segmentation, founded on industrial products, is more and more frequently replaced by a new segmentation in which products having a higher information content take an important place.

- *Changes in customer behavior:* Customer sophistication and requirements have increased over the years and are difficult to predict. Customers become more "sovereign" in their choices and decisions. To keep the loyalty of their customers, firms need to adopt fairly sophisticated means for tracking customer requirements. This is what we call the "reversing of economic logic" (Sandoval, 1989). This new logic appeared by the end of 1970s in the most advanced countries, which then entered the era of the consumer's sovereignty. This point needs some discussion. Perhaps the first to understand the new reality was the Japanese manufacturing industry, in which Toyota and its production system played a pioneer role. Japanese begun to produce for consumers according to the wants of consumers, not according to their supply capacity when ever it was possible. Figure 1.1. illustrates this new productive logic. But doing this, Japanese manufacturing industry was the first in discovering new problems such as goods quality, creating a corresponding quality policy, founded on the old Feming quality principles. One of the most popular Japanese creations was the just in time production strategy, which, in turn, called for more and more flexibility and answers in time (for more details see Womack, 1990). The improved performances of the Japanese manufacturing industry were then celebrated worldwide, the advanced countries became interested in developing such systems, and then Japan began exporting its managerial system to other countries.

- *Rapid developments in technology:* Technology over the last couple of decades has changed significantly, and very often organizations are not able to keep pace with it. Even more, companies that adopt new technology find that it quickly becomes obsolete. Thus, many companies are often very confused in terms of what to do. This is a key point addresses to study in the next chapters.

- *Strategic alliance between customers and suppliers*: Increasingly, firms are entering into strategic alliances with customers and suppliers. Again the successes of Japanese companies impressed Western companies, particularly during the 1980s. This strategic coordination of the total supply chain is now practiced by Western firms.

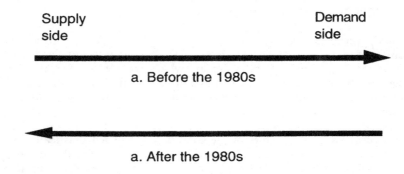

Figure 1.1. Logic sense of productive systems.

- *The changing span of the product lifecycle (PLC)*: At one time, designers were concerned only with the functionality of a particular design, giving inadequate consideration to ease of manufacturability, serviceability, disposability, maintainability, and environmental concerns. But today, designs must consider the entire life cycle of the product, and other disciplines must intervene from the beginning of the product edging. The designers' span of control and influence over a given product has evolved appreciably.

- *Manufacturing's evolving production methods*: In general, these methods may be classified into pushing and pulling. In pushing, the supply side is the more important; whereas, in a pulling system, the more important is the demand side. The classical example of a pulling system is the *kanban* principle of the Toyota production system presented by S. Shingo (Shingo, 1989) and the just-in-time (JIT) production strategy. These two systems may be combined. But *kanban* is not a universal tool, generalized to every shopfloor in Japan. For example, for similar purposes, Hitachi uses a method called OCR and Nissan Motors the action plat method, implemented since 1989.

These few points show that productive systems, and particularly classical manufacturing systems, have become more and more complex. Under these conditions, the possible alternative strategies to be adopted by enterprises, in terms of improved engineering processes, and especially time-to-market performance factors, are not clearly evident. But before studying alternative strategies in the next chapters, which are closely related to the different approaches and paradigms proposed by divers authors and/or institutions, we need to provide some context.

1.3. New productive paradigms

One of the main questions is that of the historical context in which all these business changes are taking place. This context is commonly referred as a *paradigm* in the sense of T.S. Kuhn (1962).

The dictionary defines *paradigm* as an example or pattern, especially an outstandingly clear or archetypal one. *Paradigm* is defined by J. Barker as a set of rules that establish boundaries and describes how to solve problems within these boundaries (Barker, 1990). In fact, paradigms influence our perceptions and help us to organize and classify the way we look the world. A *paradigm* is a model that helps us. From this point of view, paradigms seem to be universal components of human thought; they will always be present in our daily life and activity.

The enterprise paradigm must be defined as a set of beliefs and hypotheses that supports the activities of workers. It is then some kind of mirror between a company and its environment. This mirror serves to filter inputs that are either accepted or rejected by the company's members.

One of the main questions is What behaviors does the present paradigm induce in a company facing the new challenges generated by this new environment? From this viewpoint, one thing becomes clearer: it is practically impossible to overcome the challenges without changing the way the company is managed today. This situation influences the behaviors and reactions of people. According to D. Morris changes are always resisted (Morris, 1993). This author considers resistances as legal or normal, and under these assumptions he studies many normal believes such as business work is controlled from the top down, and human resources activity should be separated from business operation management. These beliefs are simply factors acting against changes.

If a paradigm shift must be inserted within a more general framework, it is important to question the future productive paradigms. As the future is emerging now, all components of the enterprise must work on these questions. This is a challenge not only for managers and engineers but also for every member of the company, including its suppliers. What about these future production systems?

As a first response, we take once again the traditional case of manufacturing systems. The next generation of manufacturing systems is a main object of the research and development, and some interesting approaches have been proposed as solutions (see Chapter 2). As CIM, one of the most advanced steps in manufacturing systems, results from improving of productive technology of the manufacturing system, it integrates, as a whole, the future development of these systems. But important questions need to be solved at this point. For example, what will be the characteristics of these future systems or the ability to design such kinds of systems? The most advanced countries have created special teams that are advancing solutions to the above questions. For example, the MANTECH program (US Department of Defense program) has organized a group to study the question of future manufacturing systems. The result of this study is a report on agile manufacturing (see Chapter 2). In Europe, EC (particularly through the intermediary DG XIII and DGIII) promotes many programs of research and development within the framework of the ESPRIT program such as the CIM-OSA (CIM-open system architecture) model or the European CNMA (computer network for manufacturing automation). These programs search not only for a configuration but also for technology components of the future systems. Japan has launched important programs in the field of new information technologies, one of the most welknown being IMS, launched at the end of the 1980s as an internal research and development program. The main goal of this program is to design, as far as possible, an image of the future generation of manufacturing systems. In 1991 IMS was launched also as an international research and development program. We study this point in Chapter 2.

We must also represent a paradigm in an historical trend; we need some reference points to be inserted in a trend. It seems interesting simply to recall the steps of evolution proposed by Y. Furukawa (Furukawa, 1992) because they are very future oriented. This author summarizes the entire evolution of human production systems into five eras that each correspond to a crucial transformation in human and material forces that took place within the productive system. Then there are five basic tool modifications and four human changes (the author seems to assume that the first change corresponds to the birth of humankind). Table 1.1. presents a synthesis of Furukawa's approach.

But these particular approaches to manufacturing are related to the economy and society in which it is evolving. The next section addresses to think to this important point.

Table 1.1. Main steps of production paradigm.

Eras	Workforce	Material forces
Ancient era	Human-dependent production paradigm	Pyramids
Middle era	Human-independent production paradigm Labor intensive	Hands, tools, and other mechanisms
Modern era	Human-independent production paradigm Human-skill dependent	Power machines, power tools
Present era	Ecoharmonic production paradigm Substitution for human labour Human brain dependent	Computer communication
Future era	Substitution for human intelligence	Artificial intelligence

1.4. From the information to the knowledge age

Most manufacturing developments are related to the information age paradigm. In our view, this postindustrial paradigm exists when more than 40 percent of the workforce is producing, processing, or transmitting information by electronic and telecommunications means, or is handling, storing, or transmitting information by classical means. We think today this is the reality for most developed countries and may be for most of the so-called new industrialized countries (Sandoval 1985, 1992).

But we must go beyond this simple description because this expression is becoming a commonplace in speeches, articles, and even in scientific approaches, especially in Europe and Japan. One interesting question is whether the societal paradigm is being substituted to that of the information age. Contrary to Furukawa's approach, this new production and societal paradigm should be defined as a knowledge age. In short, that means knowledge becomes as important as raw

6

materials were for classical manufacturing industry. Then all countries will be (one day) confronted with this development, even if we cannot determine a fixed date from which this transition will begin. All these processes overlap. Figure 1.2. represents this evolution involving the last three societal paradigms - industrial society, information society, and the coming knowledge society.

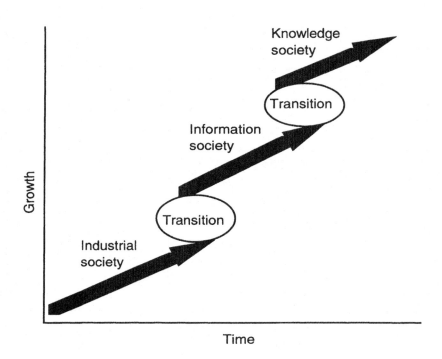

Figure 1.2. Society's evolution over time.
(Source: V. Sandoval Paper presented at the International United Nations Workshop on Transports and Telecommunications, Singapore, July, 3/5 1995)

From figure 1.2. we can observe one transition period between each phase. Human history appears then as a spiral movement beginning when human beings had scarce resources in terms of knowledge and rudimentary tools. With these resources, they created wealth and goods for satisfying their most elementary needs. But human beings invested many centuries in perfecting these tools and acquiring an always increasing know-how.

The highest productivity in traditional sectors such as agriculture and manufacturing industry creates the possibility for a dramatic reduction of employment in those sectors. As a result, the part of these sectors in the GNP has a diminishing trend over the long period. On the other hand, many new activities appear and develop. This situation creates conditions for a new era in which the main production factor become more and more the human brain supported by the use of ICT. Then information becomes a raw material, and the most intelligent machines are the productive tools.

Some thinkers consider ICT to be one of the typical characteristics of the new kind of society that is now emerging. Common expressions such as *information society* or *information economy* are used to label this phenomenon. Meanwhile, we believe that the proposed definitions extremely simplifiy the problem.

To study this we begin with the classical separation of economies into three main sectors. This theory was proposed by Colin Clark (1960) during the 1930s, and was available for Australia, but from then it has been exported to other countries and incorporated as a tool in economics thinking. These sectors are primary (agriculture), secondary (essentially manufacturing industry), and tertiary (essentially services).

Nevertheless, some attentive scientists observed that this separation was not the right one to really understand the evolution of the more advanced countries such as the United States. M.U. Porat (1977) and Ch. Jonscher (1981, 1983) separated economies into the information sector and other sectors, the first sector comprising the most important part of employment and providing the most important part of the value added. They demonstrated that the United States was already an information society during the 1970s. According to Porat, in the United States information employment reached 43 percent in 1975, and the income of the information sector reached 54 percent in 1974. His conclusion is that the United States lives in an information economy. Based on Porat's matrix, Jonscher demonstrated that around 40 percent of the income of the American workforce corresponded to the information sector, taking into account the only coordination and organization activities in companies. OECD demonstrated, based on Porat's study, that in the more advanced countries such as Canada, Germany, Japan, and Sweden, the main production sector was then the information sector.

Inspired by the analysis of F. Machlup (1972), D. Bell (1973), P. Drucker (1971), J. Masuda (1980) (in Japan) and J. Voge (1983) (in France), we proposed a separation into information sector (IS) and noninformation sector (NIS) (Sandoval, 1985) and demonstrated that 41 percent of the French workforce by the year 1982 was working in the information sector. We reasoned in terms of products and workforces invested to produce them. For us, the IS sector must include two generic products - information products (for example, a lecture or a book) and product of information (for example, a prototype of the new car involving essentially an engineer's skills).

We consider this as an appropriated tool for better understanding the current and future evolution of countries. Under these circumstances, what is really happening? What is occurring is simply a more and more important input (and in consequence, output) of ICT in productive systems affecting both IS and NIS sectors. This is the first essential point. The other essential point is that the globalization process is creating a new geography. Figure 1.3. illustrates the two sectors that are strongly influenced by ICT. This is a new characteristic to take into account in any study and, in particular, in our study about the new concurrent paradigm for competitiveness, because of its implications for organizations operating in a global market. We begin the study of these problems in Chapter 4.

In our view, information, considered as an input during the production process (production in the wider sense of any goods and services), means that the process of production, distribution, storage, investment, and consumptiom of information becomes a new activity. And this is a universal process that concerns all countries.

8

Even more we must consider a simple design of input-output information systems. That means we have a simple black box needing information to work on it. The goods produced by this system have important information input. We call this informed goods - that is, goods needing an important input of information to be produced (Sandoval, 1985).

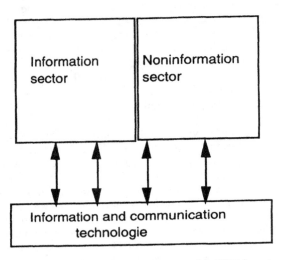

Figure 1.3. Two sectors with ICT input.

To summarize, Figure 1.4. represents the evolution of productive systems distinguishing traditional three sectors (agriculture, industry and services) and Information and noninformation activities. The figure compares gross estimated employment by sector in 1900 and 1992 for a developed country such United States, England, France, or Germany. The figure uses extrapolated data from a former study (Sandoval, 1985).

That means we have a simple black box needing information to work on it. The goods produced by this system have important information input. We call this informed goods - that is, goods needing an important input of information to be produced (Sandoval, 1985).

That means we have a simple black box needing information to work on it. The goods produced by this system have important information input. We call this informed goods - that is, goods needing an important input of information to be produced (Sandoval, 1985).

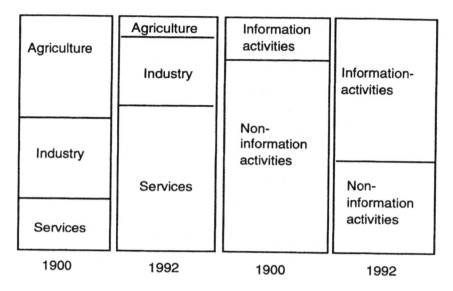

Figure 1.4. Evolution of the information sector.

The transition process from the information age to the knowledge age will occur, first of all, in the more advanced countries. This doesn't means the first industrialized countries or biggest companies will be the first to enter the new age. This means simply that the country or company fulfilling the conditions (such as implementation, and training) will enter first. For example, the high rate of economic growth and the appropriate implementation and assimilation of advanced technology can help developing countries rapidly transform into developed countries. By the way, companies from those countries can benefit from this framework and growth faster.

1.5. The knowledge factor and the global infrastructure

In this knowledge age, knowledge is more and more placed at the center of economic activity, and companies must pay more attention to it and to its implications.

The study of knowledge as an economic factor is similar to the study of goods production process, for example, in that knowledge is produced, distributed, and consumed in the same way as traditional manufacturing goods. F. Machlup was the first to study what we call the production chain of knowledge. His first work about the question is *The production and distribution of knowledge in the United States* (Machlup, 1972). This book analyzes the production sector and the distribution of knowledge in the American economy.

We can take the principal ideas contained in this study and develop them. We must then study the production, distribution, and consumption of knowledge as if it were goods. Nevertheless, from our point of view, this study doesn't remain a macro or micro study. For example, according to our definition the production of knowledge is not only a matter of the educational or scientific institutions but also must involve factories.

If you work for a living, you need to preserve your energy. One way of doing this is to make better use of your knowledge to solve advantageously many different situations in your working life at any time. This is one of the more important elements in the context of systems dominated by ICTs.

We know that the main characteristics of knowledge dissemination over the last two decades are the colossal increase of the amount of knowledge and its globalization (production and dissemination becoming planetary). The modern media play a fundamental role in all this. This dissemination is normally cheaper. You are proprietor of knowledge, you send it by media tools toward a wide public, your ownership is now shared by thousands, maybe millions of people around the world, but you remain the owner.

The world of classical information in which we lived until recently is now completed by the world of telecommunications and computer networks. Within this context, companies must be communicationless - which means they operate in open environments for communicating with each other. They must act in partnership, at first, but gradually they must open their own system to communicate even with competitors. Managing such companies is very different from traditional management, and many paradigms must be changed to be active in this new world.

Knowledge has now new possibilities for improving productive human activity. In fact, to produce, implement, and operate these networks it is necessary to have a higher quality of workforce. More and more knowledge is incorporated in physical tools, and then more and more knowledge is needed to do work productively.

Let us now to look at the peculiar paradox in that new situation. In some sense, as humans approach this new age, they should be able to enhance their own potentialities as a main vector for economic and social development. This means the possibilities for overcoming crucial problems such as underdevelopment will be increased in parallel with the involvement in information age. This is a sustainable point for many reasons, but the following two are interesting to consider:

- As potential capital, every human has his own brain, which is producing and consuming knowledge. The role of knowledge as a productive factor is reinforced as people interface directly with this new age (Sandoval, 1992; Stockfelt, 1991)

- Information must be considered to be a principal raw material during the postindustrial age. This raw material has some remarkable characteristics: it is reproducible, nearly without limitation (maybe the only limit is physics), produced at cheaper conditions because of the lower prices of the electronic components (the hardware and software) (Moore's law) (Davidow, and Malone (1993)). All this must improve the conditions for accumulation of the wealth in all countries.

But, as writes A. Leer (1996), the trouble with information assets is that they are harder to understand and differ from other commodities in many respects:
- information has an intangible nature,

- information is considered a public good and a political instrument of democracy,

- information cannot be owned (but it has an owner at its origin),
- information is vulnerable and subject to human communication skills, and
- information is expressed in tangible forms that are exclusively protected.

1.5.1. Infrastructures

Normally, scientists associate at every step of society an infrastructure, which supports the dominant sector. Traditionally, the infrastructure is an underlying foundation, which in society means things such roads, railways, power grid, and factories. However, in the case of the information society, the infrastructure is founded on computers and communication networks. But as we see in figure 1.1., this society is evolving toward a knowledge society. The infrastructure will also evolve, and include a growing range of underpinning technologies, software tools, and mechanisms, which enable better use of the information, as well better storage and retrieval (Leer, 1996).

One important point, then, is the building of the appropriate infrastructure, which supports the information and knowledge societies. In a world characterized by globalization, this infrastructure must have, normally, a global character and must contribute to the building of the global information society. Nevertheless, the solutions differ among countries. In America, for example, the first step is building the NII (national information infrastructure) and then the GII (global information infrastructure).

1.5.2. U.S. infrastructure

In September 1993, the U.S. government launched *The National Information Infrastructure(1993)*: agenda for Action aiming to give to citizens a broad range of information and information services, through innovative telecommunications and information technologies. But the information infrastructure is a global issue. So in March 1994, vicepresident Al Gore presented the U.S. agenda for cooperation by calling to establish an ambitious agenda for building the GII. This GII will circle the globe with information superhighways (or networks of distributed intelligence) on which all people can travel, as we are navigating on the Web today. These networks will allow people to share information, to connect, and to communicate as a global community. It will make possible a global information marketplace, where consumers can buy or sell products. The development of the GII must be a cooperative effort among governments and peoples and cannot be dictated or built by a single country (Gore, 1994).

The GII is designed as an assemblage of local, national, and regional networks will be a distributed, parallel computer. According to Gore, approximately 60 percent of all U.S. workers are "knowledge workers" (a similar concept was presented by Fritz Machlup in 1972), which means that people's jobs depend on the information they generate and receive through the information infrastructure.eight out of ten new jobs created are in information-intensive sectors of the U.S. economy. The growth of networks allows people to realize that information is a source of value when it is shared. When two people communicate, they each can be enriched, and unlike the traditional resources, the more they share, the more they have (this is also known as the Metcalfe's law).

1.5.3. Europe's infrastructure

Following the decision of the acceptation of the White Paper presented by President Delors (1993), the European Council setup two groups to follow the acceptance of its recommendations (1994). One group chaired by Commissioner Martin Bangeman (1994) formulated a concrete action plan to realize the potential of the global information society in Europe. The information society is viewed as a new way for people to live and work together. It is a revolution based on information which we can process, store, retrieve, and communicate in whatever forms it may take (oral, written, or visual) unconstrained by distance, time, and volume. The Bangeman report views the information society as a means to achieve many of the European Union's objectives. It proposes an action plan for reaching these objectives.

As the result, industrial companies, and more generally human organizations, are at a turning point. We examine in more detail the networking process and infrastructures at the company level in Chapter 6. For instance, the classical principles of the analysis, and even the solutions generated before, are less and less available or simply become obsolete in this new context.

Nevertheless, progress following this general approach depends on local conditions. Different countries have different degrees of development, entry into this new era is different according to the countries involved. But every country must keep in mind the general framework and operate according to their particular conditions and possibilities. Even more, the general information framework must be taken as an opportunity to reduce if not to eliminate the existing differences in development between countries and regions.

Technology must help humans to alleviate their living conditions - as individuals, and as groups. Nevertheless, the way in which technology must do it is different according to its applications. Manufacturing companies can use some technology such as intelligent manufacturing technology, and by the medium of goods, individual or groups should enjoy it. Other technologies can have a wider application, and individuals should enjoy them more directly, with fewer intermediary steps. A typical example of the latter is ICT and most of the ICT related technologies. Because of the most rapid and widest spreading occurs with the lowest costs and reusability, ICT should contribute to better solutions to social and economics problems such as inequalities inside given societies and between societies.

One preliminary discussion concerns the opportunities presented by technology and what technology is appropriate. This question is closely related to the existing technology and the use of this technology. The problem is to take advantage from technology and not to submit to it. This is related to technology transfer and diffusion.

Today this question has a new face. To explain this point, we take only two characteristics - globalization and delocalization. In reality, both the globalization process, considered by countries and international organizations as a dominant point in the new world reality, and the delocalization process affecting activities of enterprises (manufacturing, transportation, banks, and other sectors are concerned) settled in developed areas are not possible without an important implementation of the advanced ICT. These processes are generating both new possibilities and constraints - for example, the creation of developed pockets or advanced technology islands in developing countries. One problem here is how to take advantage by disseminating benefits at a wider scale.

Generally speaking, ICT contains a mixing of computer and telecommunications elements; this mixing being more or less complicated according to local conditions, the production sectors involved, or the level in which IT is acting. In general, ICT reproduces the history of computer industry once again. In short, it began in scientific laboratories and gradually expanded to other sectors, reaching by this way the majority of the human activities. Actually, ICT is entering into millions of houses, and transforming them into a mass using tool.

The next points to be consider are as follows:

- The need to apply a global market approach,

- The need to reconsider geography and time scales because of the determinant impact of telematics (in a wider sense),

- The need to reposition business and commerce,

- The need to get out a good interpretation of the electronic business and commerce in the new era.

1.6. Business strategies

1.6.1. Business collaboration

"Boundarylessness" is General Electric CEO Jack Welch's term for breaking down the barriers that divide employees (such as hierarchy, job function, and geography) and that distance companies from suppliers and customers. Welch described "boundarylessness" in the company's annual report:

Our dream for the 1990s is a boundaryless Company, a Company where we knock down the walls that separate us from each other on the inside, and from our key constituencies on the outside. The boundaryless Company we envision will remove the barriers among engineering, manufacturing, marketing, sales and customer service; it will recognize no distinctions between "domestic" and "foreign" operations - we'll be as comfortable doing business in Budapest and Seoul as we are in Louisville and Schenectady. A boundaryless organization will ignore or erase group labels such as "management," "salaried" or "hourly," which get in the way of people working together. A boundaryless Company will level its external walls as well, reaching out to key suppliers to make them part of a single process in which they and we join hands and intellects in a common purpose - satisfying customers.

Business collaboration based on boundarylessness is an important trend, and we consider it, in this book, at the starting point. It does not mean that companies will have to physically colocate expertises, which are collaborating on a same geographical site. That is no longer necessary because the networking technology has sufficiently evolved to support an electronic colocation between the necessary disciplines. It also offers the opportunity to have experts participating together on different projects in order to better make use of costly resources.

Within this context, there are different existing business strategies that could be applied depending on economic and market trends. Nevertheless, the level of risk is an important factor for selecting the more appropriate business strategy, and we know that willingness to access alone a market could be a big risk as it will mean needing to acquire all the necessary expertise. Instead of acquire the complementary expertise it is less risky to deal with other companies offering expertise and even more to share the risk. But this means building partnerships.

These kinds of projects in partnership could elaborate on, at least, two different strategies. The first one consists of cooperating as trading partners with different objectives and interests. Partners agree on the proposed project plan, and operate separately, and the initiator coordinates the project. This kind of partnerships is the most widely used today, and we know the problems encountered by applying this strategy based on weak interaction. The second strategy consists of collaborating as trading partners who agree on common objectives and interests to better satisfy customers. They prepare and agree on a common project plan, and operate concurrently in sharing information and knowledge, and the project is driven by a multidisciplinary team composed of the necessary expertise delegated by partners.

The most significant difference between these two strategies is that trading partners still having boundaries between them when they use the cooperation strategy. For example, the application of the concurrent engineering approach to manufacturing industry (we study this point in Chapter 4) has demonstrated that the existing boundaries between disciplines are the main obstacle to an efficient global business process, as problems are discovered too late when disciplines operate sequentially, each one after the other. It explains why the second strategy, collaboration, is breaking down boundaries between both disciplines and partners to have all disciplines operating concurrently for better customer satisfaction.

1.6.2. Business collaboration and electronic commerce

Internet technology is certainly one the most important steps recently made in the domain of people and their knowledge colocation by the use of electronic means. The email messaging system and the World Wide Web certainly give anyone the opportunity to share information and knowledge with the others. This networking technology is very simple and very cheap both to buy and to use when you already have a computer. The Internet is going to change the traditional way of doing business by opening access to the global market through electronic colocation. It becomes common for those having a computer connected to the Internet to plan holidays based on worldwide information on Web servers and to decide places to visit and stay. That is clearly more efficient than reading travel brochures. Furthermore, using email you can ask for supplementary information, recommendations, and even prebooking commercial information. Using this technology, people can feel close to any place in the world and that is very impressive. Then people begin to feel what electronic commerce is for any citizen in the world. It is enabling to book and prepay hotel room or service such as a teetime on a golf course, far away, after having seen the golf course pictures on their Web server, and all of that directly from their home.

The trend to business is clearly business collaboration through the worldwide network where enterprise knowledge models are available on the network to every company searching for complementary expertises. Those enterprise knowledge models will be only a part of the enterprise knowledge but sufficiently precise to have a good idea about what solutions are proposed. Electronic commerce also means the capacity to deal with or to buy complementary services available in a faraway small or medium-size enterprise as well as large enterprise. Classical trading barriers could be overcome by the worldwide electronic colocation. We can imagine in the near future, that there will be only a single worldwide common market, money, regulations and understanding around the world.

We are convinced that we are entering a concurrent society, based on boundarylessness and knowledge sharing, that will exponentially accelerate people and societal evolution on earth.

The emerging information and knowledge societies, based on ICT and telematics networks, create new opportunities and possibilities. But it is necessary to understand where and how. So one fundamental question is to know if whether the existing enterprise's paradigms or approaches are pertinent and whether they are until what limit. We begin this study in the next chapter.

References

Bangemann Martin. (1994). Europa and global information society : recommendations to the European council. Brussels: EC Report.

Barker, Joel. (1990). *The Business of Paradigms*. Burnsville, MN: Charthouse Learning.

Bell, Daniel. (1973). *The coming to post-industrial society*. New York: Basic Pinguin Books

Clark, Colin. (1960). *Les conditions du progrès technique*. Paris,: Paris. First English edition, MacMillan, 1940.

Davidow, William and Malone Michael. (1993). *The virtual corporation. Structuring and revitalizing the corporation on 21st century*. New York: Harper Business.

Delors Jacques. (1993). White Paper on Growth, Competitivness, and Employment : the challenges and ways forward into 21st century. Brussels: EC Report.

Drucker, Peter. (1971). *The age of discontinuity*. French Translation. Paris: Editions de l'Organization.

Furukawa, Yuichi. (1992). "Joint Research Program into International Manufacturing System from Preliminary Study. *Proceedings of the First International Symposium on Intelligent Manufacturing Systems.*, Tokyo.

Furukawa, Yuichi. (1992). "Paradigm shift in manufacturing systems". Paper delivered at the IEEE International Conference on Robotics and Automation, Nice, France

Gore, Al. (1994). "U.S. Agenda for Co-operation". Speech of the Vice President Al Gore at the ITU's First World Telecommunications Conference, Buenos Aires, March.

Jonscher, Charles. (1981). "Information and Economic Organization". *Proceedings of the Pacific Telecommunications Conference*, Honolulu.

Jonscher, Charles. (1983). "Information Resources and Economic Productivity". *The Economic Information and Policy*, 1 (1).

Kuhn, T.S. (1962). *The structure of scientific revolution*. Chicago, IL: Uniersity of Chicago Press.

Leer, Anne. (1996). *It's a Wired World*. Oslo: Sandinavian University Press.

Machlup, Fritz. (1972). *The production and distribution of knowledge in the United States*. (2nd ed.). Princeton, NJ: Princeton University Press.

Machlup, Fritz. (1980). *Knowledge and knowledge production*. Princeton, NJ: Princeton University Press.

Masuda, Joneiji. (1980). *The information society as post-industrial society*. Tokyo: Institute for Information Society.

Morris, Daniel and Brandon, Joel. (1993). *Re-engineering your business*. New York: MacGraw Hill. National Information Infrastructure. (1993). National Information Infrastructure: Agenda for action. Official Document. Whashington:U.S. Government.

Porat Marc. (1977). *Information economy*. Washington DC: OT Special Publication 7712-USA Dep. of Commerce.

16

Sandoval V. (1985). Evolution de l'emploi d'information- France et OCDE. Paris: Transportation Department.

Sandoval V. (1989). *EDI pour l'entreprise*. Paris: Editions Hermès.

Sandoval V. (1992). *Knowledge as economic factor*. Stockholm: ALP-Latin.

Shingo, Shigeo. (1989). *A study of the Toyota production system*. Cambridge, MA: Productivity Press.

Stockfelt, Torbjorn. (1991). *La Pedagogia de la vida del trabajo*. Stockholm: ALP-Latin.

Voge (1981). Voge Jean "Nouvel ordre économique de l'information et communication". Paris: Report Ecole National Supérieure de Télécommunications.

Womack J.P., Jones D.T. and Roos D. (1990). *The Machine that changed the world*. New York: Rawson Asociates.

2 EXISTING APPROACHES

2.1. Introduction

This chapter studies some of the relevant enterprise's approaches concerning proposals to overcome the old paradigms and strategies within networked environments. The main question here is: What kind of enterprise's paradigm should be the most appropriated to be competitive in a world characterized by both the increasing globalization and the rapid implementation of ICT. This last event covers practically the entire spectrum of human activities.

Many answers have been elaborated during the last years to the above question, but we choose to select only the most meaningfull for our purposes. In this chapter, we try to think about them. Chapter 5 presents detailed discussion in order to underline the main points of our own approach - concurrent enterprise. The present study proposes separating approaches into three types:

1. Those taking as a starting point socioeconomical aspects such as shared enterprise and intelligent enterprise.

2. Those originating in the restructuring of the manufacturing industry sector such as agile manufacturing (AM), computer-integrated manufacturing (CIM), intelligent manufacturing systems (IMS), the future generation of manufacturing systems (FGMS enterprise), learning enterprise, and the CIM-OSA model built within the framework of the European Program ESPRIT; and

3. Those founded on advanced models and virtual elements and networks such as virtual enterprise, extended enterprise, and some related cases such as fractal factory, studied in Chapter 3.

In addition to those approaches, we study concurrent engineering (CE). CE began at the same time in Japan and in the United States as a new paradigm for doing engineering in the manufacturing industries. This new approach has evolved from then and today is more complete and substantial one. CE is for us one of the main fundamentals of the concurrent enterprise. Chapter 4 presents the main concerns about CE.

The majority of these approaches consider concepts such integrated enterprise and/or extended enterprise as an important background. James Brian Quinn (1992) has presented the intelligent enterprise (IE) which is different from existing approaches, at the beginning of the 1990s. We consider this work very important for our purposes. The shared enterprise (SE) was presented by Pierre Andre Julien (Julien, 1995) as a contribution in the field of competitiveness of enterprises, but it is quite interesting because the problems studied and its consequences for enterprises, operating in the new networked environments (networked in telematics sense such as Internet).

CIM and FCIM are important to understanding main developments concerning manufacturing industry, the classical main productive system. In particular, two points are closely related to the emergency and dissemination of CE practices and the development and advances of the IMS program. Agile manufacturing is quite separate from the above approaches because its origins, scope, and impact on the actual strategy of a manufacturing company. Nevertheless, AM is very important, in our feeling, for a better understanding of virtual enterprise, which is a key point in the construction of concurrent enterprise. In fact, AM concept induces the virtual enterprise concept.

The fractal factory is an other special case because its implications for virtual environments, its relations with BPR, and its relevant importance within the context of telematics advanced networks such as Internet, Intranet, or Extranet. The fractal factory was developed in Germany by IPA (Institute for Production), and was proposed by H.J. Warnecke (Warneke, 1993). Finally, virtual enterprise is one of the latest arrivals to this world populated by approaches searching to help business strategy. This last is an important element to be used as one step in the construction of the concurrent enterprise, as we study in Chapter 3.

Learning enterprise is a particular case, and is rather difficult to put into a given classification. Learning enterprise can be taken, for example, as a daily learning or as meaning using ICT. But one thing is clear today: knowledge is considered to be a production factor. Therefore, it must be studied, modellized, and organized to improve the efficiency of productive system. In ICT environments, this is a fundamental challenge, as we argued in Chapter 1.

2.2. The shared enterprise

P. A. Julien uses the term *shared enterprise* and not *networked enterprise,* which is used by different researchers, such as G. Paché and C. Paraponaris (1993), P. Veltz (1996). This last term has multiple connotations (for example, network of enterprises, information network, resources network). In addition, this expression allows a better understanding about the idea of running a common project on condition that managers consider cooperation together as a source of profit for their companies.

According to P.A. Julien (Julien, 1995), unlike the traditional vision assumed by the economic theory, markets with perfect competition or oligopolistic competition are the exception and not the rule. In reality, there are many coalitions between firms, formal or tacits, and relatively stable but they do not constitute, necessarily, a partnership. Even an alliance between a small number of companies is not a shared enterprise. Cooperation between firms becomes a shared enterprise only if the

ACKNOWLEDGMENTS

Our thanks go to our colleagues of the European Society for Concurrent Engineering (ESoCE) and Concurrent Engineering Network of Excellence (CE-NET), especially to Petri Pulli, VTT Electronics and Jouni Similä, CCC Software Professionals who directly contributed to Chapter 7 concerning virtual shared spaces that support collaborative work on the Internet.

Our special thanks also go to our colleagues from the Industry: Fikry Garas, Taylor Woodrow; Giampiero Giarda, Alenia; Horst Genet, DASA; Peter Greenwood, Rolls-Royce and Associates; Kees Hof, Signaal; Jean Lebrun, Thomson-CSF; Mika Rytkönen, Nokia Mobile Phone; Jan Tuxen, Odense Steel Shipyard, for the fruitful discussions we had about business collaboration challenges and new generation of enterprises operating on the global market in the soon coming next Millennium. And more particularly to Roberto Santoro, ESoCE Italy; Roger Jory, Sedco-Forex/Schlumberger; and Gilles Pindat, ADP; who are the source of the practical business cases described in Chapter 6. Several other examples were part of our final reflexion such as the Virtual Research Center at NASA presented by Dan O'Neil and the Nippon CALS Research Partnership project VE2006 presented by Hiroshi Mizuta during the ICE'97 Conference in Nottingham.

Naturally, we need to thank our many longtime and newly made research project friends who contributed their knowledge and experience in the domains of Enterprise Integration (CALS), Extended/Virtual Enterprise, Concurrent Engineering and Electronic Commerce. By the way, it is certainly interesting to notice the key role of the European ESPRIT research program as an infrastructure framework that contributes to create a real European research culture. In bringing together people from different cultures and domains, it constitutes diversities making the richness that stimulates both creativity and innovation. Contributions to the CENT (Concurrent Engineering Needs and Technology), FREE (Fast and Reactive Extended Enterprise) and CE-NET ESPRIT projects were a fertile source of inspiration.

Another special thanks go to our research colleagues: Lars Bergman, SISU; Jean Claude Bocquet, Ecole Centrale Paris; Ip-Shing Fan, Cranfield University; Ricardo Gonçalves, Uninova; Antony Marinidis, ATM group; Kulwant Pawar, University of Nottingham; Vesa Salminen, FIMET; Aurelian Stanescu, University Politechnica Bucharest; Johan Vesterager, Technical University of Denmark; Frithjof Weber, BIBA; Nel Wogmun, University of Twente; for their contribution to the source of reflexion.

Finally, perhaps our greatest appreciation goes to Kluwer, Scott Delman, our demanding editor who had enough faith in us to support this project and Sharon Fletcher, his assistant, who kindly and patiently answered our questions. They gave a special attention to make this book easily understandable and without them this book would not have been possible. We worked hard so that they will be rewarded according to their trust.

Marc Pallot and Victor Sandoval

AUTHOR BIOGRAPHIES

Marc Pallot is presently Managing Director and Principal Consultant at MPC, a consulting firm specialized in Business Process Improvement. He has about 20 years experience in the domains of Design Automation, Concurrent Engineering (CE), Project Consortium, Business Process Re-engineering and Enterprise Integration (CALS). He also is president and co-founder of the European Society for Concurrent Engineering. He is coordinator of CE-NET, a European network of excellence on CE and Concurrent Enterprising, funded by the European Commission. He participates in several European projects on CE, Virtual Enterprise and Electronic Commerce. He was formerly Vice-President Product Marketing and Engineering, WiN Technology. Prior to this, he was Research and Development Director for a software house; Application Manager at Applicon Inc.; a Product Designer and CAD/CAM Application Manager at Thomson-CSF. He is a frequent lecturer on CE, Enterprise Integration and Business Process Improvement within conferences and for high schools.

Victor Sandoval is professor and researcher at Ecole Centrale Paris, one of the leading engineering schools in France. He holds two doctorates and three other postgraduate degrees. He has been involved in telematics and information technology development and implementation since the early eighties, publishing more than 10 books on these topics. He wrote hundreds of articles and short papers in these fields, and participated in many international conferences. He is currently invited by Universities in Europe, Japan and South America for conferencing, and advanced seminars. He is advising companies and national and international organizations in this field. He partipates in many research programs in manufacturing, logistics and ICT in France and in Europe.

participant companies decide to work together systematically, supported by their owns skills, convinced that each party alone will never be able to play successfully in internal and international competitions. So the situation of subcontractors must evolve to a systematic cooperation and assume formal manner (as, for example, a shared venture).

This common enterprise is supported by one simple principle: every participant company is conscious that its own efficiency is increased by the synergies created and therefore that it can create more profits. Traditional existing hierarchies (for example, between contractors and subcontractors) are replaced by cooperation and then by a systematic exchange of information that can stimulate every partner involved. So shared enterprise can be defined as a network of independent companies that cooperate together, in a durable manner, to reach common shared objectives, and that are supported by the innovation capacity and dynamism of every participant to successfull compete.

This cooperation is contrary to traditional subordination or even vertical quasi-integration, where a main company is giving instructions to all others - such as subcontractors, vendors, and providers. In the new partnership, everyone has a specialization, concentrates on particular capacities and know-how, and at the same time profits from the contributions of others. The glue enabling this partnership is the convergence of interests issued from the common goals.

For P.A. Julien, shared enterprise is very difficult to set up. First, it is necessary to fulfill five conditions: (1) to pass from hierarchic organizations to cooperating firms, (2) to change the people culture, (3) to combine competition and cooperation, (4) to systematically exchange information, and (5) to create systematic innovation that is diffused throughout the entire partnership. These conditions are quite similar to the four conditions proposed by Y. Lecler (Lecler, 1993):

1. *to pass from hierarchic organizations to cooperating firms.* The shared enterprise goes beyond simple specific collaborations for just subcontracting production parts; it must develop together some products to put into the market. This new enterprise allows a new hierarchy between companies having one or more pivot firms associated at different levels of subcontractors cooperation according to production complexity (for example, the first-level subcontractors have second-level subcontractors for simpler productions).

Note: A pivot firm is a firm playing a major role or the leadership in trading between producers and consumers.

The efficiency of this partnership comes from enterprises interacting together. Figure 2.1. shows a pivot firm and the levels of subcontractors. This system needs the important link between sub-contractors (horizontal relations) to ensure a full contribution from different skills. According to P.A. Julien, one partner must be responsive to orders, improving quality and reducing costs by innovating. He calls it the "intelligent" subcontractor.

2. *To change the people culture.* To transform traditional relations between firms, companies can share much more information about joint productions and potential evolutions in the short and middle terms. At the same time, it is necessary to accept some leadership from specialized or intelligent sub-contractors. The cooperation concerns middle and long term contracts in order to profit at maximum from the expertise of subcontractors and their development. P.A. Julien, quoting Guilhon, indicates that these contracts are around four years as a mean duration, delay permitting a return from material and immaterial investments. Japanese sign the

framework contract much more long within the context of their general planning strategy of the company (Sandoval, 1994a, 1994b; Lecler, 1993).

3. *To combine competition and cooperation.* Cooperation does not avoid competition. It does contribute to systematic research into how to improve competition across the overall network. So it is a main factor for increasing productivity. This means keeping the best practices, advantages, and sharing resources (such as such bureaucracy in the large-size organizations). More than one producer in a given sector is needed. So that an alternative is available when one network member fails. In the same way, subcontractors do not limit themselves to only one main contractor. This means encouraging legal independence of enterprises to stimulate management, and encouraging the network dynamic and information production coming from the outside sources.

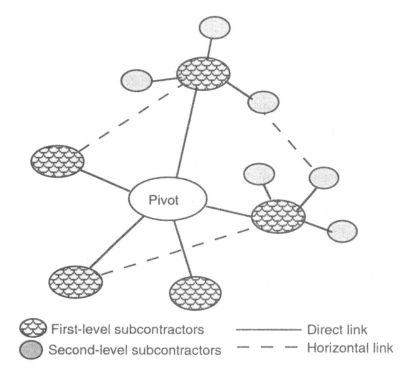

Figure 2.1. Pivot firm and subcontractors.

The intelligent enterprises convert intellectual resources into a chain of service outputs and integrate these into a form most useful for certain customers. In the industrial world, managers make their money by investing in the special skills and intellect that only highly motivated, knowledgeable people can provide and then by leveraging this intellect in the marketplace through a few best-in-world internal systems and the integrated management of outsourced activities. In fact, the core intellectual and service competencies support broad strategies and force global competition. According to Quinn, the new service technologies in the communication, information, storage, distribution, transportation and similar fields have made it possible for manufacturers to compete directly over a wider geography. 4. *To systematically exchange information.* The mutual exchange of the information (already seen in point 2.) becomes a key factor in this new form of organization. This concerns the real or potential evolution of every item and the final product, and also sharing and encouraging the partner's innovation. If, for example, one provider discovers a new way to manufacture an item, it must inform the main contractor, and other providers can adopt the new method. This process is called *diffuse innovation* and enhances the entire network, according to P.A. Julien, quoting M. Bellandi. To eliminate or reduce eventual risks (that is a contractor leaving during a critical period) and other dangers, companies must share information. This means giving information under certain conditions and receiving available information. In all cases, traders must get the advantages of the know-how and the learning capacity to improve the relations mutually advantageous for every one (Julien, 1995).

5. *To create systematic innovation that is diffused throughout the entire partnership.* Using the dynamic evolution of every company integrating the network by the new technologies (material and immaterial) facilitates taking a position in the market and being able to successfully meet the competition.

Within the context of SE, Julien puts forth the concept of creative synergy. Technologies and diffuse innovation permit a differentiation into productive components enabling the generation of a global innovation. In that case, the differences are distributed all along the production chain. This network is associated with creative synergy (remember the Schumpeterian principle of creation and destruction). This synergy starts from the transfer of information (internal and external) and diffuse innovation. All this allows a dynamic collective learning of technology on every aspect and the long-term coherence of the shared enterprise. The creative synergy acts as a communication action in the sense developed by J. Habermas (Habermas, 1985). This author explains socioeconomic changes by the exchange of information, adjusting information to those providing and receiving it. Shared information becomes energy and acts as a facilitator for internal changes, and its adaptation to external changes allows for adjustment and anticipation.

Companies involved in shared enterprises need to reengineer their own architecture in order to take into account the common interests. But this architecture might be built following the rise of the company both internal and external, respecting the rhythms of partners. It needs also a common language for the regular exchanges, founded on the creative synergy. Centralized organization architectures were built on the bases of the scale economies coming from the size side, and the scope economies coming from know-how and diversity of activities and skills. But the scale economies are limited, and the bigger the size the fewer economies are generated. We develop this point in Sandoval (1993). On the contrary, the small companies compensate for a lack of scale economies by being more flexible. The question is now how to conciliate both to optimize the entire group of companies.

2.3. The intelligent enterprise (IE)

The theory of intelligent enterprise (IE) has been developed by J.B. Quinn (Quinn, 1992), who has studied the latest developments in the U.S. economy. His approach is quite different from those prevalent at the beginning of the 1990s but we think it has a great importance for our purposes. Quinn outlines two main distinctive characteristics of the U.S. economy - the importance of services in both GNP and value-added and the role of services in the global dynamic of the economy. Nevertheless, we underline that similar characteristics are presented by the other advanced economies, and so they are not exclusive to the United States (see Sections 1.3 and 1.4). This is an important point because the scope of Quinn's approach must be applicable to other advanced countries. Nevertheless, in Quinn's view these two characteristics are essentials for building a new paradigm of enterprises - the intelligent enterprise.

To build this new paradigm, Quinn begins discussing what he calls the four myths about services. These myths are the lower-value misconception, the low-capital-intensitivity perception, the small-scale misconception, and the service can't produce wealth viewpoint. In fact, all these are wrong because services offer perpetual growth opportunities, and in the particular case of the United States, they contribute to restructuring the entire economy.

The main idea of Quinn's theory is the word *intelligence*. We will see later in more detail the signification of intelligence in production systems (see Section 2.6), but here intelligence is taken closely related to the intellectual tasks and highly skilled services within an enterprise. Thus intelligence is linked to services, and in this way, it is helping to restructure economies. One problem for company strategy consists then in determining what is the intellectual core inside company and then the skills required for preferred services. Another point is how services, based on knowledge, affect the organizational strategies. As examples confirming this assumption, Quinn quotes the cases of Federal Express and American Express.

Nevertheless, the simple study of the service enterprise, founded on a specialized knowledge, is not sufficient, according to Quinn, and then he proposes building a new kind of enterprise's paradigm, the so-called intelligent enterprise. The intelligent enterprise is characterized by the conversion of intellectual resources into a chain of services, that are provided and integrated in a manner that correspond as closely as possible to the consumer's needs. In reality, this customer's involvement determines strategy and destroys the classical industry boundaries: "These powerful service companies (the biggest companies in North America), directly connected to their product producing services, have placed ultimate consumers ever more in command of the world's production system and are able to dictate responses to their individual and collective desires. Being able to sense, produce for, and service these trends is the sine qua non for success in the new service society. Service technology has created both the need and capacity for such responses. They have also radically changed the sources and options one can call forth in responding" (Quinn, 1992, p. 21.).

This argument is directly related to what we can call *reverse logic of productive systems*, which becomes gradually a common thing in both national and international market (See Chapter 1, Section 2). As we know, this new logic appeared by the end of 1970s with markets (in the most advanced countries) entering then in the era of the consumer's sovereignty. The Japanese manufacturing industry wa probably the first to understand this new reality and to design a corresponding strategy. But the question is more complicated than this. In Japan, the manufacturing industry is an important contributor to the GNP and to the value added, even today, contrary to the manufacturing industry in the United States. The open question emerging here is this: consumers play a relevant role in manufacturing, Quinn's approach must profit from the quality or just-in-time principles extended to the services sector, that means to the entire economy.

According to Quinn, enterprises that sell rights, accountability, financial products, applied research, education, health care, consultancy, design, and so on are selling, in reality, the skills and intelligence of their own employees that are committed to produce it. But we can also add that this is also true for manufacturing, where more and more value added comes from the intellectual service activities. One way to prove this is to consider the contribution of engineers, scientists, technicians, and other skilled people to the value added generated in manufacturing companies (Jonscher, 1981) and (Sandoval, 1985). In France, for example, in the Midi-Pyrenees region managers, engineers, and technicians represent more than 50 percent of the workforce, and they are principally concentrated in the aerospace and manufacturing industries.

Focusing company strategy on core intellectual and service competencies needs some conditions. For example, this means knowing the real contribution of intellectual services to the value chain. This also means focusing on critical knowledge and service-based activities in this value chain. Or focusing its strategic investments and management attention on those core competencies where it can achieve and maintain best in the world (to keep a significant competitive advantage in the long term); create value through knowledge-based services, and rethink vertical integration by profiting fully from outsourcing and not just as a peripheral activity. But knowledge-based and service-based strategies are most effective when companies develop best-in-world capabilities around a few selected competencies that are important for customers. Quinn writes, "By concentrating its own resources on these selected areas and benchmarking other areas to ensure that it has comparability with or access to best-in-world suppliers, each company can build an unassailable strategic position" (Quinn, 1992, p.59).

This approach implies a redefinition of the basic nature of the company. Once a core service capability is developed in depth, it often redefines the very nature of the company's business in its original position in its industry. The organizational changes are important here. For example, the author discusses the infinitely flat organizations, the spider organizations, or the inverted organizations in which the interactions within the organizations are either at the local contact point or with a communications center. Figure 2.2. illustrates an example of a spider organization.

To sum up, enterprise must concentrate its efforts on specific skills, services, or relevant pieces of knowledge within the value chain in which it must be the first in world. It must be a fundamental condition for remaining competitive. Enterprise must then

- Remain the best at supplying a set of services supported by its intellectual assets,

- Search for parity with other key elements of its value chain in trying so to reach best in this kind of activities, and

- Support a selected core of skills by other defensive positions (other products) and keep its distance from potential competitors, in doing so, enterprise is becoming intelligent because the development and coordination of its intellectuals assets occur everywhere.

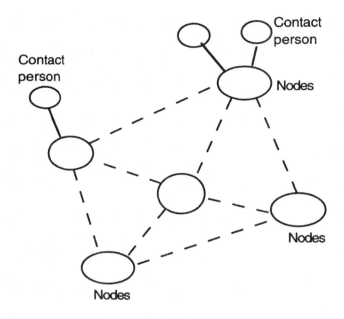

Figure 2.2. Quinn spider organization idea.

One emerging problem here is the need to keep specialized knowledge and skills to allow better management of suppliers. Only a specialized group of managers can help the company to remain in a better position. In addition, there is the emergences of new services founded on knowledge, which can be a new source of benefits.

Today most public and private companies are becoming both the base of knowledge and the coordinators of it. This means intelligent companies. The capacity to manage human intelligence and to embody it in services becomes, then, a critical factor for manager skills in enterprises. Among the challenges issued from this situation there are the following:

- The measurement of intellectual assets (from identification to definition of some metric) and

- The characteristics of the intellectual professional (discipline, no creativity, egoism, fat organization, and inverse management).

The new enterprise is then desegregated, founded on service and knowledge, concentrated around core intellectual or skilled services. This enterprise manages and coordinates priority information and intelligence in an attempt to answer customer needs. All activities are organized around it. Three key elements are fundamental:

- Simplified and reduced organizational internal hierarchy, management structures are lighter and high quality,

- Enhanced productivity and capacity to answer to the customer's needs, and

- Reduced investments and increased strategic flexibility.

2.4. Agile manufacturing (AM)

The agile manufacturing approach was developed within the context of the MANTEC (Manufacturing Technology) Project of Department of Defense in the late 1980s and early 1990s. AM is materialized in a report resulting from an industry-led consortium integrated by thirteen corporations who contributed executives to the board of this study and more than 100 who participated in two rounds of interaction with the ongoing work of the board. According to the agile manufacturing report (1991), leading manufacturing companies must build a new infrastructure to realize the transition from mass production to agile manufacturing production. This is a challenge for the competitiveness of the american manufacturing industry, and doing so can helpt it recover the leader role it lost during the last two decades, writes S. Goldman and K. Preiss (1991). The agile manufacturing report advanced the idea that by 2006, United States will enjoy world leadership in manufacturing. But to reach this level, America needs the agile companies, and this is the present challenge.

AM alters the meaning of industrial competition, as competitor, supplier, and customer/firms occupy changing roles in relation each other. Competition and cooperation become mutually compatible, and the competitive advantage is determined by speed to market, by ability to satisfy individual customers preferences, whether consumer or commercial customers, and by responsiveness to intensifying public concerns about manufacturing's social and environment impacts. In an agile company, manufacturing machinery can be programmed quickly to produce new products, in many variations. This environment will facilitate the creation of products with a high information content, and related commercial services will increasingly come to determine the competitiveness of a nation's industrial sector.

In an AM environment, enterprise must be able to bring out totally new products quickly. In this situation, reprogrammable, reconfigurable, continuously changeable production systems, integrated into new information intensive manufacturing system, make the lot size of an order irrelevant. So AM produces by order as in Japan, where mass production manufacturing produced to stock and sell, basing its production schedule on marketing projections. Because of the longevity of its evolutionary lines, agile manufacturing helps an enterprise to develop strategic relationships with consumer as well as commercial customers. Communications plays here an important role. The same comments made about IE (see above) are also available for a discussion of AM: AM is a coherent view with a new logic of productive systems.

The key point of this report is as follows:

- A new environment for industrial products and services has appeared and obligates manufacturing industry to change strategy;

- The competitive advantage, in this new system, belongs to the industrial companies that can be agiles and can answer quickly to the demand for high-quality products;

- The adaptation needs to integrate flexible production technologies with the skills of workers, and by this means with more knowledge and more flexible management structures, the company becomes capable of simulating cooperation initiatives inside and between firms.

Then the main premise of AM is a simple one to be able to answer to the increasing competition and globalization of markets, companies must develop productive systems that have a flexibility maximum. To do this, it is necessary to use the latest technologies in the field of the electronic exchange. Computers network computers, companies, administrations, research, and so on are then linked to these networks and must use the centralized and shared system.

But even if technologies are already operational in most companies, they cannot themselves generate the new system. To begin these technologies must be integrated within an organizational environment, that fully uses knowledge, creativity, and all other human resources available to the industry. But even that is not sufficient. Companies must have access to general social resources, such as appropriate training for the labor force, communication networks, adequate information, and support from the government. AM must be a result of a coordinated effort of industry, governement, and public. Companies, technologies, and its links with the social context constitute a system, a base for AM.

The increasing power of the information and communications technologies, embodied in production tools, allows the new system, with agility incorporated, to produce small quantities, reduce costs, and increase quality, contrary to mass production, which reduces unitary costs by producing a large number of uniform units. The manufacturing machine programmed quickly must produce new and different types of goods with more and more informational content, and the related commercial services are very important to remaining competitive with other industrial nations. As in SE, competition and cooperation are becoming compatibles, and the competitive advantage is determined by shortest time to market, by ability to satisfy the individual consumer's preferences, and by reactivity against the environmental problems.

Agile enterprises are strategically focused and emphasize long-term financial performance - as opposed to specific short-term performances and easily quantifiable approach common to mass production. Authority is diffused, not concentrated in a chain command; they have a dynamic structure, keyed to the evolving needs of cross-functional project teams. So agility is a strategic issue as opposed to a tactical one. According to the agile manufacturing report, AM is accomplished by integrating three resources - technology, management, and workforce - into a coordinated, interdependent, system (see Figure 2.3.)

Dan Roos (1995) proposes the following basic characteristics of the AM model:

- *Product flexibility and customized products.* Agility requires a much greater degree of design and process flexibility to achieve mass customization.

- *Multiple-use modular manufacturing.* The manufacturing facilities of an agile enterprise are design for multiple uses and are built around modular approaches.

- *Knowledge based organizations.* Agile organizations take advantage of information available to dynamically adapt processes to serve customer needs.

- *Enterprise integration.* The flow of information across organization boundaries in an agile enterprise (including suppliers and customers) allows a much higher degree of concurrent activities and process.

An agile manufacturing system is then a summation of the technologies that are replacing the obsolete paradigms. The key to agility is information - especially the rapid collection, processing, and transfer of it. But the barrier is an inflexible information system and IS people who lack understanding of the business environment.

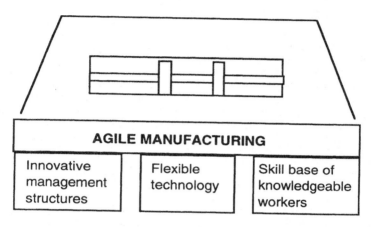

Figure 2.3. Bases for agile manufacturing.

Among the capabilities that allow a company to achieve the objective, A.G Brothers (1995) indicates the following:

- *Quality*. Produce a product that unfailingly satisfies customer expectations.

- *Mass customization*. Respond quickly to customer or market demands.

- *Features and technologies*. Incorporate new features and technologies quickly into products and services.

- *Adaptation*. Adapt to market demands.

- *Innovation*. Generate new ideas to combine with existing capabilities to create new sources of value.

- *Suppliers*. Develop close relationships with suppliers to permit shifts in deliveries quickly in response to changing customer requirements.

Constant innovation is the creation and evolution of products and services. Agile enterprises are able to manage the unpredictability of innovation by maximizing the scope for human initiative. So a knowledgeable workforce is the single major asset of the enterprise. Continuous workforce education and training are the long-term investments that ensures better assimilation of information and creative response to new possibilities suggested by it. Mass production is fixed by nature; agile manufacturing is a continuously evolving system. But this last point asks for a new social contract that avoids elite organizational values and parochial managerial attitudes. The overall system creates wealth for society, not individuals. Unlike mass production, agile production requires that every worker understand the production scheme into which his or her jobs fit. From the company's view, agile manufacturing enhances SMEs through wider access to their services that a national manufacturing network would allow.

2.5. Computer integrated manufacturing (CIM)

By the mid-1980s, the rapid and steady development of computer and telecommunications technologies introduce many acronyms for many kinds of production activities. The word *aided* appears in most of them; so the computer is a tool for aiding people. But in the acronym CIM (computer integrated manufacturing), for the first time the word *aided* is replaced by *integrated*. Computer-aided becomes simply computer-integrated. Computers not only help people but also integrate a system in its productive activity. Then the integration of productive systems begins, becoming one of the most important fields of R&D in advanced manufacturing and other activities. CIM technology is based on a set of complex different technologies adapting computer power in discreet manufacturing. R.U. Ayres (1992) distinguishes three categories of technologies:

- *Enabling technologies* (such as telecommunications, microelectronics and computers). Currently, these technologies are applicable far beyond the domain of manufacturing.

- *Transition technologies* (such as microelectronic and computer devices that have been applied over the past thirty years, but on a stand-alone basis). NCs machine tools, programmable controllers, and robots are examples in this category.

- *Technologies central to CIM directly related to computer integration*. Typical examples of these technologies are computer-aided design and computer-aided manufacturing and design (CAD-CAM), computerized manufacturing resource planning (MRP), local area networks (LAN), and so-called flexible manufacturing systems (FMS). This last is a key step for introducing CIM technology because it enables links between programmable automation at the machine level and the integration of computer manufacturing at the information level.

Nevertheless, CIM is more than a technical problem. As write H. Baumgartner, K. Knischevski and H.Wieding (1991), relations between organization, technologies and data processing must be considered as a single entity. For example, management indicates the long-term objectives, then a specific CIM concept for each company. Table 2.1. summarizes these technologies. Among these factors we can point out:

- Market demands (products, quality, and delays.),

- Technical and economic objectives of the company (reduction of manufacturing costs, improvement of material flow, information flow.),

- Degree of computerization and networking (type of hardware and software, network implementation, size of network, distributed architectures...), and

- Factors specific to the manufacturing conditions (formation, personnel, and type of machines, type of technologies, production structure, size of company).

Table 2.1. Categories of technologies for CIM.

Enabling technologies	Transition technologies	Central technologies
Telecommunications	NCs	CAD
Microelectronic	Machine tools	CAM
Computers	Programmable controllers	MRP
		LAN
	Robots	FSM

Nevertheless, CIM is more than a technical problem. As write H. Baumgartner, K. Knischevski and H.Wieding (1991), relations between organization, technologies and data processing must be considered as a single entity. For example, management indicates the long-term objectives, then a specific CIM concept for each company. Table 2.1. summarizes these technologies. Among these factors we can point out:

- Market demands (products, quality, and delays.),

- Technical and economic objectives of the company (reduction of manufacturing costs, improvement of material flow, information flow.),

- Degree of computerization and networking (type of hardware and software, network implementation, size of network, distributed architectures...), and

- Factors specific to the manufacturing conditions (formation, personnel, and type of machines, type of technologies, production structure, size of company).

Figure 2.4. gives an example of a CIM global view, including technical and organizational aspects. The number of elements involved becomes quite important, and then CIM become quite complex. At the bottom (production or shopfloor level) of this figure, there are many techniques (CAD, CAM, CAP, CAQ, FMS, FA, computation, communication, databases, maintenance) and their integration. In the middle of the figure, we can see a continuum flow going from product idea to the finished product or service. This flow includes logistics, organization, personnel, and training as resources involved for creating the appropriate outputs. We will find some these points within the context of concurrent engineering (CE) paradigm (see Chapter 4).

To implement a CIM project, an important point is the CIM concept. To create such a concept we must start from the analysis of company strategy, and it must be in phase with the main goal - to reach an economic technological optimum. So there are a variety of applications of this concept, such as, for example, a CIM concept for computer-aided integration concerning only one process or manufacturing conveyors, a CIM concept for manufacturing-oriented systems, or a CIM concept for large applications.

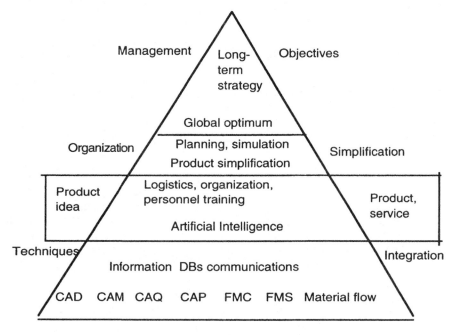

Figure 2.4. CIM pyramid: Technical and organizational aspects.

One way to realize a CIM concept is to begin by integrating the existing islands, then to continue by creating networks of islands, and finally, to replace the networks by functional fields (vertical integration) and by manufacturing field (horizontal integration). It is also necessary to integrate the production field (material arriving, storage, manufacturing parts, assembly, delivery package, delivery) and functional CIM fields (CAD, CAM, CAQ, MRP, etc.) Horizontal integration concerns at every step only one separate level in the hierarchy (for example, CAD contributes to the integration of product design and design of the means to manufacture those products, when means depend on the product design, but the implementation of CIM is different for each). Vertical integration is a top-down or bottom-up process. Then it integrates, for example, CAD, PIC, and CAM, the most common being CAD-CAM. So the integration process is based on different technologies, such as CAD, CAM, MRP, PIC, or CAP. This is available for Western manufacturing companies. In the case of the Japanese manufacturing companies, the implementation is quite different (see below).

From the above development, we can now advance a more precise definition of the CIM concept. For such a definition we simply follow J.B. Waldner (1990). According to this author, the CIM concept concerns a totally automated manufacturing system in which all functions of a company (such as commercial, production, accounting, or management) are integrated and controlled by computer systems.

2.5.1. CIM and FCIM

In the study of CIM, one interesting point is that of the CIM in the United States. Historically, the U.S. CIM was not as good as the Japanese CIM. During 1980s, the concept of flexible computer integrated manufacturing (FCIM) appeared. The FCIM concept is closely related to the U.S. Department of Defense CALS initiative. CALS (computer acquisition-aided logistic support) was launched by the Department of Defense in 1986. For this reason the first implementations of FCIM were prepared by industries tied to military activity. The most advanced U.S. manufacturing companies are involved in this program. Indeed, the Department of Defense Logistics Commanders approved the FCIM Charter on 4 June 1991. The FCIM is defined as the integration of equipment, software, communications, human resources, and business practices within an enterprise for the rapid manufacture, repair, and deliver of the items on demand, with continuous improvements in the process (Wilson, 1993).

FCIM is a full-cycle process, that begins with identifying a part need and ends with delivery of the parts to the customer. The FCIM objective is simple - to improve quality parts at a low cost and to produce at the right. The customer is happy, and the manufacturer keeps its competitive edge in a crowded, competitive business environment. The FCIM process - which capitalizes on modern software and hardware in an effort to produce a variety of similar products smoothly and rapidly - is designed to reduce the lead times, increase turnaround time, and decrease cost.

The goal of the FCIM is a continuous process improvement. To reach it, all members of an enterprise (employer, employees, management, vendors, and suppliers) must work together to eliminate policies, procedures, and processes that do not maximize the turnaround time for the production and delivery of a part to the customer. Among its characteristics, FCIM includes the following:

- FCIM builds on existing systems and capabilities.

- FCIM is modular. This means that the steps in the existing process may be automated or manual, but each step must be examined to discover more efficient and effective operating methods.

- FCIM requires cultural changes. People must develop new timeframes, establish new interfaces, and employ new skills. The intent of FCIM is to create a new environment for manufacturing products.

- Technology involves risk.

To achieve continuous improvement processes for the twenty-first century, the initiative begins with experiments within the process validation enterprise (PVE). The PVE is an experimental environment, which includes the operational functions within the Department of Defense that are required to acquire selected long-lead-time and high-cost items - from placing an order to delivery. The implementation of FCIM must be a shift from decisions based on unit cost to viewing the total time and cost; must be saved through reducing logistics costs required to meet readiness goals; must be established allowing users to spur on advanced technology development efforts through an implementation-oriented approach. This will lead to technology solutions that are linked to users' needs. Figure 2.5. depicts the PVE structure for this joint venture.

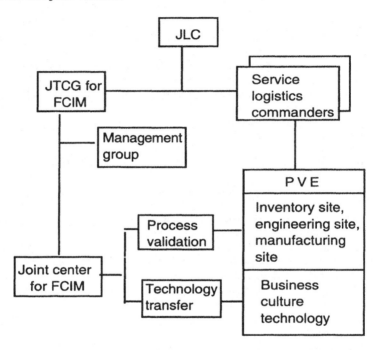

Figure 2.5. Joint technical coordinating group (JTC) for FCIM and the PVE.

Note that the development of FCIM impacts on some current research programs such as rapid acquisition of manufactured parts (RAMP), which is from then considered as an FCIM technology program.

2.5.2. Japanese CIM
Japanese view considers technology as a subject wider than a simple classification and in continuous movement toward the future. The word *kaisen* is sometimes used in reference to this kind of trend. So it is not as simple to distinguish enabling technologies or transition or central technologies for CIM as it is in Western manufacturing industry. But in practice, technologies such as NC machine tools, programmable controllers, and robots must be considered as key technologies for CIM. So they are not just transition technologies. They have a fundamental character to the supply side for responding to demands inserted in a sequence supply, and it is rather difficult to isolate them.

As we know, definitions are important in the technology field because they can clarify the scope of its application. Japanese companies sometimes give a definition at the beginning of their CIM involvement. Managers are then clear about what the target is, and this has a great influence on the people who are in charge of developing CIM and who are normally from different departments of companies.

Definition is also important for the conceptual approach to CIM. But it is difficult to set up such a definition. In fact, CIM depends on many factors - for example, market demands (products, quality, delays.), technical and economic objectives of company (reduction of manufacturing costs, improvement of material flow, information flow.), and degree of computerization and networking (type of hardware and software, network implementation, size of network, distribution). Concerning the Japanese CIM, a general definition for CIM exists at least at the overall company level (a company here means one company and many other partners trading with it). Another example of the definition concerns the Shimizu Corporation. This company is not a classical manufacturing company because construction must be considered a different process, with very specific characteristics (particular work localization, variety of inputs, time differences for input requirements, difficulty of automating some manual operations, and so on). So one question is What definition for CIM should be used in that case? In the present company case, the solution found is expressed by an acronym, which is created by substituting *construction* for *manufacturing*. This is not simple word play because it contains an essential point - that there exists a computer integrated construction (CIC), just as there exists a computer-integrated manufacturing. It has, probably, a double consequence. On the one hand, the computer is integrating a construction process as well as a manufacturing process as in the classical situation. A second consequence is more important: if the computer can integrate construction, we can assume an extension of the CIM principle (the integration by computer) to any human production activity. In other words, and this should be true at least from the point of view of definition, CIM should be a universal step or, in the Japanese view, a productive paradigm that corresponds with an era (see Sections 1.2 and 1.3)

To sum up, there exists a general approach: CIM is considered to be an important aspect of the development of manufacturing systems that companies must incorporate as a part of their own competitive policy.

CIM is founded on a set of standard components - factory automation (FA), engineering automation (EA) and office automation (OA). CIM integrates all of these components, the more important being FA. FA is principally supported by technologies such as manufacturing application protocol (MAP). These technologies are developed according to individual companies. Toyota, for example, has developed the Mecathronic Network (ME-NET) as a simplified version of MAP, restricted to the low layers of the protocol only.

2.6. Intelligent manufacturing systems (IMS)

Intelligent manufacturing systems (IMS) represents the Japanese vision for the future generation of manufacturing systems (FGMS). This section introduces the main elements of IMS.

34

2.6.1. The launching of IMS

IMS is a program for international cooperation in advanced manufacturing. It is a catalytic agent for global cooperation in advancing the state of the art in manufacturing, and existing levels of technology in many companies, including small to medium enterprises (SMEs). IMS provides a vision and structure for worldwide sharing of manufacturing technology development, including costs, risks, and benefits, in a balanced and equitable manner. The ten-year program responds to common problems in the manufacturing sector of industrialized nations - greater sophistication in manufacturing operations, improved global environment, enhancement of the discipline of manufacturing, and an opportunity for organizations of all sizes to respond to the globalization of manufacturing, thus facilitating the process of standardization.

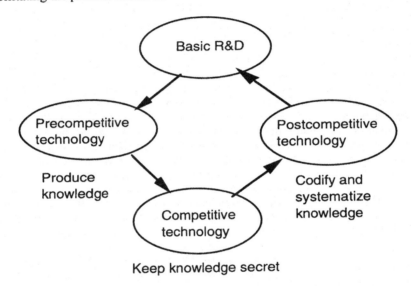

Figure 2.6. The the theory behind IMS.
(Source First International Symposium on IMS, Tokyo, 1992; IMS Web Server).

IMS is based on a theory developed by Professor Yoshikawa, president of the University of Tokyo. Figure 2.6. illustrates the development cycle proposed by Yoshikawa

The idea behind postcompetitive technology is that at some point a technology no longer plays a role in competitive capability. Further, expertise can be lost over time. Hence, the idea is to codify knowledge and in the process identify missing elements that can lead to new basic R&D. Today IMS is an international collaborative program comprising six regions - Australia, Canada, the European Community (EC), the European Free-Trade Association (EFTA), Japan, and the United States. The program began with feasibility studies involving partners coming from overseas countries. After this stage, the program entered a more advanced stage with the development of one particular set of feasibility research projects in which are now participating countries from six regions. .

From our experience with this program, the main theoretical principles of IMS, supported by the Yoshikawa's theoretical approach, can be summarized as follows:

- *The organization of manufacturing knowledge.* A study of the technological knowledge of traditional industry allows us to divide it into product-design knowledge and related manufacturing knowledge. Manufacturing knowledge will be improved in proportion to product-design knowledge and, conversely, manufacturing knowledge is reflected into product-design knowledge. This last is easy to describe because details normally are incorporated in invention rights and so become public knowledge. Manufacturing knowledge also includes many intangibles (for example, unspecified variables). This knowledge remains under the form of know-how.

- *The systematization of manufacturing knowledge.* To collect and systematize knowledge requieres accelerating the activation of the firm holding such knowledge, facilitating the technology transfer from advanced to less developed countries, and diffusing those technologies to small and medium-size firms. More precisely, following Yoshikawa, manufacturing knowledge can be separated into confidential information and nonconfidential information. Nevertheless, the systematization of manufacturing knowledge is not a simple codification of this knowledge. In reality, if countries truly want a transfer of knowledge, it is necessary to simplify and reorganize the manufacturing knowledge in such a manner that technical personnel in developing countries can easily understand it. In addition, it will be appropriate to develop machines and equipment to be easily adapted and offer them to these countries.

- *The standardization of manufacturing knowledge.* This point must be developed in parallel with the progress of the organization in systematizing manufacturing knowledge. If the development of the future production system (to be realized within five or ten years according to CIM) is now being undertaken by individual countries as well as companies, then this has a high risk of leading to a chaotic situation in the near future. If some progress has been made (for example, CIM protocol standard by MAP-TOP), it is not enough. Standardizing relevant technology and knowledge aimed toward CIM (the major production system for the future) can avoid duplication of investments.

- *The development of next generation manufacturing technology.* It becomes more and more clear that firms (especially the bigger firms) cannot continue to compete for development in all sophisticated industries without risking some negative consequences. Then cooperation appears as one solution, and IMS must play an important role, as a joint international program in handling information and results, and making them available to all people as a common asset for all countries.

2.6.2. CIM and IMS

As was shown in Section 2.5, for Japanese manufacturing companies, CIM is one step in the evolution of manufacturing system. According to this vision, CIM should contribute to the characterization and implementation of the future generation of manufacturing systems. A representative example of this progressive approach is done by Hitachi Vision which identifies the following steps (see Figure 2.7.):

- FA (factory automation),
- CIM, and
- IMS (intelligent manufacturing systems).

FA deals with flexibility and automation comprising standards for products stable planning and size lots. CIM deals with integration and information. Circulation, particularly integration must drop the inefficiency of isolated subsystems. IMS deals with a future factory prototype.

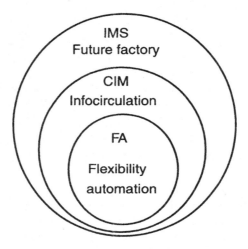

Figure 2.7. The trend toward CIM and IMS.

CIM represents a turning point in the evolution of the production paradigm (Japanese view). Here computer communication plays a fundamental role in the transition from the actual production paradigm characterized by the replacement of human labor to the future production paradigm characterized by the replacement of human intelligence.

Illustrating how CIM is an input to the next generation of manufacturing systems, Y. Hasegawa (1992) compares a traditional CIM and the next-generation CIM, which closely encompasses IMS systems. The future CIM will renovate and evolve the actual one. The author illustrates his comparison using fifteen items: internationalization, response to market, environment for product development, processing for engineering jobs, production system, production lead time, production planning, machinery facilities, communications, response to system renewal, human interface, amenity, contribution to region, response to international standardization, and response to earth's resources. Table 2.2. presents a comparative description of the main points.

Table 2.2. Item comparison between classical CIM and new CIM.

Item	Conventional CIM	New CIM
Internationalization	Regionalization	Globalization
Response to market	Flexible product output	Market input
Environment	Job-supported systemizing CAD ..	Artificial intelligence for response
Processing for enginering	Discrete partially parallel processing	Global concurrent engineering
Production system	Various kinds of production	Job-order mass production
Production lead time	Short lead time (few days)	Very short lead time (few hours)
Production planning	Stock or order production system	Complete job order production
Machinery facilities	Machinery facilities	Autonomous module facilities
Communication	Conventionnal communication system	ISDN or satelite communication
Contribution to the region	Main contribution economic	Regional industry and culture
Ecology	Productivity deals	Resolution and reduction

For FGMS, CIM must become then intelligent. An intelligent CIM is a system capable of substituting forÒ or of supporting humans in the aspects of their intelligent activities, including sensing, memorizing, thinking, recognizing, and judging. From this viewpoint, the structure of intelligent CIM consists of three hierarchical levels: management, design and factory level.

1. The management oversees the decision-making process. The essence of this intelligent system is the database linking activities such as the current and future market needs of manufacturing and of research and development.

2. Design comprises product design, process design, and production scheduling, which are not yet connected directly to each other today. Based on and linked to product models, the process and scheduling will be simultaneously processed.

3. At the factory level, the first important aspect is to link CAM to CAD. But this realization needs to happen in connection with the product model and the activity model. Y. Furukawa calls this *intellectualization*, instead of *intelligentialization* of the shop-floor components such as robots, machine tools, and others. Expert systems, artificial neural networks, fuzzy theory, and sensor fusion are the main technologies of today's intellectualization, and they will move to objects of more autonomous nature (see Furukawa, 1992a, 1992b). In the FA paradigm (substitution for human work), the technical features are the integration of nonautonomous mechatronic devices (in the sense of substitution for human manipulation) into production systems at the shop-floor level, resulting in automated factories (more reduction of direct work, high production rate, and product diversification). The CIM paradigm (incorporation of information processing into production systems) has many technical features: it must integrate all components in manufacturing - including product development and design, manufacturing and management, as well as nonautonomous hardware therein - into a single system at the corporate level, through the use of computers and interconnecting networks. One reaches then a reduction of indirect labor, marketled production, and a faster business. In the IMS paradigm (substitution of human intelligence), the technical features are characterized by the incorporation of human skills and knowledge into production systems using autonomous hardware and computer technologies, and their integration into a human-oriented, flexible intelligent manufacturing system on a global scale. One can reach then a human-oriented production, improved factory amenity, regionally adaptable production systems, the preservation of global environments, and global localized production. We can assume that CIM is not only different, according to the companies or processes involved, but also is evolving over time, becoming more and more intelligent. CIM must be considered as an input in the creation of the future generation of manufacturing systems (FGMS).

Despite critics (from those considering it a very good idea to those considering it an impossible challenge), IMS can be considered a good principle containing many ideas contributing to the creation of the new manufacturing paradigm.

2.6.3. IMS: A new manufacturing paradigm

IMS must be placed in an historical perspective. For doing so, Y. Furukawa (1992a, 1992b) uses the paradigm approach. According to Furukawa, the word *paradigm* (in the sense of T.S. Kuhn, 1962) is interpreted (in Japanese) as a generally accepted set of concepts (precepts, ideas, or facts) during a period of time, and serves as a standard for people, particularly scientists, for interpreting natural, social, economic or other phenomena (see Sections 1.2, 1.3, and 1.4).

There have been only a few changes in the social consensus, or *paradigm* on manufacturing - for example, the move from individual handcrafts into work-intensive manufacturing, or the substitution of machine tools for human work.

When mechanical means were substituted for part of human work, we have the so-called secondary manufacturing *paradigm* which remains dominant in the prosperity of industrial nations around the world.

Another *paradigm* is the replacement of human intelligence by the artificial counterpart in our time. In that situation the brain, a complex thinking apparatus, is being replaced by by artificial means. Computers have been rapidly invading factories as well as management and sales departments as data storage and processing devices, integrating in this way production activities into CIM with interconnecting information network systems. But according to Furukawa, computers not only will replace the most simple brain functions, such as memory, but also its more complex functions, such as knowledge, reasoning, and judgment. Then we will face the third manufacturing *paradigm*. As the previous paradigm, this new one is facing new problems that it needs to study to find appropriate solutions. The Japanese call this *ecoharmonic manufacturing paradigm*. But human-intensive manufacturing, the mechanized manufacturing paradigm, and the ecoharmonic manufacturing paradigm will coexist, at least at the beginning of the twenty-first century.

Then it will be necessary to research the future generation of manufacturing systems. In the Japanese view, two ideas are fundamentals: a country alone (Japan) keeps accumulating wealth by improving production efficiency using the mechanized manufacturing paradigm; a simple transfer of existing technologies from advanced countries to less developed nations will not be enough to narrow the technical gap that exists between both sets of countries.

The IMS must also emphasize a more extended use of computers to simulate entire manufacturing operations through the creation of virtual factories, as well as the scientific and technological basis for unmanned factories to spare human beings from undesirable and dangerous jobs. The future manufacturing system must pursue the following objectives:

- To help reduce the technical and economic gap between advanced nations and less developed countries by accelerating technology transfer through organization and standardization of manufacturing technologies that are sources of wealth actively;

- To promote standardization of manufacturing technologies that are likely to be dominant during the next decade so as to improve worldwide productivity by securing interchangeability among relevant technologies used in advanced nations as well as less developed countries; and

- To create a new manufacturing paradigm, taking into account factors such as human creating pleasure, and harmony with the ecosystem, including social and natural environments, far beyond present industrial concepts based on the market-oriented economy in which the sole purpose of developing and manufacturing products is to make profits.

The technical areas of IMS concern intelligent devices; autonomous control and system integration, system design, system architecture, and information integration. The proposed topics are then classified into the four following categories, assuming that production systems comprise management, design, and manufacturing - topics concerning organization of knowledge from existing excellent technologies, topics aiming at the standardization of production activities comprising management, design, and manufacturing, as well as information; topics aimied at development of future manufacturing systems commensurate with the concept of next-generation production systems; and topics dealing with the relationship between production systems and such factors as man, society, and natural environment.

2.7. The CIM-OSA model

The objective of the CIM-OSA (computer-integrated manufacturing - open-systems architecture) model is the appropriate integration of enterprise operations by means of efficient information exchange within the enterprise with the help of information technology. Open-systems architecture (OSA) defines an integrated methodology to support all phases of a CIM system life cycle from requirements specification, through system design, implementation, operation, maintenance, and even system migration toward CIM-OSA solution.

As has been shown (see Section 2.5), CIM is a new manufacturing paradigm that has been developed over the last decade. CIM has been recognized to be of strategic importance for Europe. The European strategic program ESPRIT supports a number of CIM-related projects, among them CIM-OSA (AMIC, 1993). The CIM-OSA model gives a general answer to the integration problems as illustrated in Figure 2.8.

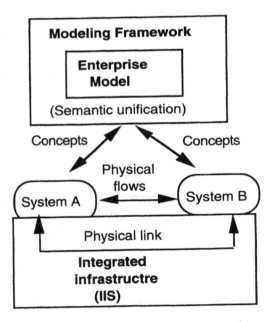

Figure 2.8. The CIM-OSA approach for system integration.

2.7.1. The CIM-OSA modeling paradigm

CIM-OSA provides an architecture to describe the real world of the manufacturing enterprise by providing a unique set of advanced features to model functionality and behavior of CIM systems at three distinct levels - requirements definition, design specification, and implementation description. This description is used to control the enterprise operation and to plan, design, and optimize updates of the real operation environment.

Using a finite but comprehensive set of modeling concepts, a manufacturing enterprise can create a precise model of its own CIM requirements using a standardized set of basic constructs and partial models and then transform this model through a series of well-defined steps into a model of the physical CIM system matching those requirements. The application of CIM-OSA results in a complete description of the enterprise, which is then stored on and manipulated by the information technology of the enterprise, as is shown in a related virtual enterprise case in Chapter 3 (Section 3.5).

The CIM-OSA architectural framework is represented as a 3 x 3 x 4 building block cubed as shown in Figure 2.9., such that each block of the cube serves as a basic modeling construct with which the requirements and solutions (or implementations) of a particular enterprise may be described.

The three directional axes of the cube provide the path for stepwise instantiation, derivation and generation:

- Instantiation is the process that captures the enterprise's requirement using a mapping against a common, neutral, supporting reference framework to achieve a consistent set of requirements;

- Derivation is the process that organizes the captured requirements so that they can be realized by a controlled set of information technology applications; and

- Generation is the process that supports the analysis and synthesis of specific aspects (or views) of the enterprise.

On the Instantiation axis, different levels of generality are defined that permit the CIM user to choose building blocks to meet particular instances of one's design needs, starting from generic requirements definition and terminating with the CIM system the particular implementation description model.

The derivation axis identifies the different modeling areas of the requirements definition, design specification and implementation description, which are to be addressed by the enterprise when developing its own CIM system.

The generation axis traverses the four modeling views - function view, information view, resource view, and organization view - considered in CIM-OSA that model the entire enterprise.

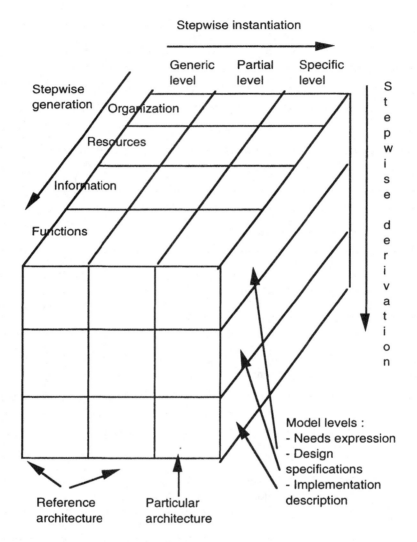

Figure 2.9. CIM-OSA views.

The CIM-OSA modeling methodology is more descriptive than prescriptive. In order to satisfy the needs of particular enterprises, CIM-OSA does not provide a standard architecture to be used by the whole manufacturing industry, but rather a reference architecture from which particular architectures may be derived. To facilitate this derivation of particular architecture from reference Architecture, CIM-OSA brings together a number of architectural principles and employs several structuring concepts.

The architectural principles and structuring concepts serve the following purposes:

- To create a modeling framework of the CIM enterprise that wholly or partially distinctly segregates the what (or model of required enterprise functionality and behavior) from the how (or model of an actual enterprise system implementation) by means of the how to (or model of optimized enterprise system design); and

- To derive a particular implementation model of the enterprise that is active during the operation of the enterprise system and is the basis for the computer-controlled execution of the modeled business processes and enterprise activities, thereby providing true computer-integrated manufacturing (Jorysz, 1990).

2.7.2. Modeling and the life-cycle of the CIM system

CIM-OSA provides a methodology for following the life cycle of the CIM system. The steps of the life cycle of the system are expression of the system design, implementation description, installation, exploitation, validation, maintenance, and stop. Figure 2.10. illustrates a comparison between models and life cycle of the systems and real world.

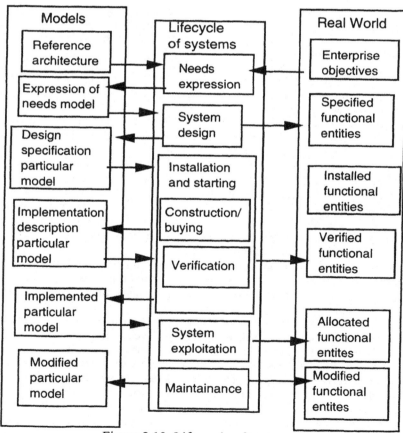

Figure 2.10. Life cycle of systems.

2.7.3. The knowledge-creating company case and the learning enterprise

A specific approach centered on knowledge has been developed by Hirotaka Takeuchi and Ikujiro Nonaka (1996). They begin their explanation using a rugby approach as a clear example underlining the role of the team in creating knowledge and ideas. In practice, project teams do most of the successful product development. Working together, team members are on the field from day one - engineers production, quality control, and sales. Whenever a problem comes up, they all pile in together. That's very different from the relay approach, in which one functional team passes the baton to the next.

According to these authors, an organization's ability to sustain innovation depends on creating and spreading knowledge among middle managers. Thus training is not sufficient, and neither is individual genius. The knowledge creation is linked to the innovation process. And the question is to determine how organizations innovate, not just once or twice but systematically and continuously. But the innovation process in Japan is different from that in the West, and here cultural difference can play a significant role. In Western companies, one individual can quickly bring a big innovation to market. Japanese companies rely on innovations from groups of ordinary people, and then they depend on middle managers' trying to push everyone in the team up to a higher level of shared understanding. Our experience observing many manufacturing plants in Japan confirms these assumptions.

More generally (see Section 2.6), the knowledge creation depends on the interaction of two types of knowledge - explicit and tacit. The IMS Gnosis Research Program based on the Yoshikawa's principles, started using this distinction. In Western companies, people are very comfortable with explicit knowledge, the sort of information that can be verbalized, written down in documents, put into computers, and readily communicated. The Japanese are using tacit knowledge, which comes from personal experience and is usually difficult to express. It is not completely rational because it is connected to emotions, and beliefs (more experience than something in the mind).

But creating knowledge requires a convergence of tacit and explicit knowledge. For profiting from the employees' tacit knowledge, Japanese companies work hard to create a feeling of unity. and this is influenced by Zen spirit: they believe that the best state of intellectual ability comes when the body and mind become one. The ideal form of communication is known as the "breath of ah-UN". Our experiences in working with Japanese managers and engineers show that only a few expression are needed to communicate and sometimes no explicit verbal communication at all is needed. We have worked many times using graphics or hand symbolic constructions.

In creation knowledge, middle management plays an important role. They help the front-line people put those ideals into practice. Even more, when information is shared freely between top and middle management, knowledge spirals up and down the organization. Project teams work when goals are very clear, and they have the autonomy they need to meet them. This kind of institutional knowledge is created when knowledge passes from the individual to the team and then from the team to the organization. So when a project is completed at a company level, the team members return to the normal hierarchy. That gives them a chance to dump all the knowledge they have accumulated from their experience into the common-knowledge base. And gradually, the experience of project teams spreads through the whole organization. That's how you achieve continuity and repeatability. This practice is very similar to that proposed by T. Stockfelt in a lecture during the Lillehammer Winter Olympic Games (1996). He argued that the new relation to be established between the coach and the team in top-level sport training, was to share experience and live together in Zen spirit.

Is this knowledge-creating company principal applicable in Western companies? We think so, reasoning on this simple approach that knowledge as a natural creative function and combination of tacit and explicit knowledge. But this needs some changes to go beyond Japanese culture. For example, in Japan, the biggest companies cannot hire people, so they are keeping the knowledge-creation process and the fundamental basis - the human resources. In the Needherlands, specialists called this the coach tramway syndrome - the coach knows all about his job, and if he disappear, this knowledge is lost with him.

More generally, the knowledge creation is in a new context created by the ICT. and this is a challenge for all businesses in a global environment.

2.7.4. GNOSIS

This is a new case of learning enterprise approach. This program is launched as an international IMS test case. GNOSIS aims to establish the framework for a new manufacturing paradigm through the utilization of knowledge-intensive strategies covering all stages of product life cycle, in order to realize new forms of highly competitive manufactured products and processes that are environment conscious, society conscious, and human oriented.

The ultimate goal of GNOSIS is to establish the framework for a new manufacturing paradigm that will overcome or minimize the problems inherent in the existing mass production paradigm, while simultaneously enabling manufacturing enterprises to become more competitive and providing the human user with cheaper, easier to use products. Thus a postmass production paradigm is proposed. This involves a new approach to manufacturing, recognizing resource limitations and the balance of nature in order to achieve a sustainable manufacturing environment. The new paradigm will be realized by the manufacture of soft products, with their associated production systems and industrial enterprises. *Softness* here refers to adaptability, robustness, and growth potential together with congeniality to the natural environment and human society. The lack of such softness in conventional manufactured products is due largely to the uncoordinated use of knowledge, resulting in conceptual blind spots - local optimization but global inconsistencies. Hence, the effective systematization and utilization of knowledge is regarded as the key to the establishment of the new paradigm.

The principal themes of the research were selected to enable this strategy to be implemented at various levels, so as to achieve results in the short to medium, as well as the long-term. Research into the postmass production paradigm goal will include conceptual themes such as social needs, manufacturing philosophy, and the economy, in addition to considering the driving forces and obstacles to it. Research into newly competitive soft products and production systems, which will form the backbone of the future manufacturing paradigm, will be supported by knowledge systematization and a knowledge intensive engineering framework, with modeling and integration themes focusing on generic representation and communication issues.

46

References

AMIC. (1993). CIM-OSA : Open System architetcure for CIM (2nd ed.). Berlin: Springer verlag.

Ayres, R.U. (1992). "CIM : A Challenge Technology Management".*Internationa Journal of Technology Managment* 7 (1-3).

Baumgartner H. , Knischewski K. and Wieding H. (1991). *CIM, mise en oeuvre de la productique.* Berlin: Siemens aktiengeselschaft.

Brothers G.W. (1995). "Consultant Information and Configuration Managemnt : Achieving Agility in Manufacturing Through Knowledge Management". In *Proceedings CALS Expo '95, Long Beach* , CA.

Furukawa, Yuichi. (1992). "Joint Research Program into International Manufacturing System from Preliminary Study. *Proceedings of the First International Symposium on Intelligent Manufacturing Systems.*, Tokyo.

Furukawa, Yuichi. (1992). "Paradigm shift in manufacturing systems". Paper delivered at the IEEE International Conference on Robotics and Automation, Nice, France.

Goldman, Steve, and Preiss Kenneth. (1991). *The Twenty-first Century Manufacturing Enterprise Strategy.* Project vol.1. Bethlehem, PA : Iacocca Institute.

Habermas, J. (1985). *Théorie de l'agir.* Paris: Fayard 1985.

Hasegawa, Yukio. (1992). "Strategies Issues for Developing Next Generation of CIM Systems". In *Proceedings of the First International Symposium on Intelligent Manufacturing Systems,* Tokyo.

Jonscher, Charles. (1981). "Information and Economic Organization". *Proceedings of the Pacific Telecommunications Conference,* Honolulu.

Jorysz, H.R. and Vernadat, F.B. (1990). CIM-OSA Part 1: Total Enterprise Modelling and Function View. Part 2: Information View. *International Journal of Computer Integrated Manufacturing* 3 (3:4).

Julien, Pierre Andre. (1995). "L'entreprise partagée": contraintes et opportunités. *Proceedings ILCE'95 Concurrent Engineering and Technical Information Procesing, Paris.*, Paris, France.

Kuhn, T.S. (1962). *The structure of scientific revolution.* Chicago, IL: Uniersity of Chicago Press.

Lecler, Y. (1993). *Parténariat industriel. La réference Japonaise.* Lyon: L'Interdisciplinarité.

Pache, G. and Paraponaris, C. (1993). *L'entreprise en réseau.* Paris: Presses Universitaires de France.

Quinn, James Brain. (1992). *The intelligent enterprise.* New York: Free Press.

Roos, Dan. (1995). "Virtual Enterprise in Agile Environment". In *Proceedings CALS Expo '95 Long Beach, CA.*

Sandoval V. (1985). Evolution de l'emploi d'information- France et OCDE. Paris: Transportation Department.

Sandoval, V. (1993). *CALS Introduction et mise en oeuvre.* Paris: Editions Hermès.

Sandoval, V. (1994a). *Computer Integrated Manufacturing in Japan.* Amsterdam: Elsevier Science.

Sandoval, V. (1994b). *Techniques de re-engineering.* Paris: Editions Hermès.

Stockfelt, Torbjorn. (1996). "Communication between Coach and Athlete". Special Lecture at the Winter Olympic Games, Norway, Lillehammer.

Takeuchi, Hirotaka, and Nonaka, Ikujiro. (1996). *The Knowledge-Creating Company: How Japanese Companies Create the Dynamics of Innovation.* Oxford: Oxford University Press.

Veltz, Pierre. (1996). Entreprise globale, Europe et le monde. Paris: PUF.

Waldner, J.B. (1990). *CIM, Nouvelle perspective de la production.* Paris: Dunod.

Warnecke, H.J. (1993). *The Fractal Company. A Revolution in Corporate Culture.* Berlin: Springer Verlag.

Wilson, A. (1993). "FCIM: Continuous process improvement". FCIM Journal, 1 (3).

3 VIRTUAL ENTERPRISE (VE) AND RELATED APPROACHES

3.1. Introduction

This chapter continues studying one central problem - the virtual enterprise (VE), as a fundamental point in our approach to concurrent enterprise. The first question studied concerns the definition of this new entity: What people do understand by *virtual enterprise*? What is its scope in businesses actually? Why we need to build such kind of entity? Is it for amusing or entertaining people? These questions are relevant if one does not know the real significance of VE and its scope and furthermore the its importance for businesses in the future. We present here a detailed examination of this new approach to enterprise. In addition, we study some other related cases and terminologies including a short presentation of fractal factory because of its implications in developing virtual worlds and its interfaces. We also presented the VE2006, an ambitious Japanese project with immediate consequences for Japanese business today and for all companies doing business with Japan, especially in Southeast Asia.

3.2. Towards a concept of VE

3.2.1. Definition

The virtual corporation presented by W.H. Davidow and Michael S. Malone (1993) is one of the first coherent studies focused on this question. But even if the authors offered a complete panorama of the virtual corporation, they did not discuss a clear definition or concept of it. Todays specialists and commentators use a similar expression - virtual enterprise. So the requirements set forward to support the VE have generated an emerging field of research and new technological development.

But, as in the case of the virtual corporation, there is no a clear definition of or common understanding about the concept. In general, VE is mostly associated with certain characteristics, with sources coming from agile manufacturing (AM) paradigm. In this last case, the ultimate expression of trust is the routine formation of virtual companies by groups of agile manufacturing enterprises. Often the quickest route to market a new product is to select organizational resources from different companies and then synthesize them into a single, electronic, business entity - a virtual company. If various distributed resources perform their business functions jointly, then a virtual company can behave as a single company dedicated to a particular project. As long as the market opportunity continues, the virtual company continues in existence. When the opportunity passes, the company dissolves, and its personnel turns into others projects. The ability to form virtual companies routinely is a powerful competitive weapon. Agility must ensure quality and costs (Goldman and Preiss, 1991).

Virtual enterprise has now become a common expression in Brussels's official vocabulary itself, in particular within the framework of the IV research and development program. In America, the last CALS Conference (Orlando, October, 1997) was centered on the virtual enterprise as a challenge for the twenty-first century, and in this particular case for the American manufacturing industry, as it is the case in the AM paradigm. In Japan within the framework of the CALS dissemination, the NIPON CALS Research Center is developing an important R&D program concerning this same topic (See Chapter 2).

Stimulated by these developments, one year ago, we sought to learn more about what people understand by VE. We did a simple survey in 1996 searching for an answer to this simple question: What is your definition of virtual enterprise, and its scope? Can you compare it with the existing enterprise? We selected some relevant answers to comment (all came from top-level scientists and ICT specialists). From this survey, we quote four definitions that illustrate some interesting feelings and perceptions about VE definition and scope.

3.2.2. Definition A
A VE is a model of a real (or conceived) enterprise that allows people to obtain useful insights into relevant aspects of that enterprise - for example, by simulation, analyzing the effect of changes, optimizing economical or technical parameters, and predicting behavior in future situations. Obviously, an enterprise can be modeled at various levels - strategic level, resource level, work plan level, product level, technical device level, and so on. Depending on what answers one wants to get from a VE, one has to choose the proper modeling level. So typically, a VE abstracts from details, which are deemed irrelevant for a given purpose.

3.2.3. Definition B (Dutch definition)
A virtual enterprise is a temporary enterprise (entity) that exists as a network of enterprises, that each pursues its own continuation and that for the duration of a project (or program) - in which market needs are satisfied by the development, production, and selling of products and services - closely cooperates and thereby intensively exchanges information.

A virtual enterprise is to be distinguished as a network organization and from supply chains. The network organization is defined from a single organization from where control and management originates (see Section 2.2). The extended enterprise, which is used in some studies, can be considered a network organization (with attention for shorter product life cycle, environmental liability, and interenterprise cooperation) (Ssee below).

3.2.4. Definition C (Finland)

A virtual enterprise is a model of enterprise that can produce a product or service whenever, wherever, in which ever form. It is a process which the best resources are gathered around the customer problem. It is managed by the customer and is dissolved when the project is over."

3.2.5. Definition D (Ireland)

A virtual enterprise is a project team comprising firms that are located independently from each other and that are bringing their diverse skills together for the purpose of completing a one-time (project based) or long-term (mission or strategic-alliance-based) aim. Examples are construction projects, the ESPRIT R&D project, marketing alliances.

3.2.6. MEI-VITAL definition

To these answers, we add a definition given in MEI-VITAL Project: Virtual Enterprise (VE) is defined as a temporary business-driven organization that is as flexible as possible to cope with project requirements such as schedule and cost, and where all trading partners should be involved in a local or global project as value-adding contributors and ideally should work concurrently. A virtual environment can exist only by the telematics networks link partners that are dispersed geographically but that belong to some productive entity. A productive entity is composed of many different components belonging to the different traditional companies in the classical sense.

Under this condition, a virtual enterprise can be considered also as a single company having geographically distributed sites. This means also that a single worker can be considered as an individual who fullly collaborates with the VE. So it is possible to extend to the concept of teleworking where each external employee or worker could be considered as an individual enterprise collaborating within a virtual enterprise. Going ahead in this reasoning, it is possible to reach an open question - the combination of the VE principle and the invariant principle of the fractals (see Section 3.4).

3.2.7. Summary defintion

To sum up, we can propose the next definition: A virtual enterprise is a temporary entity (materializing alliances) that exists through the telematic networks, and aims to share skills, resources, costs, and benefits to achieve one or more projects answering to the market opportunities for products and services. It allows geographically distributed sites and incorporates enterprises and departments of enterprises, whatever size they are, intocomponents for a given business in order to satisfy the customer needs. This definition allows us to build the concept of concurrent enterprise (see Chapter 6).

3.3. Characteristics, functions and bases of VE

3.3.1. Characteristics

Table 3.1. summarizes some characteristics and goals of VE, according to the different survey answers, as follows:

- Even if only one answer speaks clearly about simulation, most of the answers have it in mind.

- Most of the answers consider a VE to be a temporary entity.

- The goal is determined and precise. In general, it is a project.

This characterization resembles to that proposed by L. Camarinha-Matos, C. Lima and A.L. Osorio (1997). According to these authors, starting from the multiplicity of organizational variants, VE can be classified from many different perspectives. They consider the duration, configurations, and coordination as the three main characteristics describing VE. The report on agile manufacturing advanced already these points.

- *The duration.* For example, an alliance can be formed to participate in a single business opportunity and to dissolve when that objective is accomplished. On the other hand, the duration of an alliance must have a specific time span or continue for an indefinite number of business processes.

- *The configuration.* The network can follow a fixed structure or can be variable in the sense that the nonstrategic partners can join or leave the VE according to the phases of the business process. At the same time, the configuration determines the possibility of enterprise involvement in only a single or multiple VEs.

- *Coordination.* Regarding VE coordination, in some business sectors, there are only direct supplier and clients interactions. A VE coordinator must be identified, and delegation is single or multilevel.

We discuss some additional points. One of this is the virtual and real problem. One critic says that virtual exists, and is not virtual. VE exists in reality, but it exists only by electronic means, is supported by virtual telematic circuitries, and then follows the logic of this system rather than that of our real physical systems. So the virtuality extends from the networks to people working on common projects. This poses some crucial problems, such as those regarding interfaces and the redesign of the activities at different scales between companies. We do not study these problems because they are outside our purpose (in another working paper we are developing these points, especially principles and laws governing the new business spaces, generated by the ICT implementation and dissemination).

Another problem is that of the comparison between a VE enterprise and a real enterprise. VE is difficult to compare with a real enterprise. In a real enterprise, the accumulation of components is fixed for a longer period. In a virtual enterprise, the combination of parts is only temporary, in order to fulfill a specific task. Each part can overtake one or several tasks in the same way that departments in a normal company do. The configuration of the VE is done by a central institution, which has to find the best combination of parts according to the task. Some existing enterprises encompass such diverse skills and geographic locations that they are able to form virtual enterprises. However, such firms sometimes lose focus of their core competence.

Table 3.1. Some characteristics and goals (based on seven survey 7 answers).

Answer Number	Relevant Charateristics	Goals
1	Simulation tool	Optimization behavior
2	Temporary entity	Project
3	Temporary entity	Customer satisfaction
4	Virtual machine acts as a real one	Not clear
5	Temporary entity	Special task
6	Temporary entity, project team	Project
7	Temporary entity, distributed sites geographically, telematics links, networking groups	Project

Other point is the type of VE. There can be many different types according to the business opportunity, local conditions, duration, configuration and coordination, project concerns, and so on. Pushing ahead with this reasoning, we think some kind of VE algebra exists with these operations and operators and, maybe, in the near future this will be developed as business VE algebra to find the best temporary combination answering to the market demand in a given moment. This means simply the following. As VE exists because network links computers (based on computer, telecommunications, and multimedia, as a fundamentals, and using a appropriated content to be operational only within this context), then the virtual character is inherent to the networks and new business models are needed to perform in this new world.

We discuss more some preliminary points in Chapters 6 and 7. For instance, we give as an example a more pragmatic classification of VE. J. Vesterager, J. Tuxen, B.E. Danielsen and T.S. Frederiksen (1997) indicate the next two types of VE:

- Production facilities are selected from a network after an initial virtual enterprise has been established, and

- The virtual enterprise produces a limited amount of product types by means of a large but limited potential of production competencies.

Another point is the problem of the visibility or transparency of the information. This problem is quite similar to that studied in the case of shared enterprise (see Section 2.2). But here is maybe the more crucial one because the essential raw material (the input and the output of the system) is just information and information with more value added (see Section 1.3). Enterprises involved in a VE must exchange a part of their information to achieve their common goals, and support the VE functions. According to the specific role of the enterprise in VE, the problem is to separate what information will be a common asset and what not. But even this simple distinction is not always available or clear because people sharing information are, in normal circumstances, creating new information by definition. This is a natural process as T. Stockfelt (1991) underlines.

J. Vesterager and his colleagues Tuxen, Danielsen and Frederiksen, 1997, see VE as a mean to realize agile manufacturing. VE is to be perceived as a structured and well-considered constellation of parts from a network of traditional enterprises. The network has been established in order to fulfill a certain purpose. Each traditional enterprise contributes to the network with its specific core competencies (in the sense of Quinn's approach, see Section 2.3), and the network is to be seen as a potential from which different virtual enterprises can be established in order to satisfy diverse customer demands. As we see, it is quite similar to the SE (see Section 2.2).

When a customer demand meets the network, the necessary core competencies will be allocated by (following two stages) forming a virtual enterprise in order to fulfill the specific demand. The core competencies are thus forming a proper business product in the virtual enterprise, enabling the virtual enterprise to satisfy the customer demand in focus.

The network is a dynamic unit, while the virtual enterprise not, according to Vesterager. The network with its longer perspective of time will allow core competencies to leave or join, while core competencies, once selected, will have to remain in the virtual enterprise until the customer demand has been satisfied.

As mentioned the virtual enterprise is formed in two stages. First, an initial virtual enterprise is made responsible for meeting the customer demands in a constituent product and production specification considering the production capabilities in the network, but without choosing final production competencies. In the second stage, the final production places or competencies are chosen, which complete the specification merely considering own capabilities. For us, VE is a part of concurrent enterprise, so these steps are also available in what we called the concurrent enterprising process preparing to reach a concurrent enterprise state (Sandoval, 1997a).

3.3.2. Bases for VE

To be successful, a VE must be determined by the manner in which it is managed and put in relation the organization principles, the technology, and the skills. On these bases, we must be able to build the VE and, in a wider sense, virtual organizations. Figure 3.1. illustrates the bases of virtual organizations.

Organization. Processes such as network reengineering (we discuss more about this point in Chapters 6 and 7), automatization, management concerning suppliers of SMEs, and geographically delocalized subcontractor activities concerning the biggest companies become more and more important. In all these cases, companies are working supported by distributed telematics network. So this process conditions the best and more competitive organization structures. But for instance at least two factors are limiting this evolution: (1) the lack of expertise and the recognition of the existing virtual organization structures and (2) the support of technologies enabling the distributed cooperative work.

For example, the problems of integration between participants and information handling become the main factors for success of such project. Some undergoing researches try to solve these problems. The concept on integrated data environment (IDE) is one of them. IDE aims to build integrated environments allowing the different participants to access, exchange and handle information and to create the historical data repository of the projects and the elimination of redundancies. Other solutions proposed are technologies enabling agile manufacturing (TEAM). The starting point is here the lack of connection between, on the one hand, the local industry of research and innovation and, on the other hand, the manufacturing industry (at a world-class level), which should enable the results reached by the first, to be incorporated at the rigth time.

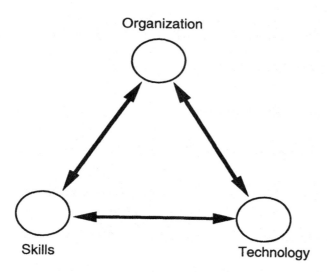

Figure 3.1. Bases for VE.

Technology. To create VE, we must integrate in a good manner the different participants. But these last are normally located in a geographic areas very different, often far one each other. Other point is interesting: the participant does not, necessarily, belong to the same company and have different cultures and, at the same time, the volume of information to be exchange is continuously increasing. Tools, technologies and information networks must help to reach an optimal sharing of the handling and exchange of the information concerning products design and manufacturing given by different partners involved.

For example, companies must use technical and commercial data exchanges as a key element for competitiveness. The impact can be appreciated in terms of time reduction at every step and at every established link, errors elimination or reduction, ROI acceleration, and a better consideration for real consumer's needs. Then to domesticate the technology, particularly, that concerning data exchange, becomes an important strategic issue.

Skills. Following our definition of VE, we can consider some consequences at the skill level. The main thing is to contribute skills and know-how. If you do not want to do this, you cannot go ahead in this field.

Telematic networks (*telematics* refers to the largest set of networks, including Internet, Intranets and Extranets) are a key point for VE and can also be a formidable tool for reducing isolation, and integrating enterprises. But habits and behaviors need to change. In fact, the work is more and more founded on collaboration. To share skills to solve a particular problem does not always means investing in heavy restructuring. This is one of the savings generated by VE: a group sometimes does something faster and better than a sum up of individual personalities and therefore contributes with more value added. We would like to underline this point: it is a typical case of the laws operating in digital spaces.

But this maxim has sometimes severe drawbacks such as the flatten of hierarchies, and the development of small groups that are more flexible about sharing resources across the networks and then getting more value. The secular barriers disappear, the hierarchies explode, and each one contributes with its own skills. As a result, young people are adapting rapidly than old people living with old habits and are able to respond with more creativity, simultaneily and consensus.

3.4. Illustration of the VE concept

This section presents some illustrations of the above conceptual development - some scenarios for car design and manufacturing.

Eric Ross (1994) considers agile manufacturing as a cooperative approach to achieve rapidity, flexibility, quality, innovation, and efficiency. Rapidity includes quick product realization, introduction, and delivery, product change, customization, and upgrade. Flexibility is the ability to produce any product rapidly and economically, in any lot size, from a range of possibilities. Quality means meeting specifications and expectations. Innovation is the ability to be first with the best new product.

Ross proposes scenarios for creating virtual companies that become agiles enterprises that in turn become VE. He starts with a case of a client seat in a car test. To perform agile manufacturing, an enterprise must be optimizing for an actual opportunity. With the best resources, success depends on the skills, knowledge, and expertise of its workforce. But the configuration for an optimal business is different according to the situation.

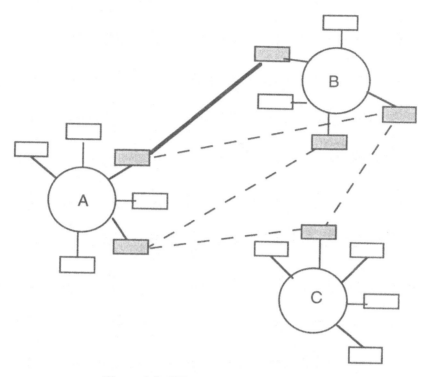

Figure 3.2. VE: market opportunity 1

For example, several companies decide to work together to pursue some opportunity. Figure 3.2. represent the functions of each company. For the first business opportunity the companies form a virtual enterprise (a temporary, intercompany organization, working as an entity for a specific mission) using the shaded functions from various partners. These decisions be made at the beginning of the business or could evolve. This configuration must optimize rapidity, flexibility, quality, cost, and so succeed.

If another opportunity appears for these companies (and for others also), the same firms can choose to pursue it. For technical or other reasons, they form a different virtual company (see Figure 3.3.). But virtual partners can change the partners for different configurations of a basic product line (in the case of Figure 3.3., company D is added to this business). From all this, Ross concludes that this a reconfigurable enterprise that enables formation of virtual companies to pursue specific opportunities. But one key requirement for the success of this paradigm is the exchange of technical information (or sharing information). Any environment involving different companies with different information systems needs a strategy, standards, and approaches for interpretability.

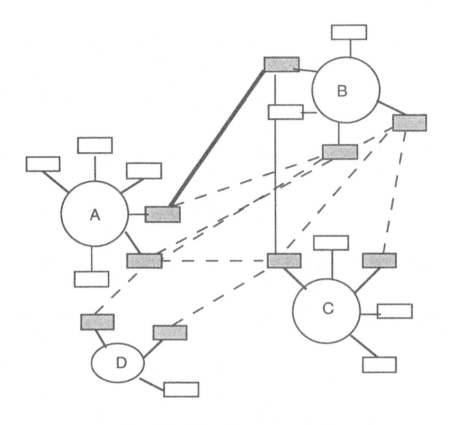

Figure 3.3. VE: market opportunity 2

These scenarios will be realized only if an adaptation capacity exists for producing and delivering quickly and economically whatever the consumer chooses. This requires an extreme flexibility, an efficient productive unity, supported by a technical interpretable information and complete integration. In this way, companies can be able to answer to the increasing market pressures (see Section 1.2).

To overcome the increasing complexity of the consumer's needs and perceptions, to deliver adequate products to the market, and to change rapidly keeping a minimal quantity at the lowest cost, companies must continue to improve their operational level. Traditionally, this improvement is concentrated on the single or separated functions of the company and on the process concerning these functions, the classical panacea being the BPR (we discuss BPR in Chapter 7). But it contributes to creating an even more complex cross-relations and making management and agility very difficult. This kind of organization finishes by constraining rather than advantaging business. So a better strategy is to improve the cross-functional activities.

Interactions between functions and organizations are often linked to the information and material flows. In all cases, the material flow has a corresponding information flow (Sandoval, 1989 and 1995) (as in the Platonic relation between a person and a shadow reflecting on the walls of a cave). But this last flow is much more complex that the first, and, in general, it is not simply linear as material flow. This problem is a typical of what we call virtual logistics: in fact, virtual logistics allows us to understand this environment, to set up the problems and to search for solutions. Information flows are normally three characteristics - they are sequential, parallel and concurrent - and these three characteristics are, unfortunately, present simultaneously most of the time. The question is how to model such a problem and how to solve it.

In reality, information, processes, and systems, which manage information, are different. Data can have a manual presentation (paper, microfilm) or electronic (in computer memories, or disks), and the systems running and managing this information can be specialized desktops, messages traveling according to the work progress, different kind of computers, and so on. If manual information can be easy to understand by human operators, it can be lost or deteriorated. Electronic information can manage these processes better, but it is not shareable by heterogeneous computer system and must be reformatted every time or even recreated to be useful in operational desktops.

3.4.1. Towards data integration

Data integration has been a problem for many years, particularly for industries managing thousands if not millions of engineering references. Until recently, computers were enable to exchange information what contributed to create a large number of information islands. One attempt to solve this problem is the CALS initiative, launched by the U.S. Department of Defense in 1986. The CALS goals are then to reduce costs, improve quality, and reduce development time of products by automating and integrating information. The main bases of this concept as follows:

- To enter information one time and to use it many times,

- To use this information throughout the lifecycle product for every manufactured good,

- To permit the cooperative work on the functions and processes (the typical example being concurrent engineering) (to be studied in Chapter 4) that are necessary for creating more competitive industrial systems, and

- To create transparent system for interfacing and accessing information, and

- To access, configure and manage the workflow.

3.4.2. Management

As management rules, Vesterager, Tuxen, Danielsen and Frederiksen (1997), studying one particular application, propose the following:

- The late selection of production competencies offers advantage because production facilities can be selected based on more detailed (constituent) knowledge about the product, thus allowing the VE to optimize the choice of the production competencies. But to secure concurrent engineering, the initial VE has to consider the critical circumstances of the production competencies.

Due to the temporary nature of the VE, a basic foundation of shared experiences, which can facilitate traditional concurrent engineering, may not exist. By means of a proper structuring of the specification, a degree of concurrent engineering can take place between the initial virtual and the potential of production competencies, thus enabling concurrent engineering despite a lack of collaborative experience. These rules can help to overcome this difficulty (already indicated in Section 3.2.).

- The fact that core competencies can join and leave the network has an important application (see Chapter 2, Sections 2 and 2 and 3). The late selection of production competencies (facilities) means that a particular production competency may have joined or left the network at the time the selection took place, but after the initial specifications have been made. It may be necessary to reduce this complexity by imposing a limit on the potential production competencies and product types that are taken into consideration.

Vesterager, Tuxen, Danielsen and Frederiksen (1997) define the terms *constituent product* and *constituent production* specification - together called *constituent specification* - for structuring of product and production specification:

- *constituent product specification.* Sufficient specification of conditions about a product's functional and geometrical or structural properties take into consideration customer demands, production engineering, and a possible functional and geometrical context of the product,

- *constituent production specification.* Sufficient specification of conditions regarding production so that the total specifications to be completed by the production competencies meeting the constituent production specification.

That means constituent specification conditions are to be specified only if they are relevant in satisfying the customer demand. This ensures that customer demands are met and that conditions critical for production competencies are maintained. The constituent conditions are formed by the initial VE. But the detailed product and production specifications are handled by the selected competencies. These competencies pass along knowledge about the detailed constraints of the production competencies (see Figure 3.4.) They assist constituent specifications by means of domain models to demonstrate the critical sufficient knowledge. The semantics in domain models are defined by means of feature technology combined with the CIM-OSA dimension of genericity. As a result, we have particular, partial, and generic features. Partial features are used for knowledge integration between core competencies, facilitating the communication of sufficient knowledge between the potential production competencies and the initial virtual, and allowing specification generic features to be used for the description of more basic and general conditions to enable concurrent engineering (see Chapter 4).

3.5 Related cases

This section present some VE: related cases and terminology.

3.5.1. The case of the Virtual Factory (VF) framework

According to A.M Stanescu, I. Dumitrache and A. Curaj (1997), the concept of VF envisions a virtual environment in which a closed-loop manufacturing process controls software system and scenarios can be successfully tested and executed without using the actual manufacturing equipment. The control software interacts with a suite of software modules that accurately simulate both factory equipment and manufacturing processes within the system. VF is defined as a system of software models and applications that perform both process management and resources management according to the multifacet production representation. A suite of simulation tools is necessary to emulate all functions of the real factory.

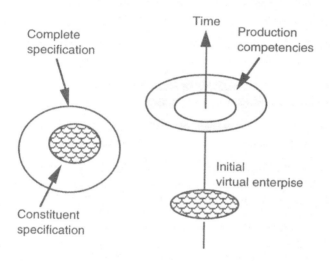

Figure 3.4. Constituent and complete specifications established by virtual enterprise.

The automation system is the integration platform-based system that maps the virtual manufacturing processes, ordered by the scheduled plan, into a spatiotemporal activity pattern. It works according to an optimum dynamic task allocation of manufacturing resources.

Physical factory is the programmable manufacturing system, comprising the heterogeneous resources - the producers set, tools set, movers set, carriers set, storage set, human set, the working-in-progress parts set.

This system must take into account a set of requirements for advanced control manufacturing system. Among these we have the robustness to preserve the structural proprieties of DEVs in the presence of internal disturbances or the decision support system autonomy to improve the role of cooperative multiagent systems within a synergetic framework of advanced manufacturing concurrent enterprise (see Chapters 4 and 7).

3.5.2. The Case of the extended enterprise in the aerospace industry

The Cranfield extended enterprise model was used to provide the organization concept of the aerospace multi-tier supplier network. Extended enterprise is a concept of manufacturing business operations that looks at all the participants in the manufacturing of a product. Extended enterprise is often associated with VE. The product owner designs, markets, and bears the ultimate responsibility for the product. It works together with supplying partners that supply the subassembly, components, and particular process integrating the manufacturing of the product. The extended enterprise is distinct from the conventional subcontracting in the sense the extent of information flows that facilitates the tightening of the manufacturing design and production (see Section 2.2). The opportunities for using partners specialized skills and knowledge in enhancing the design of the new products are very large. The supplying partners own the product and are at the forefront of their particular field of expertise. The grouping between the product owner and the supplying partners may change with different product , depending on the skill and cost mix. But the requirement for dynamic grouping of business partners places a heavy demand on the information flow, communications and standards. The impact covers information access and security, finance and responsibility sharing, together with a host of business issues as well as the technical problems involved.

3.5.3. The case of virtual enterprise 2006 (VE2006) (Japan)

In Japan, there exists an advanced project called Virtual Enterprise 2006 (VE2006). Demonstrations of VE2006 show the advantages and the limits of the existing technologies to build VE, particularly concerning the automobile and construction industries. But VE2006 will be also applied to the health care and education industries. We present some developments of the VE2006 prototype. The present objective of VE2006 is to formally describe the automobile minor-change model and, based on the formal description made for the common model among task groups, to control the business model (demonstration scenario) and to adjust of interfaces (process model and data model). These developments concern principally the business model using IDEF0, the configuration management and time management and the network management project. VE2006 is based on CALS-related technologies. Figure 3.5. gives a general view of VE2006 and its related components.

VE2006 Business Model using IDEF0 was presented by Naotsugu Hirata and Shunji Kido (1996). VE2006 supports the implementation of a smooth process operation. IDEF0 is used to express the business processes of automobile minor-change and arrange its information streams. IDEF0 is a process modeling method used to analyze a system. CALS is a concept for broadening efficiency between related enterprises that requires good communication among members in various fields. IDEF0 searches to harmonize a top-down model built with IDEF0, which envisions the future of VE.2006, with bottom-up models received from the implementors. But the full implementation of top-down model (ideal solution) under current conditions is almost impossible because of the constraints of platform, time, cost, and a lack of information on the business model. In addition, IDEF has not yet a welknown method among VE2006 members.

The role is to establish a fictitious division that manages product data and project schedule, in a carmaker and a lampmaker, through tusing today's computer environment and available computer systems. The scenario for demonstration is a visualized concurrent process of creating the engineering change proposal in the carmaker and the lampmaker based on the existing data. The solution of the integration problems arising during implementation of PDM (product data management) systems, a time-management system and television conference system are then essentials.

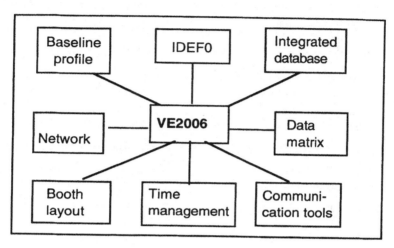

Figure 3.5. VE2006 view.

A prototype system of configuration management and time management as a virtual enterprise in 2006 was implemented. Problems are addressed that arise during implementation of PDM (product data management) systems, a time-management system, and television conference system. To realize complex and temporally limited management structures during the whole lifecycle of product data, at this time, IDEFO was introduced to describe the life cycle. The analysis of workflow was left unfinished.

3.5.4. Fractal factory case

The concept of the fractal factory was developed and introduced by IPA (Germany) as a contribution to researching new corporate paradigms. For H.J. Warnecke, R. Rupprecht and M. Kahmeyer (1995), the concept of the fractal factory is based on the common understanding that global markets as well as corporate structures and processes have grown too complex to be deterministically modeled and planned; in global competitive environments, manufacturing is never deterministic. The concept was presented by H.J. Warnecke (1993). The IPA construction begun by developing a model for corporate reengineering based on a reflection of nature incorporating a variety of fundamental theories from mathematics and, in particular, chaos research. Corporate structures and processes have been screened on the basis of fractal geometry, developed by B. Maldelbrot (1982).

Following B. Maldelbrot (1977), a fractal object is an object whose dimension is not a whole number and whose properties or some properties depend on the dimension. An object whose geometry can be described by a noninteger dimension is known simply as a fractal. Hugely complex shapes could be described in terms of

62

their appearance only, which means using some kind of cartography - for example, lungs, clouds, rocky coastlines, mountains, blood vessels, plant root, and so on. Nature's complex structures typically consist of a set of basic structural elements-so-called fractals. Figure 3.6. illustrates self-similar product fractals with standards interfaces.

In the case of factory, a fractal is an independently acting corporate entity whose goals and performance can be precisely described. Inspired from fractal theory fundamentals, the principles of the fractal factory are self-similarity, self-organization, and self-optimization. These principles are defined as follows:

- Fractals are self-similar (self-similarity is the property of a part of an object being exactly similar to the object itself), each one performs services.

- Fractals practice self-organization, oppressively as well as tactically and strategically. Fractals therefore restructure, regenerate, and dissolve themselves.

- The system of goals of individual fractals is free from contradictions and must serve the objective of achieving corporate goals.

- Fractals are networked via an efficient information and communication system.

- The performance of fractals is subject to constant assessment and evaluation.

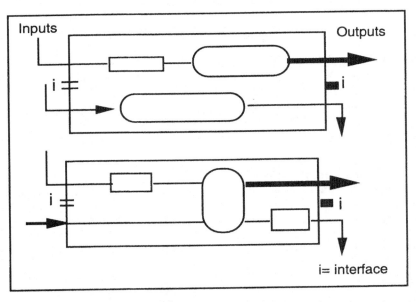

Figure 3.6. Self-similar product fractals with standard interfaces.

3.5.5. Fractal product design
Ideally, the principles of the fractal factory are to be transferred to both the design process and the actual product structure. Along with the principles of the fractal

factory, the design process will be performed by self-similar fractals, which coexist, self-organizing and self-optimizing to achieve a common goal, customer satisfaction. As we define a fractal factory, we can define a fractal product design. A product fractal is an independent module with a precisely defined functionality. Product fractals are self-similar when standardized mechanical and informational interfaces intervene. The design team of each product fractal determines and optimizes technological solutions to its function to achieve the corporate goals of overall product improvement.

In addition to that, we can underline that fractals can also be applied to management considering company as a complex system. According to Margaret Wheatley (1992), the best organizations have a fractal dimension. Observing such organizations, we can say what are its values, how business is conducted, and so on just looking at one person in this company. There exists some coherence and some predictability in behaviors. These developments are the implications of the virtual organizations, but the constructions are, probably, more simple than we imagine.

But we can envision applying the fractal theory to the business - namely, to the configuration or reconfiguration of alliances between companies. In this case, we can combine the fractals with the idea of fragile objects advanced by Pierre Gilles de Gennes (1994). The problem here is to find a good combination of the fractals's invariant principle and the forces acting to attract or repell objects in nature. To do this, we can use one (+, -) alphabet. Companies or parts of companies having (+) proprieties must attract and organize a new partnership. Others cannot do this successfully. This is one of the many issues to be explore in the field of VE.

References

Camarinha-Matos L., Lima C. and Osorio A.L. (1997). "The PRODNET Platform for Production Planning and Management in Virtual Enterprises". In *Proceedings of fourth International Conference on Concurrrent Enterprising ICE'9, Nottingham* Nottingham, UK.

Davidow William H. and Michael S. Malone. (1993). *The virtual coportation*. New York: Harper Business.

De Gennes, Pierre-Gilles. (1994). *Les objets fragiles,*. Paris: Plon.

Goldman, Steve, and Kenneth Preiss. (1991). *The Twenty-first Century Manufacturing Enterprise Strategy*. Project vol.1. Bethlehem, PA : Iacocca Institute.

Hammer M. and J. Champy. (1993). *Reenginering Corporation*. New York: Harper Busines.

Hirata Naotsugu and Shunji Kido. (1996). "VE2006 Business Model Using IDEF0". In *Proccedings of CALS Pacific Tokyo* , Tokyo.

Maldelbrot B. (1977). *Fractal, Form, Chance and Dimension*. San Francisco: Freeman.

Mandelbrot B. (1982). *The Fractal Geometry of Nature*. W.H. Freeman and Company, San Francisco.

Ross, ERIC. (1994). "Agile Manufacturing, CALS and Automative Excellence". *CALS/Integration Journal*, 3(3), p.24-28.

Sandoval V. (1989). *EDI pour l'entrepris. Paris:* Editions Hermès.

Sandoval V. (1995). "Virtual Logistics in Virtual Enterprises". In *Proceeding ICE'95, Stockholm*, Stockholm.

Sandoval V. (1997a). "Concurrent Enterprising Process". In *Proceedings of fourth International Conference on Concurrrent Enterprising ICE'9, Nottingham*. Nottingham, UK.

Sandoval V. (1997b). "Feeling and Defining Virtual Enterprise" Report sent to Directorate IIII (DGIII) (Brussels).

Santoro, Roberto. (1997). "Virtual Vertical Enterprise (VIVE)". In *Proceedings of fourth International Conference on Concurrrent Enterprising ICE'9, Nottingham*. Nottingham, UK.

Stanescu A.M, I. Dumitrache, and A. Curaj. (1997). "Multi-mode based System Design with Virtual Factory Synergetic Framework". In *Proceedings of fourth International Conference on Concurrrent Enterprising ICE'9, Nottingham*. Nottingham, UK.

Stockfelt, Torbjorn. (1991). *La Pedagogia de la vida del trabajo*. Stockholm: ALP-Latin, Pedagogiska Institutionnen, Stockholm University.

Vesterager J., J. Tuxen, B. Danielsen, and T.. Frederiksen. (1997). "Concurrent Engineering in the Virtual Enterprise". In *Proceedings of fourth International Conference on Concurrrent Enterprising ICE'9, Nottingham*. Nottingham, UK.

Warnecke H.J. (1993). *The fractal company. A Revolution in Corporate Culture*. Berlin: Springer.

Warnecke H.J., R. Rupprecht, and M. Kahmeyer. (1995). "Fractal Product Design : a Product Reengineering Approach". In *Proceedings of ILCE'95, Concurrent Engineering and Technical Information Processing, Paris*. Paris

Wheatley Margaret. (1992). *Leadership and the new science*. San Franbcisco: Berret-Koehler.

4 CONCURRENT ENGINEERING (CE)

4.1. Introduction

As concurrent engineering (CE) is an essential aspect in concurrent enterprise paradigm, we study this approach separately (see Section 4.5 and Chapter 7). The CE, in its operational implementation, involves technical, organizational, and cultural changes. Collaborative attitude, concurrent activities, new information, and communication technologies constitute fundamental enablers for this implementation challenge. Thus, CE is an enabler of concurrent enterprise. Otherwise, there is a need to characterize specific concurrent engineering implementation requirements with the classification of methods, techniques and tools available today on the market.

This chapter defines CE, identifies industrial motivations, and shows how to support multidisciplinary teams, concurrent activities, and people interactions - or, more generally speaking collaborative work. It is also assesses the suitability of existing methods, information technology (IT), and tools and presents some issues of CE-related RTD ESPRIT projects (ESPRIT is an R&D program funded by the European Union). It concludes by identifying further development needs for supporting a CE implementation across company boundaries.

4.2. Definition and motivations

4.2.1. Definition

Several names and definitions have been given to what we used to call concurrent engineering (CE), such as simultaneous engineering, parallel engineering, and integrated engineering. Those multiple names and definitions did not contribute to a clear and common understanding of the CE approach and its concepts. Parallel engineering is certainly the worst example and has introduced a complete misunderstanding about the real objective, as people thought they were already practicing CE in developing subsystems in parallel. So instead of reinventing each time a new definition, we decided, at the European Society for Concurrent Engineering, to reuse the following existing and sufficiently precise definition that

66

has been published by the Institute for Defense Analysis in 1988 (Winner; Pennell; Bertrand; and Slusarczuk; 1988):

Concurrent engineering is a systematic approach to the integrated, concurrent design of products and their related processes, including manufacturing and support. This approach is intended to allow developers from the outset to consider all elements of the product life cycle from conception through disposal, including quality, cost, schedule, and user requirements.

This definition highlights two very interesting concepts. The first one is to design concurrently a product and its related processes, which was a revolution at a time when development activities were organized in designing processes only after product design approval. The second one is the product life cycle vision at the earlier stage of a project, which reflected the customer satisfaction objective as customers more and more considered the global product cost (cost to buy and cost to use). From this definition, implementing CE means that it is mandatory to reorganize the product development process in defining concurrent activities between product and processes design. Furthermore, disciplines have to operate together and not each one after the other, in a collaborative way, for satisfying to all the requirements induced by the entire product life cycle and project objectives in a consistent way.

It also is interesting to note that operating concurrently means working together for achieving a common goal. With CE, product development does not any more rhyme with product performance but much more with product and processes performance. CE should be considered as a new product development strategy for reaching a global performance that will satisfy both customers and shareholders.

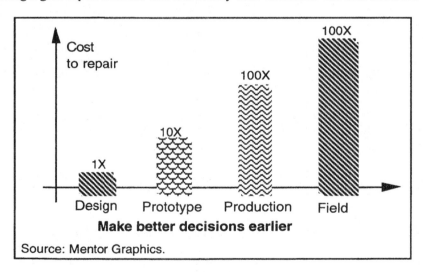

Figure 4.1. Cost to repair.

It is not easy to explain why activities belonging to a development process were sequential rather than concurrent. There are well-known roots, such as Taylorization, costs commitment, departmental budgets, and hierarchical organizations that have sufficiently influenced the organization of product development processes.

Furthermore, the company culture was seen as a kingdom, and the castle or black-box effect led for people who were competing with each other rather than collaborating. A company set an organization before defining any processes, and that further explains why improvements were based on departmental performance rather than on the global product development process or customer satisfaction.

4.2.2. Motivations

The main motivation is certainly to satisfy customers by delivering products just in time and by meeting user needs and requirements, free of bugs, not costly to buy and use (see Chapter 1, section 1.2, and Chapter 2, sections 2.2, 2.3). The other key motivation is to satisfy shareholders by increasing profits by decreasing product development costs, lead time, and recurrent costs and by increasing business due to a better customer satisfaction. Some simple graphic figures are effective in explaining the situation.

Developers know perfectly well how costly late changes can be (see Figure 4.1.). Changes during the design stage do not cost as much and are necessary to obtain a good maturity of both the product and its processes design. But then, during processes application - such as tests, manufacturing, and assembly - the cost of changes (from this stage also called late changes) is increasing considerably as there are many more folders and documents to update and components already produced to modify. Furthermore, it delays product delivery and the entire product development process. At the end, when products are in the field, the cost of changes dramatically increases while customer confidence and satisfaction decrease. Applying a traditional sequential product development process implies that developers discover problems each one after the other, and consequently the number of late changes is considerable. Applying CE in designing concurrently a product and its processes allows developers to discover problems at the design stage and consequently to avoid most late changes. Fewer late changes mean reduction of development cost as well as lead time, while it improves the overall product quality level.

McKinsey & Co. studied (see Figure 4.2.) the respective impact of development cost overrun, higher product cost, and delayed product delivery on the loss in total profit. This study did not consider one-of-a-kind product industrial sector, such as large scale engineering and construction, but much more mass production, such as automotive and electronic goods. It shows clearly that time to market is of paramount importance and that delaying product delivery could be a real disaster due to a 33 percent loss in total profit. Product cost is also an important parameter, representing about 22 percent of loss in total profit, as it is a recurrent cost, and that further explains why optimizing components acquisition cost as well as processes cost, such as testing, manufacturing, and assembly, is necessary.

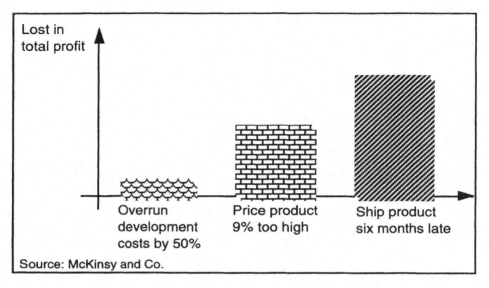

Figure 4.2. Loss in total profit.

In this case, the product development cost overrun is not as critical because it was for mass production, but in the case of one-of-a-kind it is an important parameter because it is equivalent to the real product cost (see Figure 4.3.).

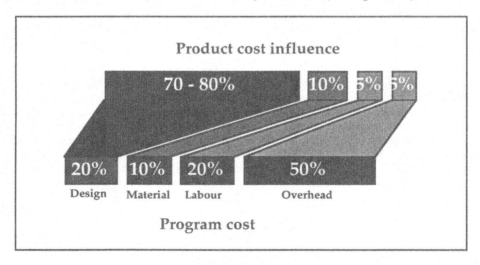

Figure 4.3. Product cost influence.

On the one hand, it is interesting to consider that design can fix between 70 to 80 percent of the product cost, while design activity represents only 20 percent of the total program cost. On the other hand, project overhead is fixes only about 5 percent of the product cost while it costs about 50 percent of the total program cost. Based on those cost considerations, applying CE to decrease project overhead (by reducing dramatically the number of late changes) and decrease product cost (by designing concurrently a product and its processes) makes sense.

The last consideration takes place in Figure 4.4., where it clearly appears that the window for cost-reduction opportunities is open only during the early stages of a project. It further explains why it is so important to design concurrently a product and its processes to have the necessary knowledge for determining the life-cycle cost. Early collaboration between developers, whose expertise is requested by the product life cycle, leads to better decisions that contribute to dramatically reduce both product cost and development lead time.

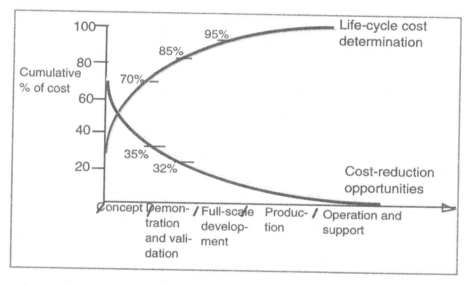

Figure 4.4. Life-cycle cost determination against cost-reduction opportunities.

4.3. CE implementation needs

Even if the definition of CE is purely common sense, it does not mean that it is simple to achieve. A full-scale CE implementation implies the following:

- Restructuring the entire product-development process by organizing concurrent activities on the basis of interaction needs between disciplines;

- Creating multidisciplinary teams on the basis of requested expertise by the product life cycle and fostering a collaborative attitude;

- Providing new development methods, techniques, and tools that allow developers to interact with each other - in other words, to support concurrent activities or, more generically, collaborative work.

This is a synthesis based on the three interrelated layers that are necessary for a successful implementation of any new approach or technology:

- An activity process,

- Personnel organization and behavior, and

- Technology support.

It is necessary to operate on these three layers because any activity process needs to be improved when a new approach or a new technology is going to be implemented to make full advantage of this change. After improving the activity process, it is mandatory to adapt personnel organization to fit with the new process requirements. Then the technology support (methods, techniques and tools) should also be adapted accordingly to the new process and organization requirements. This last layer is an important one as it makes things more practical. Otherwise, without adapted technical support any change may stay too theoretical and consequently not practical.

4.3.1. CE scope considerations

In the past most CE implementation cases have been experiments between different departments of a single company within a single geographical site. But today most companies do business within projects in partnership where developers are not colocated on the same geographical site. Even more, when involving supplier expertise, subcontractors and users in a multidisciplinary team, it becomes impossible to colocate them as they are operating from geographically dispersed sites. During projects in partnership, the efficiency of the global business process is unfortunately not equal to the sum of each company's process efficiency. The efficiency of the global process is much more dependent on how company processes will interrelate and people will collaborate (Pallot, 1994): the sum of optimum local solutions does not constitute the optimum global solution. As Jim Barkdale, CEO of Netscape Corporation says "The value created is greater than the sum of the parts involved in its generation." We called this the Netscape law.

Consequently, it is obvious that CE should be implemented across company boundaries within the extended or virtual enterprise, covering business process activities of the entire value chain (Pallot, 1993). For more details on VE see Chapter 3.

As illustrated in Figure 4.5., CE implementation across company boundaries implies structuring a coherent global development process where trading partners specify how and where they have to interact together. Concurrent activities are designed for supporting collaborative work during interactions between different disciplines that may involve several trading partners. It should be noted that the first level of interaction needs relies on knowledge sharing and mutual understanding of concepts between experts (collaborative work). The second level is the necessary interoperability between processes, which is materialized by concurrent activities, while the third level relies on interoperability of tools and platforms.

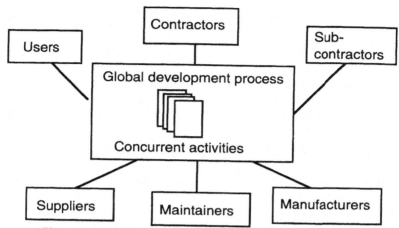

Figure 4.5. CE implementation across company boundaries.

Figure 4.6. is an illustration of the interaction needs between different disciplines, such as system, electrical and mechanical engineering for product design, and test, manufacturing and support engineering for processes design. For each subsystem or part of the product, there is a multidisciplinary team composed of experts required by the subsystem or part life cycle. Each expert could be a member of different teams, depending on its own workload, in the same project or in different projects. Interactions between people are necessary either in the same team or between different teams, depending on the common properties they are sharing (suc as weight, volume, or thermal dissipation).

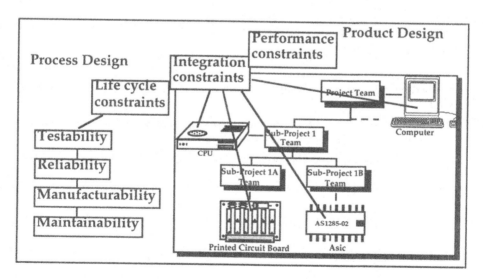

Figure 4.6. Interaction needs between disciplines.

Another important aspect of CE scope is that its concepts are focused not only on product creation and innovation but also on creating innovative processes (that is new manufacturing or assembly techniques) that allow decreasing recurrent costs.

4.3.2. Capability assessment method for CE

What to do? How to migrate from traditional engineering toward concurrent engineering? What are the objectives? What are the criteria and priorities? How can the current situation of this development be assessed? And how can possible scenarios of progress be evaluated?

Several capability assessment methods exist today, and most of them are based on the five maturity levels of the software development process defined by the SEI (Software Engineering Institute, USA). These are RACE (CE Readiness Assessment) created by the CERC (CE Research Center, USA) (CERC, 1992), and extended RACE models such as AECE by the Eindhoven University of Technology (Deg, 1994) and RACENT by the CENT ESPRIT project. Other assessment methodologies focus on the innovative climate and the organizational values for the CE development practice (Bergman, 1995).

This kind of capability assessment method should be considered as vital to identifying and planning an appropriate strategy of CE implementation including organizational and cultural change. Furthermore, it convinces employees and the chief executive to make a rational analysis of the current situation and support clear objectives toward the targeted situation.

Past experiments have demonstrated the influence of the three layers (activity process, personnel organization and behavior, and technology support) on full implementation of capabilities. I also strongly recommend avoiding the use of weak definitions of maturity levels such as "advance tools", which does not mean anything due to time progress and mixing incompatible criteria on a same chart. The best solution for a clear picture is to overlap the three layers in order to check whether capabilities are coupled in a coherent way.

Figure 4.7 shows a capability assessment chart using two overlapped layers that provides the following:

- An overview of the product development working methods and IT support tools applied by a project team during the operational work based on specific level evaluation;

- An evaluation of the coherence between working methods and IT support tools (strategic and tactical point of view); and

- Different possible improvements for implementing CE from the current situation.

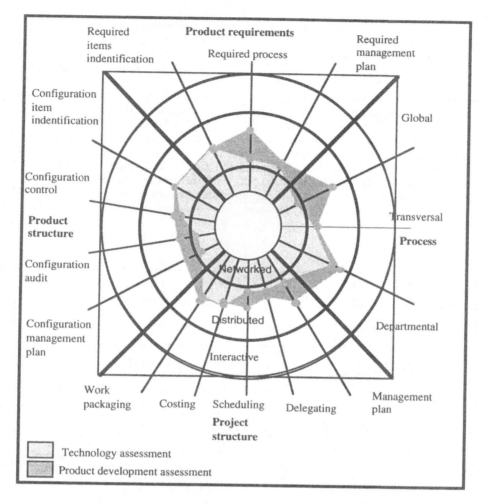

Figure 4.7. Capability assessment chart using two overlapped layers.

This assessment technique could also be used as a product development benchmarking application or as a way to compare different situations met within different industrial sectors.

4.3.3. Activity process modeling and analysis

How to model and analyze the current or as-is process development is a logical need where existing process modeling techniques and tools, such as IDEF0 (Integrated DEFinition), satisfy part of the requirements. How showed opportunities for improvement be identified to defined the targeted or to-be process? A subtle combination of assessment methodology and modeling technique could allow this. Regarding process activities considerations, it is possible to state that CE should be implemented using a BPR (business process reengineering) approach where the challenge consists of identifying, defining and implementing concurrent activities (Pallot, 1994).

The name IDEF originates from the U.S. Air Force program for integrated computer-aided manufacturing (ICAM) from which the first IDEF definition emerged as ICAM DEFinition language. Then, with an expanded focus and widespread use as part of concurrent engineering, total quality management, and business-reengineering initiatives during the IICE program (information integration for CE), the IDEF acronym has changed to Integrated DEFinition language. Doug Ross is the creator of IDEF0 functional modeling - activity or process centered analysis. IDEF0 includes three different types of diagram (see Figure 4.8.) - namely, context diagram, decomposition diagram, and finally tree structure diagram. The context diagram defines the starting point of the process to be charted, then decomposition diagrams are used to represent the different levels of activities, and the tree structure diagram is the navigator between the different levels of decomposition.

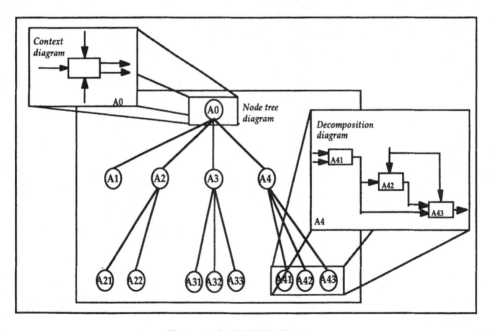

Figure 4.8. IDEF0 diagrams.

IDEF0 is based on ICOM labels (see Figure 4.9.):

1. Input is transformed by an activity.

2. Output is produced by or results from an activity.

3. Mechanisms are the resources (person, facility, machine, or other agent) performing the activity.

4. Control describes rules to apply during an activity, but it is not transformed by it.

Comparing the needs for process capture and characterization in a case of CE implementation with the IDEF0 process modeling technique, it appears that IDEF0 does not satisfy to all the needs. Nevertheless, IDEF0 is widely used in industry as a de facto standard for process modeling and constitutes a good basis on which to add complementary capabilities for CE implementation needs.

Most of the problems encountered so far are consequent to the IDEF0 macroscopic, static and synthetic view of the process model.

What are the problems encountered in process modeling?

First of all, people should be able to understand easily the process model, and with such a simplified approach, some aspects and drawing components are missed to face reality. In fact, the IDEF0 process modeling technique is certainly the simpler and more efficient modeling technique today for specifying activities and its related information flow, including feedback loop mechanism from one activity to other.

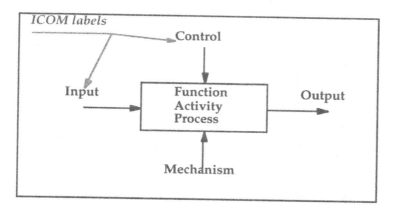

Figure 4.9. ICOM labels.

But IDEF0 does not allow specifying the activity starting and ending conditions or the events that occur when people apply the process model. IDEF0 experts would answer that ICOMs rules condition the activities and strictly follow the IDEF0 principles. But if we consider an activity at the upper level (context diagram) and then its subprocess and related activities at the lower levels (decomposition diagrams), applying the ICOMs conditioning rules will lock the lower activities until all the conditions will not be satisfied on the upper level. This kind of problem reflects exactly the traditional sequential process that has been applied during many years following the Taylorization of activities.

Second, CE means replacing sequential activities by parallel activities but by concurrent activities. This particular type of activity is much more difficult to identify and model precisely. The IDEF0 process modeling allows the specifying of traditional sequential and parallel activities. Nevertheless, if a process addresses the specification of concurrent activities, some complex iteration mechanism need, and constraint consistency capabilities, then IDEF0 appears as a limited modeling technique. In fact, IDEF0 does not provide such important capabilities covering (for example) CE implementation requirements.

Third, do not beleive a model is a realistic view. Most of the process modeling experimentations have shown difficulties in adhering to the reality of the current process. During the modeling stages, participants are slowly but surely deriving an idealistic process by putting aside what could appear as weak points, dreaming of a perfect process, remembering only positive points, forgetting negative ones, and so on.

This kind of problem shows clearly the need to, at least, simulate the process and at most implement the process to have a full guarantee that the process model represents the reality.

What are the further needs for process modeling? A list of further aspects follows:

- Macroscopic/microscopic modeling;

- Events-driven activities;

- Concurrent activities;

- Consistency of constraints;

- Project management;

- Process model validation;

- Idealistic/realistic view;

- Interoperability.

For each one of these a summary discussion is provided in the following paragraphs.

Macroscopic/microscopic activity modeling. A macroscopic activity is well illustrated by the IDEF0 context and decomposition diagrams where the principle is specified and not the sequence. There aren't any specific condition and precedence rules (except the ICOMs rules) within the IDEF0 technique. Nothing allows predicting whether if an output will be produced before another one and consequently whether an activity will start or end before another one.

A microscopic activity - or a simple task - is the lowest level of the process model granularity and is characterized by the tool application procedure where each task sequence is well defined.

Leaving the macroscopic modeling world and entering into the microscopic world illustrates how it is vital to have conditioning rules that enable the execution of task sequences. Past modeling experiments have also demonstrated how it is inefficient to stay on the macroscopic modeling level because at the end people use tools to execute tasks. Tools and tasks should be correctly integrated within the overall process model to avoid a disruption between the two worlds. When this kind of disruption occurs, people will not consider the overall process model, but will stick to the tool application procedures, and there are no guarantees that the overall process will be correctly applied.

Events-driven activities. The majority of the process activities start as necessary inputs and preliminary conditions to execute the next activities. Nevertheless, other activities could be started because a specific event happens during the execution of the process. Events play an important role within a process execution and the IDEF0 modeling technique does not allow modeling those events.

The IDEF0 modeling technique does not allow specifying the starting and ending condition of each activity. Figure 4.10. shows an enhancement of the IDEF0 modeling technique by drawing the necessary events for the process execution and their impacts in conditioning starting, suspending, canceling or ending activities. At least, each activity generates specific events concerning it - starting, canceling, suspending, or ending the activity. Other possible events concern the availability or maturity of output information, time limits, use of information, and all characterized actions within its decomposition diagram. These events could be used to condition other activity execution.

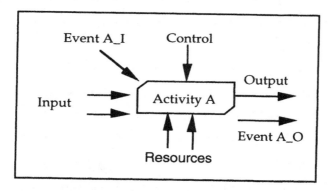

Figure 4.10. Example of a model using events.

Concurrent activities. Using IDEF0 it is easy to represent sequential or parallel activities, but what about concurrent activities? First of all it is necessary to define sequential, parallel, and concurrent activities.

1. Sequential. As shown in Figure 4.11., activities A and B have a strong constraint in execution and consequently activity B starts only once activity A is completed to provide the output information O1 to activity B. The starting condition of the activity B is S=O1.AND.XO1. This means B is a waiting information O1 and XO1 (external information coming from another activity specified in another diagram) before being executable.

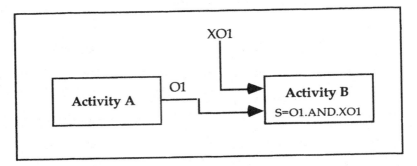

Figure 4.11. Example of sequential activities.

2. Parallel. As shown in Figure 4.12., there is no common constraint between activities B1 and B2. They both start after ending activity A and can run simultaneously without any information exchange.

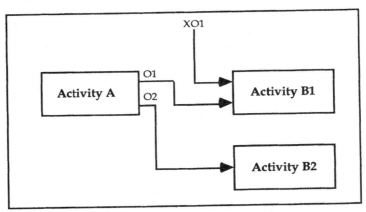

Figure 4.12. Example of parallel activities.

3. Concurrent. With reference to Figure 4.13., activity A is sequential with B1 and B2. Activity B1 is concurrent with B2 because they share common elements and constraints. There is, at least, one constraint between activities B1 and B2, and both activities should not wait for the completion of the other. There is reciprocity between activities B1 and B2, and both activities will receive information in input from the other.

The events generated by activities B1 and B2 will synchronize the information exchange and co-ordinate the linked concurrent activities. There are two possible starting conditions for activities B1 and B2. The first one is the input information AO1 and XO1 necessary to start the execution of activity B1 and input information AO2 to start the execution of activity B2. The second one, input information B2O1, will start again the execution of activity B1, and the related event information B2X will specify, for example, restarting B1 from scratch in using AO1, XO1, and B2O1 or in applying B2O1 with current information of B1.

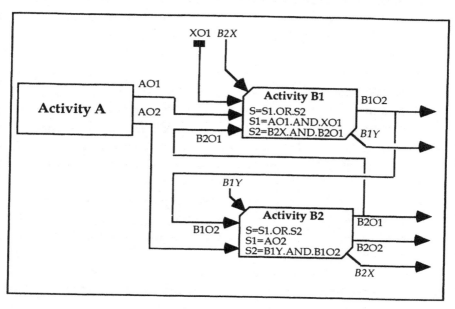

Figure 4.13. Example of concurrent activities

By this way, it is possible to influence each concurrent activity with information coming from the other linked activities without waiting for their completion. Consequently, it will not be necessary to reexecute all the previous work and so on with the reciprocity. This approach is intended to considerably help to set common constraints between those activities at the earlier stage of the work.

4. Other consideration about activity conditions. We should be careful in interpreting the drawing of the process model while two activities have a direct output-input constraint, such as the sequential activities shown in Figure 4.11. It does not necessarily mean that the second one have to wait for the completion of the first one as it has been explained before. Why?

Simply because inside the macroscopic activity (on the first decomposition level) there could be several other activities on the following decomposition levels. And one of the first activities on the second decomposition level could generate the output destined to the second activity of the first decomposition level. As shown in Figure 4.14, the activity predefine system hardware is then split in six activities inside its first level of decomposition diagram. On this level it appears the output information DO1, DO2, EO1, EO2, FO1, and FO2 of the respective activities define mechanical functions (D), define electronic functions (E), and define integration functions (F). The connection between the two decomposition diagrams is represented by the output information AO1 and AO2 of the activity predefine system hardware. At this point, we have several possible scenarios of connection:

- AO1 is connected to DO2 and AO2 to EO2.

- AO1, AO2 are two bundles respectively composed of two nets of output information DO2 and FO1 for bundle AO1 and EO2 and FO2 for bundle AO2.

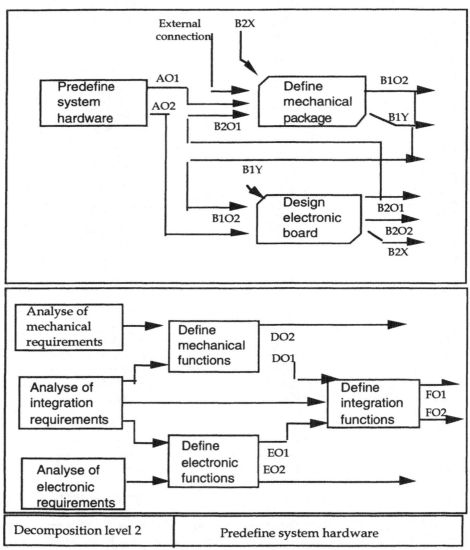

Figure 4.14. Example of starting conditions on several decomposition levels.

With the first scenario, two concurrent activities (design mechanical package and design electronic board) will not have to wait the completion of the activity predefine system hardware as DO2 and EO2 are not produced by the last activity (see Figure 4.14.).

Consistency of constraints. Another important requirement has to do with the consistency of constraints applied on what has been produced by the process or activities. While the constraints of the process by itself are well characterized within the enhanced IDEF0 model, nothing characterizes the constraints on what is produced by the process.

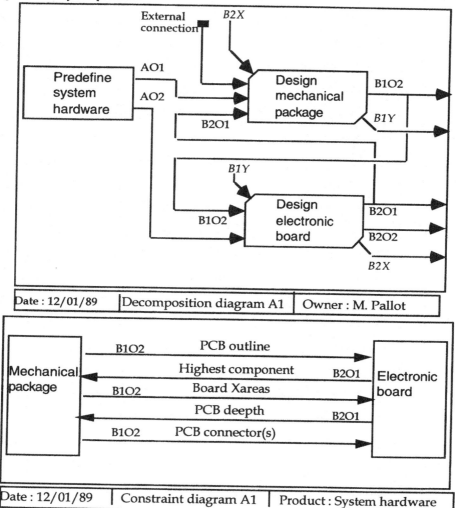

Figure 4.15. Example of constraints specification.

Constraints on the objects produced during the execution of the process could play an important role in setting up the priority of activity execution and on iteration.

If, as is shown in Figure 4.15., two objects (mechanical package and electronic board), produced by two activities (design mechanical package and design electronic board), share a common constraint (B102 and B201), it is necessary to check the consistency of this constraint within context of the two activities. This particular checking could consist of synchronizing tasks depending on the two activities to adjust the shared common constraint.

Project Management. We should consider a process as a set of value-added activities that respond to the needs and requirements of at least one customer. Project management aims to ensure and guarantee the respect of vital business parameters. These parameters are time to market, cost to buy and cost to use, and quality (life duration, usability, maintainability, operationally).

How can a process modeling technique help project management?

On one hand, the IDEF0 modeling technique, in today's version, does not really provide any information to help the project management tasks of planning and estimating the cost of necessary activities. Project managers have to use techniques and tools that have no relationship to the process modeling technique and tools. On the other hand, duration and cost are vital parameters in defining the processes to apply during a specific project, which does not have necessarily the same constraints of the other. It is of paramount importance for a project manager to identify, define, and control the duration and cost of the activities and the cost and quality of the product. The processes should constitute the basis of the project plan and cost estimation as they provide information about necessary resources and the execution of each activity. Further decomposition diagrams should allow refining, step by step, the preliminary estimation of the cost and duration.

The IDEF0 modeling technique should provide the capability to express the conditions for starting or ending an activity and also its duration (time-based, single-run, cycle-based, event-based) and related cost.

Figure 4.16. shows an example of IDEF0 diagram enhancement for project management where each activity has its own estimated cost for accomplishment of estimated duration and estimated consumption of resources. Other project management attributes could be the product components cost, the product services cost (estimated as an activity process), and so on.

Process model validation. One IDEF0 modeling feature is describing the process following a tree structure from large macroscopic activities down to more microscopic activities level by level. A specific team could be dedicated to model the subprocess of each specific activity to obtain a model of all the subprocess in a shorter time.

Then it is necessary to integrate all subprocesses within the main process. At this stage it is difficult to know whether the overall process will actually reflect the reality or will tend to be an idealistic view ignoring some constraints between several sub-processes.

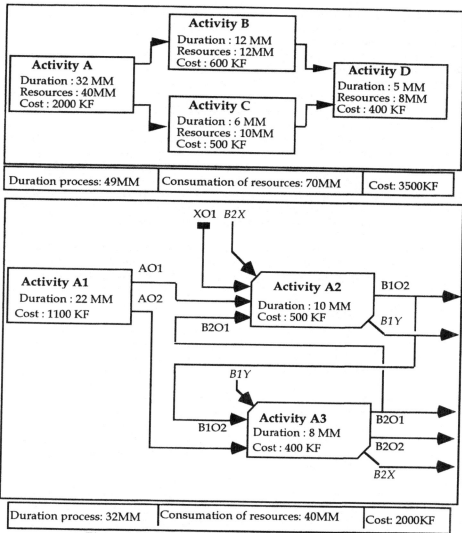

Figure 4.16. Enhancement for project management.

Within IDEF0 it is possible to check the coherence of the flow based on names of ICOMs and activities through all the levels of the description of the global model. An automated simulation of the global model will check inconsistencies and flag them. But even if the process model is coherent, nothing can guarantee it will be compliant with the work that people achieve in the reality of business.

So far the only method known to solve this problem consists of implementing and applying the modeled process within the information system. Then people use this automated process to do their jobs and consequently debug the modeled process until it reflects the necessary work to achieve.

This approach (consisting of implementing and applying a process) has other advantages. For example, everyone will apply the same process (impact on quality) to provide a support for people who conduct the process (impact on duration and commitment), to enable the distribution of information to the process " players " (impact on duration and quality). People belonging to projects are more and more on different sites but participating in a virtual and distributed team in geographically dispersed sites. Processes establish the common denominator for all involved people and, at the same time, represent the working contractual commitment and the way to achieve their challenge.

Today, existing workflow tools allow simple processes or application procedures to be implemented. Processflow tools, in the near future, will allow a full implementation of the processes to directly distribute information to people (distribute the right information to the right people at the right time in order to enable them to execute the right task), better coordinate activities, and simplify the synchronization of information exchange. Processflow tools will provide more capabilities for supporting interaction between people despite constraints within the processes.

As shown in Figure 4.17., automating processes is the best way to validate and guarantee full respect of the process models during project applications. The processflow tool will automatically distribute the right information to the right

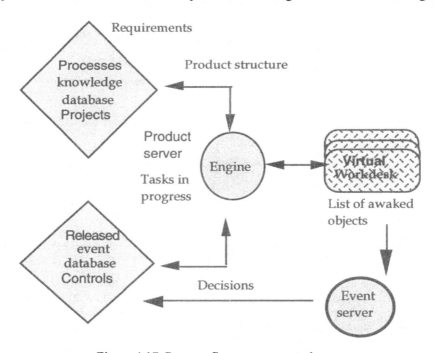

Figure 4.17. Process flow or automated processes.

people in processing the knowledge information (who is in charge to solve what constraints using which data) in combination with the events generated during the working activities. The graphic user interface is supported by the concept of a virtualworkdesk where people will see available information, activities, and tasks status. This tool will guide them in their interaction needs with other project participants.

Interoperability. Several people from different disciplines and companies, working together within the same project, do not need only to exchange information. In fact, they share a common business process while each company applies its specific capabilities to execute its own process.

The necessary interoperability is not implicit and should be specified according to common business process needs. Using IDEF0 to model the common business process provides a common language and consequently a common understanding of the requirements. But only, half of the way is achieved.

Even if the common business process shared by several companies forming the consortium is a good basis to specify interaction requirements, it represents only one part of the interoperability problem. This transversal process is inputted by the company's specific process, where people use specific methods, rules, and tools. That means each individual process should have the capability to exchange outputted objects, events, and related information (metadata) to manage the process application in order to coordinate activities and synchronize exchange of information.

It is necessary to specify and standardize metadata (limited to the domain of information for managing the processes) and events at the modeling stage to share that information between the trading partners. Metadata and events communication should enable the implementation of the necessary interoperability between activities and tasks.

4.3.4. Multidisciplinary teams
Multidisciplinary teams, recognized as one of the main elements involved in effectively implementing CE, have their greatest relevance in the first phases of the development process, when key decisions are made about subsequent development steps. Allocation of responsibility and delegation of authority to team members should be clearly identified to increase efficiency for the team and assess contributions by individuals.

We should not forget an innovative climate as an important parameter of a successful CE implementation. The multidisciplinary team concept, where each team owns at least one activity process and is composed of all necessary expertise involved within this process, has demonstrated a particularly good potential for innovation and efficiency, as far as objectives are clearly understood and commitment is verified. But then does a multidisciplinary team become really effective? Here we are back on cultural change and collaborative attitude considerations, and that means having the availability of skilled personnel, training requirements, and IT solutions for virtual or electronic colocation (that is, a virtual integrated team) (CERC, 1993). Multidisciplinary teams should also involve user, subcontractor, and supplier expertise for solving all product life-cycle requirements. The assumption should be, "Together Everyone Achieves More." Figure 4.18. illustrates this process.

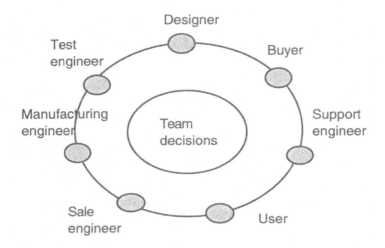

Figure 4.18. A Multidisciplinary Team.

4.4. The integrated working environment and product information

4.4.1 Integrated working environment

The technical support of multidisciplinary teams is their working environment. How can people, having complementary skills, interact with each other if they are using tools that do not communicate? Here industrial companies are facing the nightmare of the computer industry where curiously there isn't any intertools interaction protocol to facilitate communication between different applications. The only solution is to select most of the tools from the same vendor. But this is a restrictive, costly, risky, and limited solution. All needed applications are not necessarily available from the same vendor. Another solution is to have a tools integration framework initiated by CFI (CAD Framework Initiative), such as SIFRAME (Consens, 1995) and other well-known CAD vendors, enabling communication between selected tools that could be provided by different vendors. Tools are more and more compatible with different platforms and may intercommunicate via API (application protocol interface) using the object interoperability technology such as ORB, OLE, and other DCE. Technical data interchange is still a big problem. Standards such as EDIF and STEP are making an important progress, and STEP is considered to be the solution for the near future, but its orientation toward specific application protocols makes it more or less limited to the same application framework. Otherwise, Internet technology (including webservers, navigators, messaging, phoning, and other electronic boards and multimedia conferencing tools) brings much more interoperability, communication, and collaboration capabilities for an electronic colocation of people belonging to multidisciplinary teams.

CERC vision. The ideal CE environment is actually realized by implementing a generic set of services that all organizations can benefit from and all domains of engineering can exploit. The fundamental capability is threefold:

- Whenever a product developer is ready to share data, it should place it in a workspace accessible to all the developers;

- The existing applications should be integrated loosely (via direct file-out and file-in procedures) or tightly (via direct exchange over the network among communicating programs), according to the feasibility and the need; and

- The developers should have a coordination framework through which their work is made to influence upstream and downstream activities and through which progress toward a design satisfying the requirements can be assessed.

Management and monitoring of constraints throughout the product life cycle identify possible conflicts at the earliest possible time.

Standards? What standards ? Who is able to imagine what the situation will be tomorrow when many companies, associated within the same program, and using incompatible PDM and workflow systems, will try to communicate?

According to Martin Dickau, translators may be developed, similar to the gateways used to allow different networks and different mail systems to interact. Standards defining workflow system control mechanism and state information may emerge, enabling interactions in the extended or virtual enterprise that are not exactly available for today.

Translators are certainly not appropriate for a medium or long-term solution, even if they are temporarily used as a short-term solution. User groups have to push the adoption of a unique intertools communication protocol.

While the cultural evolution requires a long time to be assimilated (Alvin Toffler, Powershift, 1990), information and communication technologies are emerging at the light speed. Implementing technical concepts should be easier than surmounting cultural barriers, but market needs are driving the way, paved with money, from research technology to industrial application.

MEI: a common synergy. Adopting MEI's architecture means that each application would be able to share metadata using a common events' server to control access to each application entity and command (see Figure 4.20). Moreover, it provides the capability for managing product development activities when product development processes are described and applied. After all, wouldn't it be logical to have a common work instead of many years spent by vendors and user companies reinventing the same bases or redeveloping time and again the same interfaces?

If we want to break the infernal application interface loop, the MEI architecture could be the right approach to cooperating on standardization activities and on public domain technology. This initiative should provide a common synergy for vendors and users, for the benefit of all.

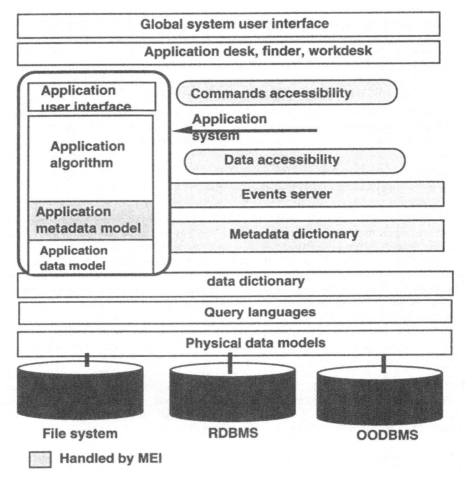

Figure 4.19. MEI architecture.

4.4.2. Product information

Product modeling is a major element in CE implementation. A single but multiperspective model has been shown to be effective in answering identified needs. Current IT tools allow partial description of specific product features and standards because product and data exchange do not cover all related aspects. Increased integration of these factors and tools has been addressed as the priority in achieving effective product modeling.

Integration of different models in a single but comprehensive product description by multidisciplinary teams constitutes the main requirement. Current capabilities and IT tools are too restricted to isolated CAD-CAM applications and PDMS (product data management system). People still have to find the right data they need to use for achieving their tasks. Nevertheless, several R&D projects on digital mock-up or virtual prototyping have already tested this technology enabler for supporting interactions between disciplines such as hardware and software cosimulation where software is tested on virtual hardware prototypes. In this innovative domain of virtual reality models for supporting concurrent design activities, VRP and VIRPI projects are representative of the European investment in this market.

VRP and VIRPI in the Finnish TEKES R&D program. Virtual prototyping services for electronics and telecommunication industry (VIRPI) is a project funded by the Technology Development Center Finland (TEKES) and Finnish industry as a part of a larger Finnish national program in increasing efficiency in product design. The project is scheduled for two and a half years starting from the middle of 1996.

The main goal of the project is to transfer virtual prototyping technology to the Finnish electronics and telecommunications industry. The project consists of both public research work and confidential development work carried out for individual companies.

The public research effort is focused on (1) defining the general virtual reality prototyping (VRP) - based product development process, demonstrating and evaluating a VRP environment implemented by VTT Electronics and (2) defining and demonstrating a distributed virtual reality prototyping system and distribution of the existing VRP knowledge to the industrial partners. (The VRP project is fund by VTT Electronics and will end in December 1998).

The VIRPI project proceeds in close cooperation with the VRP (virtual reality prototyping) project, the main goal of which is to develop virtual prototyping techniques and a supportive environment for product development in the area of consumer electronics and telecommunications. The objectives of the VRP project are as follows:

- To develop a virtual prototyping environment with basic functions;

- To develop an integration framework to connect external simulation environments and existing software and hardware to virtual prototypes;

- To create a component management system to support reuses of virtual prototype components (Java, C++, OpenInventor, VRML, audio files, textures, and so on).

Concurrent Design Environment. A European consortium is preparing a concurrent design environment supporting the collaborative processes and design constraints management in providing the following capabilities (see figure 4.21):

- Distributed virtual reality models;

- Distributed simulation models;

- Virtual prototyping;

- Distributed constraints; and

- Constraints consistency management.

An effective collaboration through the use of shorter interaction loops on different design options or alternatives could be defined as a kind of three-level structures:

- A first level representing project information and events shared between trading partners' experts;
- A second level based on shared concepts between trading partners' experts; and

A third level based on shared decision-making mechanisms.

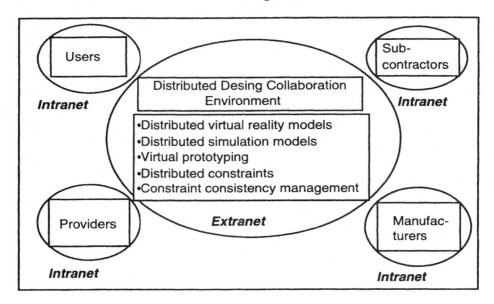

Figure 4.20. Distributed concurrent design environment.

Multidisciplinary design collaboration in geographically and temporally distributed situations can be very problematic due to the different perspectives and goals of designers. In order to collaborate efficiently, it is inevitable that the complexity addressed by new potential ways of collaboration should be supported by new collaboration technologies. Networking of enterprises starts by the need to work cooperation toward a common objective. Objectives and resources for design activities have been communicated. Tasks should coordinate, and an awareness of ongoing work should be maintained.

Collaborative virtual prototyping is an area that can be seen as supporting the partners of a common project to understand their objective. This happens through visualizations of a concept, with 3D virtual prototypes, functional, sounds, and even haptic feedback. Collaborative virtual prototyping offers designers the means for instance, for discussing and testing a design of a mechanical device with electronical and software functions distributed to the collaborating partners. Various facilities can be implemented to support this situation, such as three-dimensional telepointers, synchronized model windows between workstations, highlighted model parts, libraries of successful previous designs, and so on.

For asynchronous communication and coordination many facilities use the virtual prototype as a starting point. The awareness of design teams about latest design decisions can be support attached to the model. Figure 4.21 shows basic services in our collaborative prototyping system experiment, which is a synchronous model that runs on many workstations, shared in the 3D telepointer.

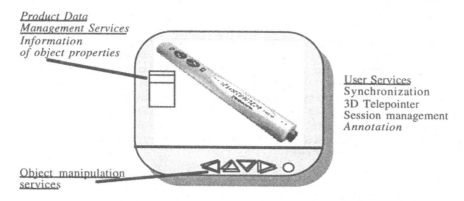

Product Data
Management Services
Information
of object properties

User Services
Synchronization
3D Telepointer
Session management
Annotation

Object manipulation
services

Figure 4.21 Experimental Collaborative Virtual Prototyping system

The World Wide Web and Internet are natural substrates for this system. The architecture is based on the premises underlying these technologies. To ensure compatibility, use is made of the latest software technology for networked environments - Java and VRML. General architecture is a client server solution, as shown in Figure 4.22.

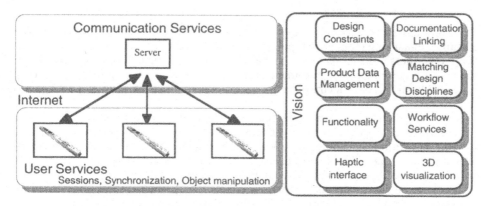

Figure 4.22 The general architecture of an experimental system.

Existing documentation in partner companies can be found in combination with, virtual prototyping with functionalities, design constraint management, support for synchronous collaboration, and latest interface technologies a fluent support for collaboration design work.

Constraints Consistency Management. Design of large complex artifacts involves the efforts of many engineers with expertise from different disciplines. Structuring a system into subsystems and parts helps to solve the design complexity. Different teams of engineers work concurrently on these subsystems and related processes, which later merge together to build the complete system. Due to the interacting nature of the subsystems and processes, we need to make sure that whenever there are selected alternatives or changes, we use proper management of constraint consistency. Communication of information to involved people as well as appropriated coordination between them becomes essential.

For answering these needs, a specific R&D project has been engaged to develop and prototype a constraints consistency management environment, including the capabilities to do the following:

- Formalize the constraints belonging to parts and related processes (such as testing, assembling, manufacturing, maintaining, and so on);

- Describe the interdependencies between objects;

- Define potential alternatives and their relationships;

- Analyze how an alternative satisfies the constraints;

- Check the constraint consistency when changing part of an alternative;

- Provide interaction support for identifying and solving unsatisfied constraints; and

- Identify the necessary skills and responsibilities for discussing, analyzing and negotiating alternatives.

Involving customer, subcontractors and suppliers. Involvement of customers (for instance, enhancing rapid prototyping capabilities) and other actors in the industrial loop (suppliers, subcontractors) can be effective in reducing reworks and better assessing requirements and features of the product under development. Associated involved legal and proprietary information management issues have to be examined and solved.

Involving the trading partners at the earlier stage of a project allows reduction in reworking and early agreement on the main issues involved in developing a product. Current networking technologies allow interfacing between customer, contractors, and suppliers. Capabilities and means for effective interaction and interfacing have been recognized to exist inside and outside among companies.

Tools for wider preliminary analyses - including price function and feasibility issues depending on modifications of product features are needed. Infrastructures and protocols to manage interactions should be identified and developed - that is, standardization, security, and management of data, information, and knowledge sharing between companies.

An effective approach should look at IT and infrastructures for CE as a whole. A CE oriented environment integrates tools enabling coordination of concurrent activities and tasks, synchronization, sharing and exchange of information, structured involvement of teams and product/process breakdown structure management.

4.5. Available methods, information technology (IT) & Tools

Other concepts related to CE exist in the information technology field and partly support CE. Those concepts are well known as groupware, workflow, product data management system (PDMS), and more generally speaking as computer support for collaborative work (CSCW). However, they are more generic than CE, which is addressing the product development domain, and are less directive on methodological and organizational aspects than CE. CSCW mainly consists of using IT to support communication for non colocated people. Groupware is a set of software functions for supporting working groups with shared calendars and video conferencing, but it does not really provide any capabilities for declaring operating rules necessary to define how people will operate on a same consistent object. Workflow systems are used to implement simple procedures for tasks and documents distribution, such as automating task sequences related to a document. PDMS is intended to manage product data and their consistency across different departments (Pallot, 1995).

All this IT has the ability to influence a reengineering of the development process through transversal application. This constitutes a link with the concurrent engineering approach where engineers should have real-time interaction support to check the consistency of the diverse constraints they have to solve.

4.5.1. Methods
Except for the CE readiness assessment, no methods have been really and specifically created to support CE. Formal methods such as DFM, DFA, and more generally DFx have been developed to support process analysis during product design. They are often integrating computer aided tools, but then there is a need to reconcile all the conflicting constraints. Other methods are helpful, such as BPR to reorganize the development process, QFD (quality function deployment) to manage product and processes requirements, WBS (work breakdown structure) and OBS (organization breakdown structure) to manage both product and project structures. The question is. How shouldthose methods be integrated to elaborate a coherent CE framework?

4.5.2. IT and tools
In fact, IT vendors sell generic tools that industrial companies have to integrate to satisfy their business process requirements. Furthermore, to obtain a necessary level of interoperability between different skills, enabling a kind of concurrent or collaborative work, requires investing on process model and information infrastructure standardization. The CALS initiative, has been presented as a possible approach toward enterprise integration, based on interchangeable or shareable digitized data. CALS operates as an enabler of CE implementation by providing simultaneous data access to the different disciplines involved within a project (Hall,

1990). CALS promotes the idea of "Create data once, use them many times". It is mandatory to avoid duplication of data and consequently to have coherent work contribution from the different disciplines. See also CALS principles in Chapter 3, section 3.3.

The present IT helps to elaborate an information infrastructure supporting business processes in linking people and integrating tools and data in a coherent way. These are IT such as distributed databases, mutlimedia, tools integration frameworks, virtual reality, CSCW, groupware, networking capabilities including TCP/IP, client/server architecture, and WWW on the Internet (Pallot, 1995).

There are also tools supporting, more or less, the work of multidisciplinary teams as recommended by the CE approach, such as, for example, product data management systems (PDMS), workflow systems, virtual prototyping, process modeling, video-conferencing, and electronic whiteboards (Pallot, 1995). Regarding process modeling and analysis some tools are available on the market, such as IDEF. About tools integration there is plethora of solutions available on the market where each CAD-CAM vendor expects to integrate with its competitors, while standardization is slowly progressing in this domain (ECIP, CFI). Concerning virtual prototypes, it is a fact that prototyping helps to debug a product before it enters into the production mode. These techniques and tools avoid a number of late modifications costing a lot of money and also allow better negotiations between all the disciplines, either from product or processes design, in choosing a solution that satisfy all the constraints.

Videoconferencing and electronic whiteboards permit to distant parties to have a real-time explanation of what people intend to do and how they plan to do it. This is fully complementary with virtual prototyping, where the first technique provides the context and the second one the simulation of technical solutions without having to really produce anything.

As mentioned before, CE-dedicated tools do not yet exist, but some capabilities required for CE implementation do. Table 4.1 shows that most advanced tools are not very well integrated into a coherent framework and have a limited capacity to support a CE approach implementation. The table illustrates CE domains, IT and tools, and an assessment according to the strong and weak points of each IT and Tool.

4.6. CE related projects

Through its ongoing European information technology research program ESPRIT, the European Commission has undertake innovative research projects in the area of CE with the aim of developing the information technology tools European manufacturing will need to remain competitive internationally (see Table 4.2).

Within the CE-related ESPRIT projects, a concept of CSE (concurrent and simultaneous engineering) has been developed where simultaneous engineering deals with concepts for enabling access to the engineering and design results that are produced in successive product development phases.

Table 4.1. CE/ IT tools.

CE Domains	IT Tools	Strong points	Weak points
Management of product and process require-ments	Quality Function Deployment	•Assessment of process efficiency •Automatisation of simple process •Tasks plan, schedule	•Complex multilevel elaboration •No consistency procedure
Managment of concurrent activities	•Activity •Modeling •Workflow •Project management	•Assessmrnt of priorities •Global view •Requirement tracking	•No concurrent activitiy model •No flexibility •No progress tracking •No task coordination
Sharing information	•PDMS	•Data repository •Data consistency •Structure coherence	•Too much static •No data distribution •Mechanism
Alternative assessment	•Virtual prototyping •Rapid prototyping	•Touching and playing with virtual models •Physical prototype in a short term	•No standard except VRMLon the Internet •Expensive and limited applications
Interactions Support •People •Tools •Systems	•Messaging, video confe-rencing tools •Framework •API linkage	•Common understanding •Facilitation tools integration and communication •Multiplatform	•Weak demonstration support •Not yet standardized •Too specific •Too many standards
Sharing knowledge	•Conferencing •MultiMedia	•Facilitation electronic colocation •Demonstration	•Limited capacity •Not mature
Sharing events	•Messaging notification •Protocol	•Intermediate notice	•Limited distribution capacity •No propagation mechanism
Product and process modelling	•CAD/CAM •Virtual reality •Models •Virtual prototyping	•Simulation and analysis fonctionalities •Multicheking	•Limited integration capabilities •Requires important computer resources

The ATLAS project, Bringing Worlds Together, is a typical test case of enterprise integration applied to design and project management activities enabling CE practice in the domain of LSE and construction. The data integration is based on express models compliant with STEP (Standard for the Exchange of Product Model

Data) or ISO10303 (Product Data Representation and Exchange), while a tool-integration framework has been used to facilitate the interoperability. The concepts of the tool-integration framework have been developed within the Jessi Common Frame project and enhanced during the CONSENS project and also used in the ADVANCE projects.

The ATLAS project has initiated a number of application protocol projects including AP228 (ATLAS, 1995).

The FIRES (Feature-based Integrated Rapid Engineering System) project has been focused on a design for manufacturing application. The objective of FIRES was to prototype a new generation of computer aided engineering tools that supports the rapid modeling, analysis, and manufacture of complex mechanical parts. Parts are represented by a neutral, feature-based data structure that has been developed from the STEP standards (using resource models and application protocols, AP213, 214, and 224) and related initiatives. The FIRES architecture comprises three key functional modules - namely, the feature-based modeler, the process planner, and the analysis interface. The FIRES consortium largely contributed to the STEP Application protocols refinement and validation, such as AP213 and influenced the development of AP214 and 224 (FIRES, 1995).

The SCOPES (Systematic Concurrent design Of Products, Equipment and control Systems) project has been centered on the integration of product design to manufacturing operations such as assembly workshop. This project issued a suite of integrated tools to support the integrated design of product and assembly factory. It includes product design for assembly, assembly planning, resource planning, simulation, scheduling and flow control, shop floor control, and monitoring (SCOPES, 1995).

Last but not least, the CONSENS (CONcurrent and Simultaneous ENgineering System) project has been specifically designated to analyze organizational aspects and structure of existing engineering processes at typical engineering sites. It implied a transfer of end-user requirements into rules and methodologies for achieving concurrent workflow in the design and engineering process.

The last issue has been the development of CSE environment prototypes, which has been used at several industrial sites. Clearly, it contributes to the development and experimentation of the CSE integration platform, including a tool-integration framework within CSE implementation test cases.

Within the first CSE pilot project of product development, a decrease of resources of 23 percent has been observed. A potential saving in further product development of 20 to 30 percent in development time and costs has been estimated. The software architecture consists of the following components - a desktop, an object management system, common basic services, a design management system, and an advanced engineering services and application tools (CONSENS, 1995).

In fact, each project corresponds to a specific area of CE:

- ATLAS for sharing product models based on STEP;

- CONSENS for experimenting a CE implementation methodology, including the development of an integration platform (SIFRAME);

- FIRES in the design for manufacturability area to concurrently design a product and its manufacturing process including CAE-CAD-CAM integration architecture in using feature based models;

- SCOPES in the design for assemblability area to concurrently design a product and its assembly chain.

Table 4.2 List of CE-related ESPRIT projects.

Project number	Acronym	Title	Start date	Duration
6090	FIRES	Feature-based Integrated Rapid Engineering System	01Jul92	37 months
6562	SCOPES	Systematic Concurrent design Of products, Equipments and control Systems	01Oct92	37 months
6896	CONSENS	CONcurrent and Simultaneous Engineering System	26May92	38 months
7280	ATLAS	Architecture, Methodology and Tools for Computer-integrated LSE	18May92	42 months
8148	ADVANCE	Advance coommon basic services for Distributed CE applications	01Fev94	30 months
9810	CENT	Concurrent Engineering Needs & Technology	01Jan95	12 months
20408	VEGA	Virtual Enterprise using Groupware tools and distributed Architecture	01Jan96	36 months
20501	CEDAS	Concurrent Engineering Design Advisor System	01Nov95	24 months
20587	TOCEE	TOward a CE Environment in the building and engineering structures industry	01Jan96	36 months
20598	MATES	Multimedia Assisted distributed TeleEngineering Services	01Jan96	24 months

The ongoing CE-related ESPRIT projects are (see Table 4.2) as follows:

- CEDAS, ESPRIT project 20501 (Concurrent Engineering Design Advisor System). This project will develop an advisor systems technology through the implementation of a groupware system, which goes beyond the current state-of-the-art in printed circuit board (PCB) design systems. The groupware system will support concurrent design, by a product-development team, of a PCB and the processes by which it will be manufactured, tested, deployed, and maintained.

- ELSEWISE, ESPRIT project 20876 (European LSE Wide Integration Support Effort). ELSEWISE is a user group reference project for large-scale engineering (LSE) companies. The aim is to study user requirements in product data technology and to develop a vision of future business needs.

- MATES, ESPRIT project 20598 (Multimedia Assisted Distributed Tele-Engineering Services). The objective of the MATES project is to establish a distributed work environment, which enables knowledge and development intensive projects to be performed efficiently, independently of the physical location of its participants. The purpose of such an engineering environment is to aid all persons involved in the product creation process in all their activities to specify, design, construct, and maintain a product.

- TOCEE, ESPRIT projects 20587 (Toward a Concurrent Engineering Environment in the Building and Engineering Structures Industry). The very specific situation in the construction industry is that many designers, engineers, suppliers, and manufacturers participate in the construction of a one-of-a-kind structure and have to be coordinated. The total of the participants in the design and construction process of a building can be interpreted as a virtual enterprise that has been set up just for the given projects.

- VEGA, ESPRIT projects 20408 (Virtual Enterprise Using Groupware Tools and Distributed Architecture). The VEGA projects aims to establish an information infrastructure, which will support the technical and business operations of the virtual enterprise. Groupware tools and distributed architectures will be developed in compliance with product data technology standardization activities in line with the current trends adopted by international industrial groupware specifications coming, for example, from the OMG (object management group).

As mentioned earlier, there isn't today any dedicated and specific technology that has been developed for CE implementation except the capability assessment. It is obvious to say that activity modeling, tool-integration framework, PDMS, workflow, and other groupware tools were not developed to address CE implementation needs but for a much more generic IT market. Nevertheless, it should be stated that important work has been already done to understand the exact needs for CE implementation. Also effort actually has been spent in developing specific CE technologies such as the concurrent virtual prototyping and the constraints consistency management environments that will efficiently meet crucial interaction needs such as design tradeoff.

Implementing concurrent activities within the product development process is another vital need for CE implementation. No modeling and analysis technique to globally identify dependencies between activities exists today. Such an activity modeling technique and tool should enable people to determine whether the activities have to be defined as being sequential, parallel or concurrent.

Methodologies and tools to efficiently manage product development dependencies along the product life cycle and verify their consistency. Furthermore, it should help in identifying the interaction needs between the different expertises and in studying the impacts of changes.

Develop a collaborative attitude and more appropriate rewarding system that could better motivate people to work together and not only to review individual people but much more to assess a team efficiency and how each individual contributes to that team.

Due to the increasing complexity of development processes, it is consequently more and more difficult to coordinate tasks and synchronize the exchange of information. To solve this situation it is mandatory to define an intertools interaction protocol (IIP) offering the ability to distribute the right information to the right people at the right time to enable them to execute the right tasks (Pallot, 1993).

Electronic colocation is also not specific to CE implementation, but according to the current business trend, more and more projects are involving trading partners operating from geographically dispersed sites as well as teleworking.

4.7. Conclusion

As mentioned before, design interaction that supports collaboration between product and processes design disciplines is a centerpiece of CE implementation. It relies on the interoperability between heterogeneous environments where Internet technologies are widely opening the door of the information and knowledge society.

For many years we thought that BPR practices were relevant for CE implementation, but then we discovered that BPR theory focused only on the business process, while the CE approach affects other processes, and behavior has a paramount importance. New product development projects involve several types of process such as management, development, support, and learning processes, and it is not only the development process that needs to be adapted for supporting CE concepts. Some people thought CE concepts were well applied by industry and no longer represented a competitive advantage. We learned a lot in studying economical, cultural, and technical impacts as well as needs for CE implementation, but we still have to progress on the way to mastering it. Furthermore, CE should also be implemented across company boundaries, and CE concepts are transferable to a methodological approach of collaborative work.

That means we have to build up from our CE implementation knowledge within this extended domain of concurrency for competitiveness where concurrent enterprises operate on the global market like fishes in the sea.

References
ATLAS.(995). "ATLAS Esprit Project 7280: Exploitation of results." October 1995, Brussels..
Bergman, Lars, and Öhlund Stern-Erik. (1995). "Development of an Assessment Tool to assist in the Implementation of CE." Paper presented at CE'94, McLean, VA.
Concurrent Engineering Research Center (CERC). (1992). "Process and Technology Readiness Assessment for Implementing CE." Concurrent Engineering Research Center, West Virginia University, Morgantown, WY.

Concurrent Engineering Research Center (CERC).(1993). "Technology and organisation for Implementing CE Concepts : a Virtual Integrating Team."Concurrent Engineering Research Center, West Virginia University, Morgantown, WY.

Consens.(1995). "CONcurrent and Simultaneous Engineering System. Consens Esprit Project 6896 : Exploitation of Results." August. Brussels.

Dickau, Martin. (1993). "Workflow System Communication." *CALS Journal* (Summer).

Fire's. (1995). "A Feature-based Integrated Rapid Engineering System. FIRE'S ESPRIT project 6090. Exploitation of Results." Septembre. Brussels.

Gilbane, Frank. (1993). "Integrating New Technologies: Workflow Systems." *CALS Journal* (Summer).

de Graaf R. (1994). *Assessing Europe's Readiness for Concurrent Engineering,*. Eindhoven, The Netherlands: Eindhoven University of Technology.

Hall, D. (1990). "Implementing the Concurrent Engineering Process." Paper presented at the CALS Phase II Conference, Society for Computer-Aided Engineering, Costa Mesa, CA, March.

Pallot, Marc. (1993). "Enable Interaction Using Meta-Data Within a CE Environment." Paper presented at CALS Expo'93, Atlanta, GA.

Pallot, Marc. (1994). "Integrating Business Process Knowledge to Achieve Concurrent Engineering Support." Paper presented at CALS Expo'94, Long Beach, CA.

Pallot, Marc. (1995). "Assessment of Available IT and Tools for Concurrent Engineering. The Cent Esprit Project 9810." Paper presented at CERT'95, Rome, October.

Scopes. (1995). "Systematic Concurrent Design Of Products, Equipments, and Control Systems. Scopes Esprit Project 6562: Exploitation of results." November. Brussels.

Toffler, Alvin. (1990). *Powershift.* Bentahm Book, NY.

5 ASSESSMENT OF THE ENTERPRISE APPROACHES

5.1 Introduction

This chapter assesses the different enterprise paradigms or approaches presented in Chapters 2, 3, and 4. Based on the analysis made in Chapter 1, one conclusion was the need for building a strong basis for a foreseeable future within the context of competition acceleration, market globalization and rapid diffusion and implementation of ICT. This becomes an important challenge for enterprises (and, in general, for all organizations). In particular, we underline some difficulties for applying classical principles and solutions to be directly to this new rapidly evolving context. But at the same time, the emerging information and knowledge societies, based on ICT and telematics networks, generate new opportunities for businesses and have an enormous potential for economic growth.

The question is then, Where is this potential (in the new value chains)? How we can exploit this potential? One major question is to know whether the existing enterprise's paradigms or approaches are pertinent or not and, if they are, to what limits. Under these circumstances, the assessment proposed here tries to position enterprises and constitutes an important step in the discussion and presentation of the concurrent enterprise approach. Thus our approach starts from texisting realities as an invitation to think about the actual limits, without neglecting any positive element existing in the dominant ideas. We do not propose to reinvent something completely new, never seen. We try only to set up some principles that will concern more and more companies in the world. This construction is emerging from our own experience and knowledge, principally with European and Japanese companies. This assessment allows us to put on the table an even more important problem, which is the evaluation of functions, weaknesses, and problems facing companies on the field of cooperation between them. The second part of this chapter presents this discussion.

5.2. Enterprise approaches: a general view

This section discusses the assessment of main paradigms or approaches developed below. First of all, we present some developments concerning the main ideas of each approach, and we try to summarize this discussion in a few matrix presentations. This kind of presentation seems to be appropriate for identifying similarities, differences, and the inadequacies of the different approaches.

5.2.1. Shared enterprise

First of all, we underline that the concept of shared enterprise or network of enterprises is not useful for enterprises. It is costly and risky. These costs, for example, are increasing costs for managing and coordinating the cooperation, loss of key information, opportunistic behaviors, inequitable dependence, overinvestments, and so on. These costs and risks must be compared to the advantages of choosing between this new organizational form and the market for realizing the firms' transactions. At least, this concept requires different conditions, such as some mechanisms of competition, a share of pledged information and diffused innovation, for developing a creative synergy and keeping this synergy for all partners, as P.A. Julien (1995) proposes.

SE has in principle a limited application: this concerns, principally, the companies undertaking the risk and supporting the eventual costs of involvement. For example, it is not appropriate for standard products or if the client must define the product's characteristics or a strategic product. But if the product is complex and under the influence of gradual innovation, needing long negotiations for the design and the development of the product's parts, it is a better solution to create a partnership. In that case, the client and provider take part in the design of one part of that product. Partnership is also important when the delivery delays are crucial, assuming that the JIT system exists everywhere (client and provider).

Nevertheless, the SE model rerquires a complete change in the old habits of internalizing production and stocking raw materials. Best management of the all phases means having better differentiation of competitors. So the advantages are not always clear or are not available for all companies and for all transactions.

As an example, we can cite the important internal management costs, particularly personal expenses for managing the rising of the insertion; the coordination and negotiation costs; the risks of losing leadership or flexibility because partners do not understand some individual transactions; the possible losses of information concerning market evolution (a key element for strategies of companies); the risks of losses because of the errors or delays of partners.

These inconvenience must be balanced with the advantages:

- The reorientation of skills and mission for better meeting the consumer's needs;

- The minimization of materials investments (installations, equipments, stocks) or concentration on the essential aspects;

- More scale economies in sharing the diagonal synergie between a large number of firms

- Fewer costs per transaction (for example, providers) compared with the actual market prices.

5.2.2. Intelligent enterprise

This kind of enterprise emerges from a reality observed by J.B. Quinn. It is clearly designed for the powerful service companies (the biggest companies) and is directly connected to their producing services. They have placed their ultimate consumers ever more in command of the world's production system, and they are able to dictate responses to their individual and collective desires. These companies must be able to sense, produce for, and service these trends as a key condition of success in what J.B. Quinn calls the new service society.

A key point here is to use related knowledge and services and organize activity around them. The knowledge-based and service-based strategies are most effective when companies develop best-in-world capabilities around a few selected competencies that are important for customers. Now the problem is to concentrate resources on selected areas and then benchmark other areas to ensure comparability. It is necessary to convert intellectual resources into a chain of service outputs and integrate these into a form most useful for certain customers. Even more in the industrial world, managers make their money investing in the special skills and intellect that only highly motivated, knowledgeable people can provide.

As we see, this kind of enterprise is, on the one hand, very oriented (to exploit intellectual resources) to answer to the real evolution of productive systems, and, on the other, is of quite limited scope. In fact, IE concerns principally the biggest companies, the service sector companies, and, inside companies themselves, only the intellectual resources are the most relevant to leverage company to reach the IE paradigm. A company becomes intelligent by supporting the selected core of skills by other defensive positions (other products) keeping its distances from potential competitors.

However, these limits cannot avoid some interesting points, such as those concerning organizational changes. In fact, to be IE, a company needs to think seriously about its own structure, organization, and management. Taking only the extreme case of the infinitely flat organizations, one can imagine the consequences and the needs for involving and motivating management at every level of company activity.

5.2.3. Agile Manufacturing

AM is a kind of enterprise built step by step, following a long-term strategy. This is then the opposite to the tactical and operational level of planning company strategies. So many considerations concerning the long term, but maybe nonacceptable for tactical or operational planning, are interesting to consider here. The company must invest in ICT in order to reach some agile state in the future. Agile manufacturing concerns, as its name says, the only manufacturing. It is conceived as a strategic tool for recovering American industrial competitiveness. This is the main message contained in the agile manufacturing report that U.S. industry has received well.

Is this message available everywhere in a global world? Is this message available for sectors other than classical industry? These questions are the open ones. Concerning the first question, we think AM has became more than a simple challenge for U.S. industry. In a global market, with an accelerated ICT input, AM goes beyond, and then most companies in the world should be interested in becoming agile, too. This concept is then becoming more and more universal within that context.

We know that in an AM environment, enterprise must able to bring out totally new products quickly. Thus reprogrammable, reconfigurable, continuously changeable production systems, integrated into new information-intensive manufacturing system, make the lot size of an order irrelevant. This is quite a wider challenge for companies competing in a global market.

Another interesting point in AM concerns authority. Authority is diffused, not concentrated in a chain command. A dynamic structure is keyed to the evolving needs of cross-functional project teams. But this requires changes in present management behavior, including in the corporate culture.

Finally, we underline that AM is accomplished by integrating three key resources - technology, management, and workforce - into a coordinated, interdependent, system. The main force of the AM message is maybe here: without a knowledgeable workforce it is not possible to build any agility. In a certain sense, this idea is similar to that of Quinn's intelligent enterprise approach in which the intellectual core plays a determinant role for company competitiveness and strategies. Nevertheless, this agility is linked to the ICT implementation and by this way reaches the VE paradigm.

5.2.4. Virtual Enterprise

VE is one of the last arrived (do not confuse VE and virtual reality, which is a specific ICT technology). VE must be considered as a fictitious entity or even as a simulated entity. It is fictitious or simulated because of the use of advanced ICT tools and the appropriated networks. Until recent years one could simulate or create fictitious entities using isolated computers. At present, with VE the problem is more complicated. Using computer software and, principally, operating network environments, we must link different (maybe dispersed) "real" entities in order to create a new one - a virtual entity.

Related to VE we have virtual factory that is a fictitious or simulated factory integrating its all components as a design process, manufacturing process, testing process, and so on. In fact, VE is wider than virtual factory. In addition, VE must concern all productive entities and not only the manufacturing one. In this sense, is larger than the IE, AM or even SE. VE has then a more universal character. For us VE is a key element in the building of the concurrent enterprise, and it is one step in the concurrent enterprising process addressed to build concurrent enterprise, as we shown in the next paragraphs of this chapter and the next chapters.

5.2.5. CIM, IMS and FGMS.

CIM is considered to be an important aspect in the development of manufacturing systems that companies must incorporate as a part of their own competitive policy. But the CIM evolution differs by country. In Europe this evolution has produced the welknown model CIM-OSA (some aspects of this model have been exported to other countries such as Canada). In the United States early efforts were not successfull. It is only in the 1990s that CIM has developed under the name of FCIM, which integrates the flexibility dimension into the model.

In Japan (this country implemented one of the more advanced and complete CIM models), CIM is founded on a set of standard components as follows - factory automation (FA), engineering automation (EA), and office automation (OA). CIM integrates all of these components, the more important being FA. FA is principally supported by technologies such as MAP (manufacturing application protocol). As we shown in Chapter 2, the Japanese CIM approach reaches some kind of standardization, at least in the step and technology implementation to be followed for building it, becoming then a tool for company competitiveness. But the general concept and components is implemented and developed differently according to the involved companies and activity sectors.

In general, in Japan CIM is considered as one step in the evolution of a manufacturing system. According to this vision, CIM should contribute to the characterization and implementation of the future generation of manufacturing systems, which means that it has an important role in the building of the IMS, following the next steps FA (factory automation), CIM, and IMS (intelligent manufacturing systems). Nevertheless, the CIM contribution to the IMS passes through a development called new CIM.

IMS, incorporating CIM, is a more ambitious challenge: it is the base for building the so-called future generation of manufacturing systems (FGMS), the main characteristic being intelligent machines operating on the shop-floor. IMS is an international challenge, contrary to AM, involving the majority of the advanced countries. At present seven test cases are finished, and some agreements to continue the research are already finalized. But IMS remain quite limited to the manufacturing industry and even more to the industry belonging to the advanced countries, even if some declarations are made in the sense of sharing knowledge on a large scale, including the entire world manufacturing industry.

We must underline another point concerning CIM: it is based on the ICT needing strong developments and investments, and it is costly, as we have seen in the case studied in Section 3.6. In addition, these technologies (an example of exception is the application of MAP protocol) are not designed for open environments. To overcome this last problem, the Japanese begin to develop the open CIM. But another problem intervened here: the open environments are today characterized by the domination of many emerging standards related to the Internet, and Intranet environments, and the CIM must incorporate it to be really operational. In other words, CIM by Internet and Intranet is one of the present (and even more future) challenges facing the manufacturing industry in achieving the implementation the integrated computer technologies from manufacturing shop-floor to the engineering, administration, and management of company.

But for our purposes, CIM and IMS are interesting because they concern the most advanced aspects of the manufacturing industry. And from this sector is emerging, more and more clear, the strong needs of reorganizing companies. This point drives us to other point studied in Chapter 4 - concurrent engineering. A priori, there is no relation between concurrent engineering and CIM or FCIM. Nevertheless, the new forms of engineering are important for achieving the goals of these two systems in manufacturing. Even more important, they become a key issue for setting up the most efficient productive systems. To be competitive this industry must work in concurrent engineering from design to manufacturing itself.

Finally CIM-OSA is a complete tool for modeling CIM in enterprises. This tool has many applications, and it is normally a subject of R&D in Europe and in other countries such as Canada. Nevertheless, CIM-OSA has given relevant results permitting, for example, the export of this technology and related technologies. CIM-OSA remains then closer to the European experiences, and, in addition, it concerns only the advanced manufacturing industry. From our perspective, CIM-OSA is then quite limited as a global paradigm. However, some aspects of the CIM-OSA model ask for some adaptation in the new environments such those of virtual enterprise and what we propose in this book - concurrent enterprise. For example, CIM-OSA is a good tool for modeling, and may contribute to the necessary developments in this field within the of virtual enterprise. In this case, specialists say Virtual Factory as we see in Chapter 3, Section 3.5.

We discuss now these paradigms in more details doing a comparison between them. Table 5.1. illustrates some business aspects compared according to the different approaches. This comparison takes into account the concept, goal, scope, strategy and structure (organization aspects) of the business. We can see that most of the resultats are different according to the approach. As we see, the concepts do not generally overlap each other, but we think the most important is that of VE, followed by that of SE and IE. AM is quite a substantial one, but it is clear that in the business environments dominated by the ICT and globalization, a company must be agile. The agility is then something like a state to be reach at every stage of business - some permanent quality and not something transitory or occasional. The scope is also different. We can summarize these by saying there are three types:

- Scope is limited because of the industrial sector concerned or the skills concerned;

- Scope concerns principally the manufacturing industry (because the answers coming from a explicate demand); and

- Scope is very large for every company, which is the VE.

The strategy is also different. In general, it is possible to separate long term strategy from those work on the project base. Duration might be short or middle or even long term; this seems to be implicit in the conceptual approach. Finally, on one point these enterprise approaches agree: companies need reorganization and must wait for a reduction of the hierarchies.

Table 5.1 Business aspects compared according approaches.

	Concept	Goal	Scope	Strategy	Structure
SE	Sharing resources	Creative synergy	Limited to some companies	By project	Reorganization and adaptation
IE	Intellectual core and services	To be the best	Sector limited	Intellectual and services related	Reduce hierarchies
AM	Agility	Fastest reaction and variation	Manufacturing sector	Long term	Reduce hierarchies
CIM	Integrate factory by computer	Total production integration	Manufacturing sector	Long term	Reorganization and adaptation
IMS/ FGMS	Intelligent integrated manufacturing machines	New manufacturing paradigm	Manufacturing sector	Duration variable	Complete change
FF	Fractal invariance principle	Reduce complexity of nondeterministic manufacturing models	Manufacturing sector	Duration variable	Remodel factory's components
VE	Existence by telematics networks	By project	Very large rank of enterprises	By project	Complete reorganization and adaptation

Table 5.2. illustrates a comparison between approaches based on the importance of ICT, cooperation, innovation, and customer needs. Customer needs are present everywhere, confirming one of the assumptions made in Chapter 1 (Section 1.2). ICT is not concerned directly by two SE and IE, but it is an essential point in the remaining approaches. In fact, ICT became a factor for understanding and building strategies. Learning, is taken here as general input and not in the sense of the learning enterprise (Section 2.6.).

Table 5.2. ICT inputs in different approaches

	Customer needs	Cooperation	Innovation	ICT	Learning
S E	Yes	Internal cooperation and competition	By new synergies	Not concerned directely	Dynamic and collective
I E	Yes	Restricted cooperation	Intellectual core innovation	Not concerned directely	Limited to core services
AM	Yes	Cooperation and competition	For long-term strategy	Essential point	Important issue
CIM	Yes	External competion, strong parts solidarity	Technical and organizational	Key input	Technical and organizational
IMS/ FGMS	Yes	Cooperation and external competition	Technical, organizational, and socio-economical	Essential point	Knowledge transfer and sharing
F F	Variable	Not envisioned	Not involved directly	Essential point	Not envisioned directly
V E	Variable	Highest-level cooperation	Key input and output	Essential point	Knowledge transfer and sharing

Finally, innovation and cooperation are also present in most of the approaches. Innovation is a key input for every approach (with the exception of FF, but the goal of it is modeling flows). Innovation must have three connotations - as a source (new synergy's and intellectual core), as a technical element, and as a part of strategy. We can underline that VE is in an intermediary position: innovation is a key point as input and as output. Cooperation may be internal, external (in the sense of openness), restricted, or highest. This last point is important in allowing us new kinds of comparisons. The next paragraphs study in more detail this question.

5.3 Why and How approaches must be used in Concurrent Enterprise

Before studying cooperation and collaboration in more detail, we summarize some points concerning the above developments in the enterprise approaches. The objective is, on the one hand, to underline the main ideas and, on the other hand, to build a graphic permitting us to see why and how we will benefit from these approaches to setting up our own about the concurrent enterprise.

This Table 5.3. allows us to get out some intermediary conclusions that must be considered as the important inputs for the beginning of this study. We retain the most relevant ideas of each approach. Thus, from SE, we can keep the idea of sharing resources and knowledge; from IE, we can keep the idea of reevaluating the role of intellectual resources and services; from AM, we can keep the idea of agility; from CIM, we can keep the idea of integrating manufacturing system that combines

Table 5.3. Synthesis.

Enterprise-type	Some Key Aspects
SE	• Partnership hability • Value added from diagonal synergies • Capacity to share resources, costs, and risks • Skill reorientation
E I	• Intelligence: enterprise's core • Intellectual services, key for competitivness • Intellectual services: key for value added • Desaggregated enterprise
AM	• Flexible, rapid, agile • Magement of innovation, flexible technology • Knowledgeable workforce • New paradigm
FGMS	• Knowledge organization • Knowledge systematization • Knowledge standardization • Ecoharmonic paradigm
VE	• Flexible fictitious entity • Interfaces adaptation • Strong input of ICT • New paradigm

with concurrent engineering; from IMS, the idea of using of more and more intelligent tools but in cooperation and innovation. Finally VE is a key input in our system with concurrent engineering. From this last point, we can simplify by saying that concurrent enterprise is VE plus concurrent engineering.

Table 5.3. summarizes some of the key ideas contained in the different approaches. Chapter 4 presented a sound development of CE. This development was particularly centered on the to way to do it, the role of IT tools, and the limits and advantages of the present system. This chapter starts by arguing that CE is an essential basis to concurrent enterprise.

Figure 5.1. gives a vision of why and how the main ideas, goals, and some organizational points fit in the concurrent enterprise approach. In fact, we start from all the studied approaches, and we use what we consider the best of them as input for our own purposes. Thus concurrent enterprise must be founded on the maturity of these elements.

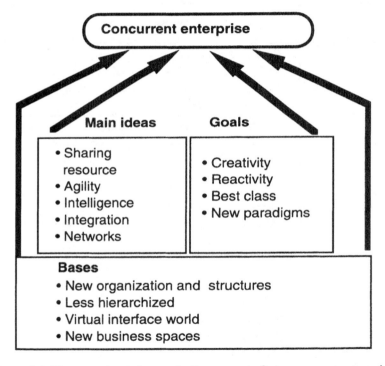

Figure 5.1. Ideas, goals, and organization aspects for concurrent enterprise.

Figure 5.2. illustrates another problem: the role played by customer needs, ICT, innovation, and project issues. As for most of the approaches studied in Chapters 2, 3, and 4 the customer's needs are present everywhere. In reality, they are determinants for the emergence of this new approach. But other approaches also considered this,; the difference now is the indispensable consideration of ICT, innovation, and working together on a given project.

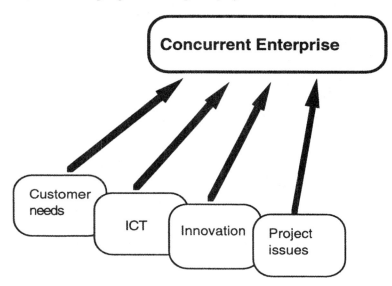

Figure 5.2. Customers, technology and strategy.

Figure 5.3. illustrates one of the last problems - and maybe one of the most interesting to consider when we study concurrent enterprise. It is cooperation and collaboration. The fundamental differences between Concurrent Enterprises and the remaining approaches come from this point. And this is available for all approaches, including CIM, IMS, CIM-OSA, and learning enterprise.

Figure 5.3. illustrates cooperation at two levels - internal and external. Companies have always cooperated or tried to cooperate in the past, but this cooperation today, and even more tomorrow, must be supported by networks and must live in the new virtual spaces. This is one preliminary problem. Companies can prepare for this eventuality. One other problem is collaboration, which is more than simple cooperation. Collaboration must exist principally thanks to the networks, but it is an essential issue for all companies. But the question is remaining the same at every time: How are companies preparing for entering this New World? What are problems face companies?

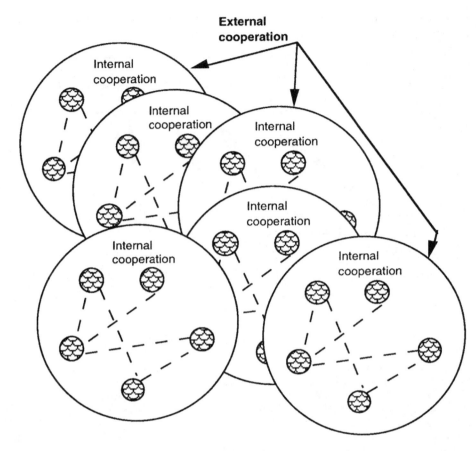

Figure 5.3. Internal and external cooperation.

5.4. Weaknesses and cooperation assessment

To be competitive in a global world dominated by ICT, enterprises must exchange information and enrich knowledge. Only in this way should they be able to be creative and innovative and arrive at the market at the right time. But to do it, they must cooperate and then collaborate, which means sharing knowledge to be more innovative and creative. In this way, they also should better use time and capital. Capital (including knowledge assets) in common ensure that they will be able to go behind the market and operate in a concurrent manner. For this last it is necessary to build an appropriate infrastructure, the fundamental support for interactions, as we will see in Chapters 7 and 8.

The development, production, and support of industrial products is more and more often realized by a group of companies, together forming a consortium, each with its own expertise and each performing a set of dedicated tasks. By concentrating on corebusiness, each individual company becomes more competitive. But whether a specialized company will survive will heavily depend on the effectiveness of operating within such a consortium and its global efficiency. There are different economic motivations that justify this trend, and accessing a larger market in being selected within such project consortia particularly motivates SMEs. It also contributes to reduce both the economic and technical risks.

In this chapter current cooperation is examines future trends are explained. It answers the question of how to enter a new collaboration partnership by using the results of the FREE project.

5.4.1. Traditional approach to project cooperation
In order to reduce lead-time and cost, many companies have already introduced the principles of concurrent engineering. This means that different disciplines no longer design sequentially a product and its related processes but design them more or less in parallel (concurrently). However, cooperation with suppliers or any trading partners currently still uses a sequential global design approach where partners exchange formal documents.

This is why the next step is the implementation of and earlier design collaboration between partners such as suppliers (often SME) and main contractors. This implies that concurrent engineering can be implemented across the borders of companies and nations. Together with this tendency, the interdependencies between companies grow, and the quality of the communication link between trading partners becomes crucial. It's not the company's local processes that should be optimized once again, but the new business system at the consortium (global project) level that has to be managed. Unfortunately, in this area hardly any supporting models, techniques, and methods exist.

5.4.2. Encountered problems
We can summarize some of the main problems encountered by the companies (particularly the manufacturing companies) as follows:

- While each trading partner has its own language, its culture, its business, management and supporting processes, its legal and security regulations, the project (consortium) organization should act as a single coherent and efficient business entity even when companies reside at geographically dispersed sites. But the problem is now the globalization of the market and the need for a global business, and what could be an advantage becomes quite a inconvenient.

- It is welknown worldwide by practitioners of projects in partnership that increasing the number of partners directly increases the project complexity and consequently the global project overhead. This leads to an increased burden in project costs in such a heterogeneous environment.

- Besides the cost and effort, it takes time to simply setup a minimum project policy level including information exchange procedures between partners.

- Duplication, inefficient work share and cost share, and ambiguity in task responsibilities are traditional welknown major risks. Within such a heterogeneous environment communication is always a big problem that is considerably increased when operating from geographically dispersed sites.

- Last but not least, within a single company it is already difficult to fully profit form lessons learned, but during a partnership project no dedicated structure exists to support a learning process.

5.4.3. Major weaknesses

The performance of the global business process within a project consortium is unfortunately not the sum of each partner's performance but rather their ability to work together (see Chapter 1). Among the weaknesses facing companies, we can underline the following:

- Most of the project overhead is generated by important weaknesses, due to the lack of a common model for operation, such as incompatible processes and organizations and insufficient interoperability between project activities and information systems.
- In the interperson relationship, within these consortia, lack of trust between persons can cause an inefficient operation in the long term.
- Timely and costly engineering changes are direct consequences of a traditional sequential design process of trading partners that lacks early design collaboration.
- It constitutes another major weakness on the global efficiency road either in missing cost-reduction opportunities and increasing project complexity both in monitoring project costs and schedule as well as managing documents update and distribution.
- Today cooperation between trading partners is too restrictive based on commercial and contractual rules that lock the necessary iterative design collaboration loop between varying expertise and interfere with the human resource management.
- No project space that can be shared between the trading partners as a common denominator for being able to work efficiently together. Within traditional cooperation, companies exchange formal documents that have been elaborated with their own policies and procedures even if they are not necessarily compatible between them. We give some developments about electronic documentation in Chapter 6.

These weaknesses are important incentives to reduce project overhead as it represents up to 50 percent of the entire program cost. This can be measured with the proper metrics.

Another incentive is more strategic as it concerns the big potential for cost-reduction opportunities during the early design stage of a project. In fact, the design stage of a project fixes up to 70 to 80 percent of the total product cost while it costs only about 20 percent of the program cost. This influences dramatically the life-cycle costs and the reduction of the lead time while improving the global quality and customer satisfaction. A recent study shows that most of the large projects are not on time and whithin budget. This opens the way to new operating approaches to overcome these problems.

The new approach is rather based on short collaborations between partners to maximize global design capacity. This collaboration is based on shared working spaces regulated by unique project policies and procedures for all the partners even if each partner can decide to use again its own policies and procedures outside of the shared working spaces. One example of this is the European Project FREE which recognizes two layers of exchange - the formal layer for commercial and contractual deliveries and the maturation layer for project preparation and product/ and processes design such as studying together needs and requirements, as well as elaborating specifications or exploring alternatives. The two layers have to be synchronized on agreed mechanisms, such as reviews and baseline management, to move the document from the maturation layer up to the formal layer.

The FREE architecture is built up from a conceptual model considering the three following views - process, organizational, and technological

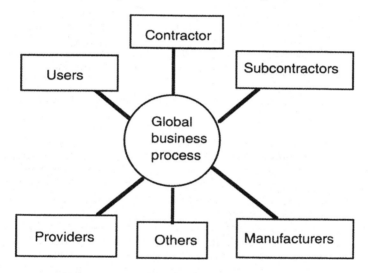

Figure 5.4. Creating an adaptative value chain.

Each view is built up from base practices and recommends necessary capabilities. For the initiation of the business case and improving effectiveness of the virtual organization, there is the method for capability assessment. During the operational phase, performance measurements are used to monitor efficiency and to provide suggestions for improvement. It is possible to contribute to the creation of the global adaptive value chain, as is illustrated in figure 5.4.

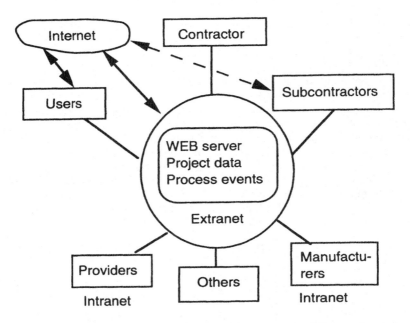

Figure 5.5. Internet, Intranet, and Extranet enabling tools.

Table 5.4. illustrates the relationship between traditional technology and IT by comparing different items, information scope, actors and concurrency level. It distinguishes two levels of concurrency - weak and strong. This table shows the differences in working practices in several cases. We can see, for example, the traditional parallel work, using traditional technology, and the parallel work, using IT technologies. The role of human operators is also different.

Table 5.4. serves as a basis for crossing the global business value-added chain with IT - in this case, with Internet, Intranet, and Extranet technologies. Figure 5.5. illustrates this case, presenting a general view about the interrelations plan between global value chains of businesses and the networks, represented by Internet, Intranets, and Extranet. All these nets have similar common standard protocols and have their own scope. But this way allows us to study some business cases and put on the table the problem of the electronic commerce that is discussed in the next chapter.

Table 5.4. Traditional technology and IT supported

	Item	Traditional Technology	IT
Information scope	Project	Drafts, folders	Document management, product and process models
	Company	Archives, microfilms	Data-warehouse
	Country	Libraries	National information systems
	World	Journals, conferences	Global IT nets
Actors	Person and person	Speech, phone, fax, mail	Email, video-conference
	Person and application		Visualization, virtual reality, GUIs
	Person and machine	Direct manipulation	
	Application and machine		NCs tools, robotics, remote sensors
Concurrency	Weak concurrency	Parallel work	Parallel work
	Strong concurrency	Expert's experience, intuition	AI, case-based reasoning

References
Julien, Pierre Andre. (1995). "L'entreprise partagée": contraintes et opportunités. *Proceedings ILCE'95 Concurrent Engineering and Technical Information Procesing, Paris.*, Paris, France.

6 BUSINESS CASES AND ELECTRONIC COMMERCE

6.1 Introduction

This chapter studies some business cases and briefly electronic commerce. By studying business cases, we can examine advantages, problems, limits, and constraints that are encountered by the enterprises that try to put in practice the most advanced productive paradigms. We selected three cases. The first studies the Virtual Vertical Enterprise (VIVE). This is a current research problem involving several European countries. The principal merit of VIVE is the integration of SMEs. Virtual Enterprise (and then concurrent enterprise) is a problem not only for the biggest companies, but because of the nature of the involved technologies for the largest set of companies.

The second case concerns the oil industry. According to our experience, this is one of the best examples of an increasing use of ICT that finishes by the creation of virtual enterprises. The problem is very concrete but can be solved in a modern environment with a ICT background.

The third case concerns the electronic document. This is also a very important case for understanding how different companies must work together around a common thing (some kind of common denominator) called an electronic document. We present a paragraph about this document.

This case shows some limits, and we would establish a link with electronic commerce, a fundamental element in this new era. We make a short presentation of electronic commerce.

6.2. Business cases

In this section, we comment on three cases.

6.2.1. The virtual vertical enterprise (VIVE).
The virtual vertical enterprise (VIVE) is presented by R. Santoro (1997). The VIVE project aims at developing a framework to build the virtual vertical enterprise, by exploring opportunities offered to SMEs by electronic commerce and cooperative working technology. The VIVE concept and its implementation is based on the following:

- The consortium of a new entity, the business integrator, capable of:

1. Identifying market opportunities,
2. Specifying the required business processes, the enterprise integration infrastructure (communications, information sharing means,...), the skills, and the capacities for the VE to be created,
3. Soliciting and supporting suitable SMEs to enter the business venture,
4. Ensuring that adequate information management support is available to SME partners throughout the VE operational life;
- The development of robust methods for selecting and adapting ICT solutions to enable the operation of such distributed business venture.

The project brings together all the players necessary to the implementation of the SME VE concept:
- The business integrators, in this case played by two regional technology transfer centers - Democenter from Italy and Richelieu from France - both which are involved in support and promotion activities for local SMEs;
- The methodology service providers, developing the required functional organizational and technological infrastructure - in this case, an engineering consulting company, CE Consulting from Italy, and a computer system company, Siemens Nixdorf from Germany;
- Two business operators with a specific task to validate the generalized methodology proposed by CE Consulting - Alenia Missili from Italy and ITCC from Greece, participating as an associate partner to CE Consulting;
- A number of SMEs, engaged in the planned pilot projects - OCS, Oil Control, and Ansaldo Ricerche from Italy, and Soditech, HEF and RBC from France;
- A number of SMEs, large enterprises, IT providers and regional centers that are interested in the exploitation of the VIVE concept, that contribute to the definition of organizational and technological requirements for the SME VE through the participation in interest groups.

The projects will deliver methodologies and technologies for the creation of a VE among SME and will be conducted through four different phases:

1. A definition phase that will result in the reference architecture of the VE:

a. The product breakdown resulting in the needed skills and technologies,
b. The corresponding business process model, identifying the roles played by each partner and the flow of all activities,
c. The general ICT infrastructure to support the products and processes from individual SMEs;

2. An implementation phase, which will produce the prototype infrastructure to implement the identified requirements on real business cases, two pilot cases have been identified in the mechanical and molten carbonate cells for batteries sectors;

3. An experimentation and evaluation phase for running the industrial test cases, providing also suggestions for further specific R&D initiatives to relevant National and European bodies, focus on:

a. For the mechanical VE, on the cooperative design of new products families and on the network extension to suppliers and customers,

b. For the molten carbonate for batteries, on the integration of different competence in the development cycle of the product, including R&D and manufacturing of single components, in order to improve the overall performance of batteries cells,

4. A consolidation and generalization phase that will provide an assessed implementation strategy and methodology for re-deployment of SME VE concept on new business opportunities.

The first three phases correspond to the main steps in the VIVE methodology, as outlined in Figure 6.1.

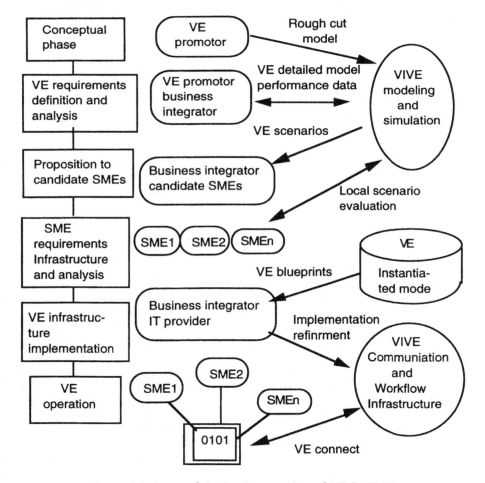

Figure 6.1. Steps of the implementation of VE in SMEs.

The main results of the project will be as follows:

1. A general model for VE operation;

2. A modeling and simulation tool and method capable of
    a. Supporting the allocation of functions to individual entities, allowing for simulating operations of the VE,
    b. Supporting analysis of compatibility of current work environment and operations infrastructures in SMEs with the planned operation environment of the VE, and supporting planning actions to overcome identified gaps;

3. Two industrial implementation test cases, resulting in two operative VEs;

4. Assessment of methods and technology for redeploying SME VE concept and application results on new business opportunities for similar applications;

5. Generalized requirements for concept adoption in a wider range of market sectors and associated methodologies and technologies.

The interest groups will contribute to the definition of organizational and technological requirements for the SME VE. Four interest groups will be built:

•   Regional centers devoted to support to enterprises and technological innovation, interested in redeploying project experience in their local environment;

•   SME interested in participating in the creation of VEs;

•   Large enterprises interested in increasing through to VIVE concept their efficiency in the acquisition of supplies;

•   IT providers, interested in evolving their own solution to suit the VIVE operating scenario.

6.2.2. Collaborative working case in the virtual enterprise

The oil search case (Jory, 1995). How CE is applied between trading partners? This concerns a shared information from Web servers, CD-ROMs, and real-time measurements about oil field services. The client, an Oil Field company, calls Schlumberger to answer to this key question: Is there any oiling in my concession and can't I retrieve it in profitable way? Schlumberger will put together a solution and propose to this client a suite of combined services.

First question: Where should we drill the hole? To answer to this question, Geco-Prackla (a Norwegian company) is providing seismic services. Work consists in emitting acoustic signals, either from a boat or from a land truck, and analyzing echos at the surface with geophones. From these measurements, the client gets a better idea of the underground geological structure, and it is now possible to determine where there is a reasonable chance to find a profitable oil reservoir. Once a possible oil field is identified, Sedco-Forex (a French-American company) is called to provide the necessary land or offfshore platform and the necessary rig equipment. This company provides MDS (management drilling system) drilling parameters that are monitored in real time (depth, rate of penetration, mud pressure, mud flow in and out, fluid levels in tanks) to help the driller control the drilling process. The company provides also the drilling management systems such as daily drilling report, equipment maintenance, inventory control, and health and safety DBs during the process.

Dowell is in charge of providing mud, cement, and fracturing services. Anadrill provides measurements while drilling, logging while drilling.

Wireline and Testing provides logging and testing services. Once the pipe string is pulled out of the hole, logging tools are carried down to the bottom and pulled back up while collecting formation evaluation data. Data is transmitted to the surface through an electric wire and monitored by an acquisition system at the worksite. Perforation tools are then introduced to perforate formation at the right depth and shaped charges are fired to facilitate the evacuation of the oil.

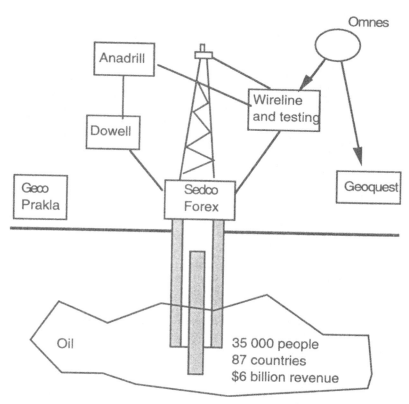

Figure 6.2. Schlumberger Oilfield Services.

Data recorded at the wallsite is sent to land, by satellite or through magnetic tapes, to be processed and interpreted. Geoquest provides interpretation services. Data are analyzed on graphic workstations, and results are used to take further decisions on the drilling process. Reservoir modeling is completed by collecting data from different wells. The information is used to understand how to optimize the extraction of oil out of the whole reservoir. Two approaches have been used to combine the data: the geoshare half allows information to be converted from a given data model into another. In parallel, work is under way in cooperation with oil companies and other service companies to implement a common data model for all DBs: this work is completed within the scope of the Petroleum Open Software Corporation (POSC).

More than 35 000 people are working for Schlumberger Oilfield Services in eigthy eight countries. Companies have been joining the group with equipment, traditions, and methods. In such a context, integration of people and systems is a challenge. Communication between research and engineering centers and field operations is critical. OMNES is in charge of supporting communication systems for the whole group. This company has been formed as a joint venture between Schlumberger, Cables, and Wireless. Data management is possible in the long run only if a common data model is adopted. Figure 6.2. illustrates the whole oild field services and processes and the place of different companies involved in it.

The integrated enterprise. Integrated enterprise can be seen as a biological cell. Organs that are the six service companies (also called «sister companies» or «Product line» perform the various functions. The corporate information is fed into the electronic document management systems. BASIS (business applications solutions in Schlumberger) is the name of the project in charge of installing the ASP management package across all product lines. It acts as the kernel of the cell. It will integrate all vital functions such as finance, logistics (material management, maintenance, sales and distribution).

The integration enterprise exchanges information whith its environment: a technology watch group works in Austin to deliver the lastest news from world-wide organizations to the Schlumberger technical community according to predefined profiles. The client link component investigates new client needs, and stores them in the EDM. The Schlumberger technical community consults the set of pending requests and proposes technical solutions. The client link team consolidates the answers and setup packages to be proposed as new services. The integrated project management team (IPM) is a virtual company, which is set up at the worksite to perform a given task with the client. Schlumberger human Resources and equipment from various product lines are put together to work for a limited period (one month to one year) with client, vendors and subcontractors. Figure 6.3. illustrates the Integrated Enterprise including a Virtual Company as a part.

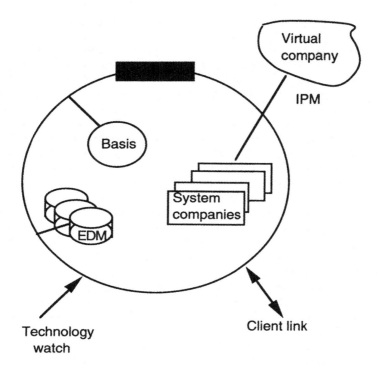

Figure 6.3. Integrated enterprise.

The integration is made by levels. First, at the worksite, various Schlumberger and nonSchlumberger service companies can connect their acquisition systems to the rig area network to share measurements and allow a global supervision of the drilling process for the various partners. Company man, tool manager, rig superintendant, driller, mud engineer, mud loggers, electrical and mechanical engineers, and warehouseman can get the right information coming from different partners at the right place at the right time.

Several DBs are used in rig sites:

- *DBD (drilling DB).* All daily information related to operations (drilling activities, mud and bit characteristics, daily rate, personnel on board);

- *CAM (computer aided maintenance).* PMS (preventive maintenance tasks are scheduled and maintenance jobs are documented);

- *SICC (Schlumberger inventory control system).* Inventory management; and

- *STB (stability program).* Computing rig balance criteria.

CD-ROMs will be distributed to all rigs with documents, quality procedures, maintenance procedures, operation manuals, training manuals, and vendor lists.

Second, worksite information is consolidated at the company level in districts, regions and headquarters. drilling DBs information is used to perform well

126

performance Analysis and produce statistical information on drilling processes. This information is used in return to enhance service quality at the rig-site. Maintenance and wharehouse status are used in the distribution center located in Houston. Information stored in the Web is made available to the all authorized locations connected to the Schlumberger network.

The third level of integration comprises outside partners such as clients, vendors and subcontractors. This is typically the case during the integrated services where all partners need to exchange mails and reports on a continuous basis. Under certain circumstances, restricted mail accounts have been open for nonSchlumberger customers who have worked with Schlumberger projects for several months. Figure 6.4. illustrates the different levels of IT integration.

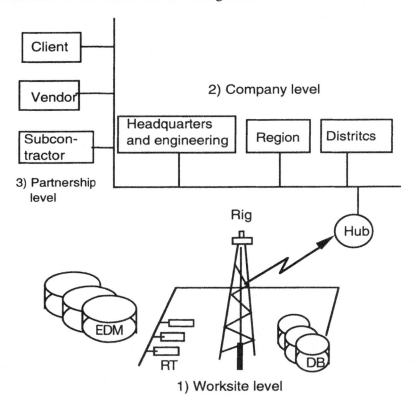

Figure 6.4. Integration levels.

In addition to that, integration must be also done geographically. Sedco-Forex operations are organized in the four main regions such as North and South America (regional office Caracas), Europe and Africa (regional office in Montrouge), Middle East (regional office in Dubai); Asia (region office in Singapore). Each region controls a certain number of districts. There are twenty-first active districts at he time of this experience.

Worldwide communications are done through SINET (Scl Information Network), which is now operated by OMNES. Thanks to this network, every workstation or PC is able to communicate with anyone in the company located anywhere. Figure 6.5. shows main points of the network in Europe, Africa, and Asia. The figure illustrates a simplified western hemisphere network.

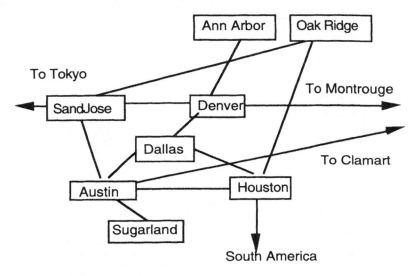

Figure 6.5. Simplified western hemisphere network.

IT trend. As many other companies here Schlumberger went through several stages of integration, following IT trends. The "do it the first time" motto with the QUALITY program was established in all Schlumberger organizations. A company-wide study was initiated to define global solutions.

The first result of the QUALITY program was to implement a standards management system, covering all activity domains. Immediately after, Time to Market became a critical issue. New solutions were then investigated to reduce the production cycle for wireline tools. The product cycle for wireline tools was reduced dramatically (four to two years) by implementing CIM (computer integrated manufacturing) techniques from 1982 to 1985. Cost CIM was very high (multiple CAD systems, numerical command machines, link to MRP system). The new target was then to reduce design and manufacturing costs by all means.

To reduce cost, the main priorities given by top management were to reuse internal software modules, choose outsourcing as much as possible for new developments, and downsize current computer equipment (1989 to 1991). These organization changes required a new effort to maintain team efficiency in a distributed environment. How to work together?

In 1992, Concurrent Engineering concepts were considered and selectively applied to integrate resources and activities among the different product lines. In 1994, a global study for integration of finance, logistics and personnel management across all product lines was initiated. The SAP product was selected. The new priority is to simplify business processes. Thus the need for business process

128

reengineering is the new issue. Facing this new challenge involves more than pure technology: human factors are now recognized as critical.

At this point we come back to the individual - the partner.

Each Web server is handled by a central system administrator and by distributed Web collectors, who are in charge of loading do and creating the project HTML links. Webs can be geographically dispersed. They will be located at the region offices to load documents generated by the region. Users can be anywhere on the Schlumberger network. Figure 6.6. illustrates this situation.

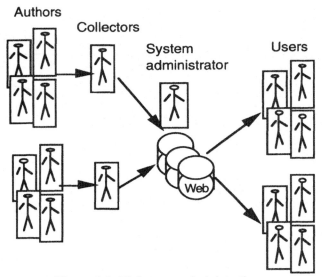

Figure 6.6. Webserver administration.

The CD-ROM generation begins by collecting source documents and their conversion into a common internal format. Collection can be done from a digital format or from paper documents. Acrobat PDF format has been selected as the internal common format representation because it is

- Compatible with all existing packages,

- Handles text and graphics,

- Uses a compact format, that is well adapted to remote communication,

- Has a powerful search capability (full text search and index)

- Includes a powerful scanning package (Acrobat Capture),

- Offers a sophisticated display function at user end but no editing (good for ISO 9001),

- Includes annotation for reviews feedback,

- Has a very easy consultation interface. The page-based display, although less powerful than the text-based display of SGML packages, is easier to handle by the user.

Acrobat files are enriched with header information (Author, Title, Subject, and Keywords) for future index search. Hypertext links are created for future easy navigation. After validation, the documents are loaded into the Webserver, which acts as a repository for corporation documents.

Once all documents are stored on the Web, part of them will be copied on to the CD-ROM. The index is generated (for fast thorough header criteria), document-encrypted CD-ROM master is printed and tested in-house. The distribution is implemented through controlled procedure.

The real time measurements are acquired though the rig area network (RAN). Various acquisition systems that can belong to independent Service Companies are connected to the network. Communication protocol is WITS (wellsite information transfer standard), which Clients have promoted. Acquisition systems are WITS servers. A WITS collector receives the data from all servers and broadcasts selectively to WITS clients. Only a minimum data value does transit on the network. Screen manipulation (numerical and graphical display zoom, logs, log editor) is handled locally by the client machine. This allows remote rig supervision through a simple telephone line using SLIP (Serial Line IP).

The company partner now needs to handle multiple, continuous, dense information flows. Adaptation to this new environment requires more than powerful IT tools. Migration strategies must be carefully designed, and tools must be used selectively. Human factors such as nonverbal communication and team spirit, play an important role. Figure 6.7. illustrates information tools at the worksite.

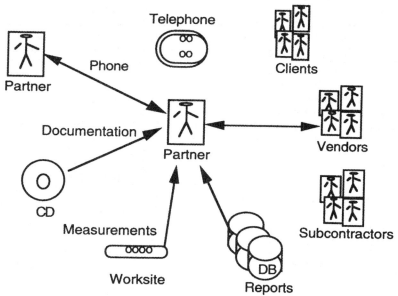

Figure 6.7. IT tools: Worksite view.

Here are a few problems encountered today:

- *Long messages sent by mail.* Just realize that receiver may receive an average of fifty mailings per day. Chances are very high that they won't be read. This situation is ideal for creating human frustration.

- *Communication exclusively through mail.* Messages can be missinterpreted easily.

The client server architecture let the user fetch the information he needs when he needs it:
- General training must identify key useful locations among the zillions now available and must navigate efficiently to discover new ones;

- Electronic mail can be used to get news, events, announcements and short answers;

- The Web can be consulted about documents that have been announced by mail.

At the worksite, remote communication is often difficult, and people must rely on local facilities. Documentation on CD-ROM is very easy to use. Real-time measurements are essential to control the drilling process. But comprehensive archival is most of the time a waste of resources. Nevertheless, one-hour archival may be useful to play-back to analyze causes of an accident. DB recording and reporting must have a very simple user interface. In most cases, the phone or short wave radio is enough to keep real-time communication with the base. Data can be transferred to the base on a daily or weekly basis.

The logistics partner is one of the most loaded in terms of data flows. His job consists essentially in communications. He now needs help from a computer tool to handle the complexity of internal and external exchanges of information. Finally, the management of so many interrelated objects and data flows has become the new challenge of the 1990s. The problem is to have powerful integrated products that can be customized to company business architecture to get a better control of complex finance/logistics/human resources issues.

6.2.3. The VERIPLAN Case.
Documents circulation concerning building drafts for the modular extension of the CDG Airport (Paris). Figure 6.8. illustrates the business partners and the main issues of the draft exchanges. The biggest projects are always running in a particular context: the need for the long previous studies, for a number of separated parts, and for the continuous trading adjustments between partners involved. This situation generates the need for continuous modifications and updating draft which, in turn, generates additional tasks. This last point is very important because in the case studied here, the additional costs are increasing by more than 10 percent over the original budget.

Thus one fundamental question is to solve the problem of drafts circulation between partners by creating a more fluid technical information exchange within the ADP and between the ADP (Paris Airport Company) and contractor companies, when they are

- Exchanging CAD data,

- Unifying documents exchanges to avoid any duplicated circuits (paper and digital), and

- Improving efficiency of draft verification and the technical coordination.

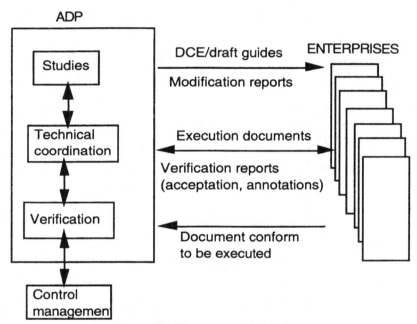

Figure 6.8. Documents circulation.

All this must contribute to improving the quality of new studies, facilitate the integration of modifications in the actual documents, and ensure the project conformity to the previous planned studies and reduce the cost of additional tasks. To do it, the VERIPLAN architecture illustrated in Figure 6.9. was designed.

The main functionalities of these systems are as follows:

- *Exchanges.* Load and unload signatures of messages; official design and recording of the undergoing operations;

- *Technical coordination.* Added value, main draft computation, drafts comparisons, and draft synthesis;

- *Verification circuits (very essential).* Diffusion graph management (paper documents and digital documents), control of the delays verification by computer;

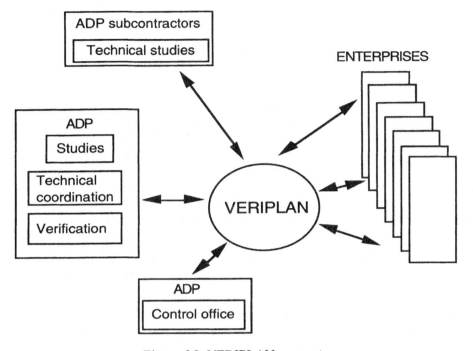

Figure 6.9. VERIPLAN concept.

- *Verification.* Consultation of ADI (recording, documents, workplan) and emission of verification reports.

The software included network Novell Netware at the physical level of the network, Windows environment, relational DB Oracle, groupware Lotus Notes, and the editor AUTOCAD. Figure 6.10. illustrates the VERIPLAN general architecture of exchange organization allowing different exchanges between partners.

This project has spent two years becoming operational (1992 to 1994). From February 1994 to May 1995 the majority of companies were connected to the VERIPLAN, and then they were able to operate in a virtual enterprise environment concerning the drafts exchanges and its verification. As the result, this system is used freely and easiest but some difficulties appeared. Among them we can underline the nonconformity of some CAD drafts to the exchange format rules; the defaults of connection management at the beginning and the nonadaptation of traditional companies to do business and trading in this new virtual environment. Nevertheless, the VERIPLAN contribution is important: new comfortable working conditions; productivity increasing in CAD, verification, and coordination; availability of digital documents; and important money savings.

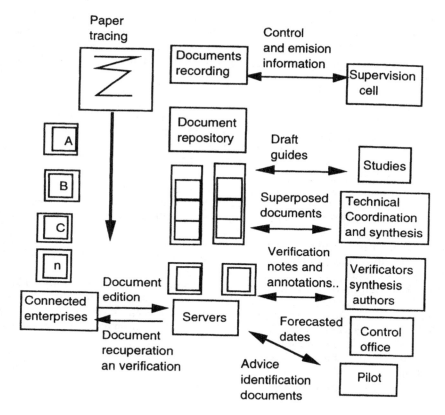

Figure 6.10. exchange document organization.

6.3. Electronic commerce (EC)

EC has three major inconveniences to overcome in the new environment:

- It is sometime confounded with the electronic data Interchange (EDI).

- It is also assimilated to CALS. CALS was born in the United States as computer-aided logistics support, and then it began commerce at the light speed. This has probably installed some confusion in the spirit of businesses that, by nature, needs a stable approach.

- Security is a headache not only for companies but also for governments because the problems involve and the challenge all nations.

EDI has now reached its maturity in most developed countries, and normally there is a convergence between standards used for doing electronic exchange (administration, commerce and transportation documents). Also a lot of know-how has been cumulated during the last fifteen years in this field. Nevertheless, EDI is not a practice that has been generalized to the entire set of companies doing business, and then it must become rather a limitation. But whatever appreciation we have concerning EDI, no EC policy can ignore EDI, and therefore must design including EDI.

CALS, even some misunderstanding exists concerning the acronym, is now known worldwide. For example, it is migrating from its original military industrial use to civil industry, as shown in the increasing, and massive, involvement of the Japanese manufacturing industry. In this country and in other Southeastern Asian countries, CALS is used not only for advanced manufacturing but also for the construction industry (it correspond directly to Japanese needs in this domain). But we cannot assimilate CALS and EC.

Curiously, people do not seem to be aware of other technology, which is also interesting in EC. STEP and related technologies are revising the electronic exchange for CAD, CAM, and manufacturing purposes. In our view, EC must also integrate this reality.

But EC becomes a planetary challenge thanks to the development and rapid spreading of the Internet technology and some related technologies such as networking computing.

In fact, Internet technology is increasingly becoming a space that not only links individuals inside organization, but also links the enterprises together. Thus individuals are linked to organization and individuals each other, leading to a dramatic increase in access and reach. This allows people to tap into the network and collaborate from anywhere, creating possibilities for teams to work on projects remotely and then disband when projects are finished. This situation results from the evolution of IT, which is creating a network-centric computing environment, characterized by a new dynamic. Figure 6.11. illustrates this new IT evolution.

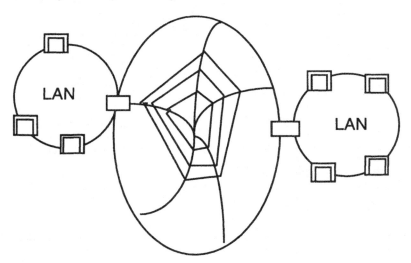

Figure 6.11. Network-centric computing.

But this evolution must be accompanied by a corresponding evolution in organization and in access. Organization must now become more and more extended and based on the virtual components of the business. Access must also be possible for anyone, anywhere, and at anytime. Networking computing allows the establishment of an effective organization regardless of physical boundaries but also the building of networked companies that extend into the value chains of their customers and suppliers and vice versa.

The potential for improved efficiency is very significant. Jim Barksdale, president and CEO, Netscape, explains that desktop-centric computing was marvelous for spreadsheets and word processors and for improving the productivity of the individual. But network computing, by hooking everything together, improves the productivity of the team so that the team is actually more than the sum of its parts. Smart companies do good jobs of networking, and they now have open standards-based tools to do that without having to go back and replicate or replace every desktop computer they've got or rewrite every desktop application.

Networking computing affects business. It will act as an EC facilitator. Thus, banks can offer secure transaction services that can be used at home at the customer's convenience. Health-care professionals can collaborate on a complex diagnosis real-time, regardless of physical location, as Rostchild Parisian Hospital is doing in cancer stomach surgery. Distributors can respond better and more quickly to retailers because they wil have real-time information about customer behavior, which is unpredictable, even for the most sophisticated existing econometric models.

A good example is Federal Express, which is taking advantages of networking computing to improve business processes. This company uses the Internet to allow customers to track the status of their own packages (a dream for many researchers in the logistic field a few years ago!). This has increased customer satisfaction and reduced expenses. But the question is more interesting because Federal Express, as well as other companies doing business by Internet, should think about other kinds of information they can unload onto the network to benefit their customers.

The networking computing profoundly impacts the evolution of ICT. This world birth from convergence of computing, communications, and content. Figure 6.12. illustrates this situation. This figure shows the closer interrelation between communications, content, and network. Each element become part of the same set.

Nevertheless, the Internet is difficult for business because it is hard to determine who is out there, and the number estimates also vary significantly. But what is more certain is the number of computers and networks providing Internet accesses. But people become accustomed - as they did with the telephone - to a new way of communicating and to practical life on the network. Some estimation considers that by year 2000 around half a billion individuals could use the Internet, and that traffic could exceed that of voice telephone at that time.

But what is impacting and provoking a veritable revolution is the Web. The Web began as a pull technology and it is becoming more and more a pull-push technology. For instance 65 percent of new users seek business or other relevant information. Not only is the number of users growing, but the characteristics of the users also are changing. Web users are increasingly time-pressured and looking for relevant information. There are higher expectations for quality of content (timeliness, relevance, and appearance).

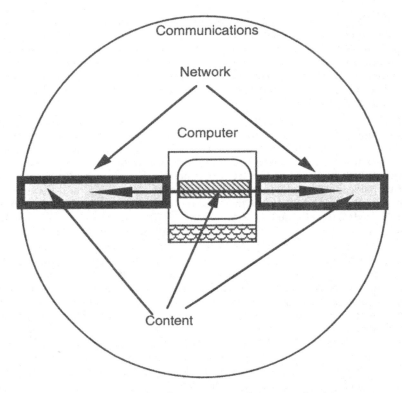

Figure 6.12. Network, content, and communications.

Similar situation pccurred in France during the early 1980s when the Teletel system was implemented to substitute for the electronic directory of France Telecom. At that time, people understood that the tool was more than a simple electronic directory, and then they offered thousands of services and created more than 32 000 new jobs. But the a massive telematic culture was created in the country, where by the year 1988, 6,5 and half millions of terminals were used by more than 18 million of households and companies.

Based on the Web explosion, many companies are now creating their own Web servers with an assessing home page and then thinking that they are now entering the EC era. But in reality, a simple home page may have a beautiful colors, but is, unfortunately, not electronic commerce. Nevertheless, it is preparing the future.

Concerning the strengths and weaknesses of the Internet today, it is in stake of rapid transformation. The Internet will

- Soon be the world's largest, cheapest, fastest, and most secure marketplace,
- Have half a billion users by the year 2000,
- Have a global reach,
- Have the most secure transaction environment,

- Provide a myriad of new services,

- Create a new Internet paradigm, and

- Become increasingly fee-based as value, ads and subscription services bring people tailored services and the possibility for business transactions.

The business focus will centered on gaining strategic advantage, reengineering processes, competing globally, leveraging internal and external information, and coping with complexity. Information technology will center on supporting a business focus, evolving role, providing global access, supporting multieverything, managing distributed computing, and controling complexity and cost.

6.4. Networking documents

This section studies the electronic document, which is the main support for electronic commerce in a wider sense, described above. To study this richest domain, we choose the networked document and its management.

6.4.1. Definition of document

According to the most commonly held view, a document is a piece of paper with printing on it. It's the thing that gets run through the copier, and it's the thing that gets sorted into piles that eventually get placed in folders.

Another view takes the document as being the end product of a process of gathering information and putting it into words and pictures. Here the costs are much higher, for one must factor in the intellectual labor.

A third view takes the document not as the end product of a process but as the means by which processes are accomplished. Status reports, forms, memos with comments, engineering change requests, product specifications, bills of materials, schedules, and so forth are the way organizations make their processes work. And even when the process has the manufacture of a document as its aim, the document itself can be understood as always in process.

When we speak about networking documents, we understand they are the electronic documents. An electronic document has a general definition: it is a document supported, processed, and permitted to be distributed by electronic means. But documents have a long history, which began when humans invented the first alphabet and were able to write about their history. But wide spread distribution of documents began with Gutenburg and his printing invention. Today we we live ina documented world. But the electronic document is quite different from the preceding one. First of all, an electronic document has a different format, the electronic pages are different, the recording system is different, the updating is different, and so on.

Nevertheless, the electronic document represents an important opportunity for improving administration in organizations. This kind of work represents an important part of the overall activity if we take it as an isolated activity. If we talk in a wider sense, these figures are even more important. For example, most of the working time of engineers, managers and technicians consists of writing or consulting documents. And these three positions represent an important part of the overall workforce.

A networked document management system is a scaleable entity, consisting of many types of technology that are increasingly recognized as important. Implementations of networked document management systems currently exist, and some are more sophisticated and advanced than others.

The confluence of several types of technology, along with the growing acceptance of several key international standardards, now makes it possible to create networked document management systems, that manage and leverage this key corporate asset. This affect the corporate information system, which has to have assimilated the single largest quantity of data left undigested on the planet - an amount that in most instances outweighs the current contents of the entire information system. Further, because the data are of a different type than information systems normally handle, and the type happens to be rich and complex, incorporating it into the information bloodstream requires learning, thinking, planning, and imagination.

6.4.2. Types of information
One can divide the information in an organization into the following categories:

- Transaction data are the high-volume, low-cost pieces of information that are managed by database managers. A single datum usually is of little strategic value, although the transaction management system as a whole may be absolutely crucial. Some types of transaction data systems include order administration, payroll, and inventory.

- Office documents are the memos, notes, letters, agendas, and other pieces of paper that fill our inbrays every morning. While a single office document may have a great deal of significance, they tend to have little lasting value. After you read one, you typically file and forget it.

- Strategic information is a separate type of datum, based on a set of transaction data and office documents that has critical value to the organization. This information is used as the touchstone for processes as they proceed and is what gets handed from one group to another as the processes are handed on.

- Technical information are drafts, CAD or CAM documents, specifications, technical manuals, and so on. Almost always it is an important part of the way products are designed, manufactured, and sold (product specifications, engineering change orders, assembly instructions, product catalogs). This information plays a crucial role in the manufacturing industry and in its relations with the other sectors.

6.4.3. Strategic document processes and problems.
Strategic documents are driving core business processes. It should be clear how positive or negative effects on these document processes could have immediate and long-term effects on competitiveness. That's why industry analysts say that corporations spend 8 to 12 percent of revenues on publishing.

Strategic documents are expensive because they are part of expensive processes. Although the processes necessarily vary according to their purpose and surrounding environment, typically they include many steps. Anything that can simplify, speed up, or reduce the cost of this process (a simplified diagram, which fails to express, for example, that a review process may involve dozens of people including some of the highest-paid executives in the organization) will benefit the organization.

As we explain in Chapter 1, documents belong to a specific category of products: they are information products, and must be considered as we consider any material goods during its production process.

This looks only at those corporate processes that have documents as their product. The fact is, however, that almost all business-critical processes use documents, even if they don't produce them. Further, documents are the way processes are handed on to other processes. Enhancing the distribution process - and making the information on them reusable - can greatly improve the velocity of these processes, even though they are not traditionally thought as document processes.

But the benefits go beyond cost savings, all the way to increasing competitive advantage. Managing strategic documents can shorten time to market, increase the quality of products (by rationalizing quality control procedures), improve services (by giving service personnel immediate access to information), and raise customer satisfaction (by increasing the quality of product and service). In addition, it can - to put it loosely - make an organization smarter. The document database every organization gathers is the repository of the enterprise's best thinking. A networked document management system can enable the organization to leverage that asset.

6.4.4. Benefits of managing strategic documents
To understand the benefits of a document it is necessary to examine its production and distribution processes and relate it to the the goals for a particular kind of document. Any document (administrative, commercial, or technical) can

- Shorten time to market,

- Cut costs,

- Reduce inventory,

- Improve quality of access,

- Improve the quality of the contents, and

- Improve the timeliness of the contents.

These benefits can directly affect competitiveness. For example, simply being able to put accurate, updated information into the hands of every field person can easily make one direct salesforce measurably more effective than another.

6.4.5. Characteristics of the networked document management
The networked document management system should possess the following characteristics:

- Openness,

- A client server environment,

- Comprehensiveness,

- Applicability to the entire life cycle,

- Easy to use, and

- Extendable.

The main top-level processes to be considered are input enhance, and output. To study these points, we take the case of the strategic document.

Input. Strategic documents almost always synthesize data developed elsewhere in the organization. The data may come from people creating contents directly in strategic documents, or it may come from work done previously with word processors and graphic packages or with other applications such as molecular design, financial modeling, or CAD. It may also be drawn from a database or from a repository in the HTML format we discuss below. The data may also be in rich-media formats such as video, animation, and sound.

Enhance. In the usual information-processing model, the word *transform* or *process* is used. But because this is not the mere alteration of one type of data into another, but is instead an adding of value to the input, we choose the word "enhance" instead. The enhancements consist of several different sorts: the incoming data are packaged into objects, objects that have to be managed, synthesized documents, and so on.

Output. A networked document management system is nothing but interesting unless users can easily get output from it. There are two main classes of output recipients - human beings and machines. Machines need their information in electronic form and need it to be structured or tagged in ways that the recipient application understands. The networked document management system obviously needs to be able to supply that type of output, whether it's an industry standard such as HTML or in other and possibly proprietary formats.

Humans can get their output on paper or online (thta is, on their computer screens). There are several business reasons why we are seeing a boom in online documents. The reasons fall into two broad classes, cost and value:

- Paper documents are expensive to produce, distribute, and inventory.

- They are very expensive to update, since that frequently means republishing an entire document set even though only a small percentage of it has actually changed.

- It is very hard for users to find information in paper documents, especially as a number of document increases.

- They are the same for every user although users may have different needs and preferences in terms of both contents and format.

Online documents can solve all these problems, but only if they are more than electronic paper. Electronic paper can help bring down the cost of dealing with documents. But a more thorough reengineering of documents for online distribution can increase the value of the documents as well as lower the cost associated with them.

In particular, within the context of the manufacturing industry, one question involves sharing product information. This is the case of the concurrent design.

The concurrent approach assumes an ideal environment, where engineers from different disciplines work on the product design simultaneously. After an initial conceptual model has been defined, several engineers should be able to work at the same time on the product definition, modifying or adding details to the design and also running application programs (such as stress analysis, and cost analysis, process planning). To fulfill integration requirements, two conditions are needed:

- It is necessary to have defined and modeled all the knowledge related both to the product (taht is, shape and functional behavior) and to the enterprise that has to produce it (such as available resources and tools).

- It is essential to define a mechanism that manages the coordination between the processes to be performed, since the different actions are not independent. Moreover, since the database is shared, access to the data should be synchronized in such a way that modifications made by different experts do not produce inconsistent results or invalidate specific functional requirements.

The product models have been widely investigated for representing and supporting all information about the product life cycle in such a way that all the involved activities may find the information they require, while redundancy is avoided and consistency after modifications is maintained. Traditional CAD modelers are not sufficient in this respect. But the automation of the analysis and production processes cannot be directly performed on the geometric description of the parts, since it is in terms of low-level entities completely unrelated to the functionality that the object serves and the production operations.

Since in the concurrent design perspective it is necessary to guarantee the possibility of evaluating at the right time the modifications proposed by the different actors of the design, it is important that all the feature-based representations are always available and coherent. Moreover, since not all the parts can be of interest for all the contexts, it is important to communicate the occurred modifications only to all the really interested actors. For example, let us suppose that, for economic reasons, the expert in charge of the machinability evaluation proposes to modify the open pocket of the object in a figure 1 in such a way that the size of the stiffeners is reduced. This change does not affect the handling context, while it can modify the structural behavior, thus only the structural analysis expert need be notified to decide whether the modification should be accepted or refused.

As we see, the electronic document is linked to the most divers activities and to the EC. EC represent the framework in which trading partners (in the example, the designers) must operate. concurrent enterprise is also emerging within this framework.

In this environment, the enterprise must be evolving continuously. Enterprise becomes an evolving entity and, in this way, a flexible and adaptable organism in a living world Amdahl's Law). As a new approach to enterprise competitiveness, we think first of all in terms of strategy. Then we think in terms of tactical and operational solutions to be undertaken, according to the local conditions in which every company integrating a partnership is evolving (a good example is the European FREE case). This is a new way for enabling an enterprise organization to answer to continuous changes occurring through market mode, product position, and economical and social situation. But at the same time, it is easy to imagine the flexible organization as a global generic business process and projects as operational business processes generated by the generic business process, belonging to different enterprises geographically dispersed. It explains why this is a virtual organization and why information and communication technologies (ICT) play here a crucial role in supporting interoperability among all the trading partners. Otherwise collaboration means the ability to share concepts, and this should not be underestimated even though the only available technology are today at the very low level of video-conferencing system and whiteboard.

As VE, concurrent enterprise does exist only for the duration of a given project and should have a customized organization performing of the project objectives to be as efficient as possible. A Concurrent Enterprise is virtually created for the first-class achievement of customer satisfaction. But it must be a flexible organization.

This flexible organization provides the capacity to launch concurrent enterprises as customized business processes fitting perfectly with project objectives. It is a kind of learning system where the global enterprise model evolves with lessons learned during project execution and its business environment. It is not just a question of knowledge management but how to create knowledge from value added collaboration with users, providers, and trading partners.

In addition, concurrent enterprise must be a learning organization. There is a kind of three-level structures in this global shared system that supports a modern nonmonolithic and effective organization. The first level is information, the second is discussion, and the third is decision. Facts, events, figures, and so on characterize the first level and provide the entities for learning. Conversations represent the second level of conceptualization, which support the social process that progressively generates the creation of new organizational knowledge. Processes, methods, procedures and conclusions are the elements of the third level supporting knowledge treatment that provides decision-making mechanisms.

This electronic value chain creates a new basis for business. As was shown in Chapter 1, this is called NII, GII or the information society inthe cas of Europe. More commonly it is also called cyberspace. In Paris, we call it *Hypermonde*, and for seven years we have thougth and discussed the principles, laws, and consequences of this new space for business (Club de l'Hypermonde, Paris). concurrent enterprise exists in this space - the space of the electronic commerce era. The Figure 6.13. illustrates the main bases of the concurrent enterprise - evolving enterprise, VE and concurrent engineering. The next chapter examines in more detail this new approach toward enterprise, centered particularly on the case of the manufacturing industry because it is the more advanced and its needs are more important.

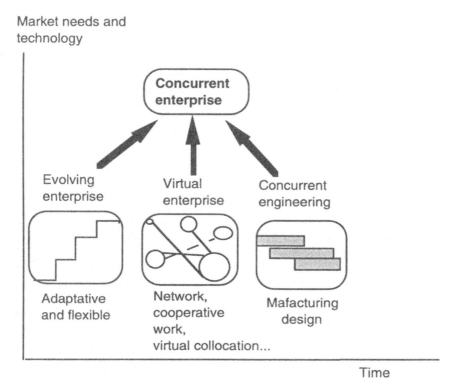

Figure 13 A view of Concurrent Enterprising Process

References
Jory, Roger. (1995)."The Oil Search Case." In *Proceedings of the ICE'95, Stokholm*. Stockholm.
Santoro, Robert. (1997)."VIVE Project." In *Proceedings of the ICE'97, Nottingham, UK*. Nottingham.

7 CONCURRENT ENTERPRISE

7.1. Introduction

This chapter also could be called "concurrent organization" because concurrency for competitiveness is a specific point of view of concurrency for performance where competitiveness means to be more efficient than competitors. "Concurrency for Better Performance: Toward the Concurrent Organization" would also be a possible title. It further means that we had to address the theoretical basis represented by concurrent organization and to compare it with other existing organization types.

Here, we should also honestly confess that the theoretical basis is not yet very well stabilized and still in its infancy even if we clearly foresee it applied to a particular aspect of the fractal theory in the collaboration and interaction domains. As the theoretical basis is not yet mature, we thought it was too early to try to widely deploy it in a concurrent organization chapter. Instead of a specific chapter, there is a short paragraph describing concurrent organization in this chapter, which is the application of the Concurrent Organization theory. A concurrent enterprising chapter follows it, which is the process that should be used to transform an enterprise into a concurrent one.

By enterprise we mean all activities having to produce something that should satisfy customers in the broad sense, such as television news, marketing projects, research projects, and new products development, just to cite a few of them, where creativity and innovation based on people and knowledge interactions are the main success factors. For sure there are number of economical and technical criteria to consider for a successful story such as being cheaper and faster than competitors while continuing to deliver first-class quality products in order to attract prospects and satisfy customers. As making profit is also an important economic criterion in satisfying shareholders in order to keep the necessary investment on board, it is recommended that solutions be optimized at the lower cost level. Concretely, it means that a concurrent enterprise should have the capacity to identify, deal, and operate concurrently with needed complementary competencies that are timely, costly, and risky to acquire to be successful with a specific target.

7.2. Cooperation, collaboration, and concurrency

Cooperation and collaboration are strategies, while concurrency is a tactical approach to being more creative and innovative in a faster and cheaper way. Here, cooperation means working separately to achieve something in common where partners' goals are not necessarily the same. Collaboration means working together to achieve common goals. Creativity means the capacity to have new ideas, and innovation means the capacity to implement new ideas. Cooperation is a good strategy if you don't want to share your ideas with someone else, but then the level of creativity and innovation is quite low due to this restricted amount of knowledge. Collaboration is a good strategy if you are not afraid to share your ideas and open to other ideas in order to reach the best level of creativity and innovation based on a larger amount of knowledge. As concurrency means adding forces in a complementary and simultaneous way to achieve a common goal, then it is easy to understand that it is a good complementary tactical approach or way of operating with a collaboration strategy. Concurrency is also synonymous with boundaryless organization as it has been demonstrated with concurrent engineering implementation that broken down barriers between disciplines enable collaboration (see boundarylessness in Chapter 1).

7.2.1. Concurrent organization

To survive in a fast-changing world, particularly in different domains, the adaptation capability should be higher than ever before. The adaptation capability combines the learning mode with creativity and innovation potential. Otherwise, survivability doesn't mean that someone or something has to live for eternity but lives for a given life cycle where learning and teaching are daily concurrent operations between the old, current, and new generations. In fact, new generations really constitute the surviving mechanism. While revolution has shown a tendency to push back to chaos (like reengineering), evolution is built on capitalized knowledge (like the learning organization). Then the opportunity is to rapidly progress in operating concurrently. It's like having a piece of the key, but some others own the complementary pieces, and you do not know them, and no one knows he has a piece of that key. Let's imagine that anyone can build up some models of all the pieces he has and put him or her on a global network. Here we have the connection with fractal theory, as some pieces should inevitably attract some others due to the fact they have something in common. Humanity constitutes one of those possible networks even if the interaction potential is quite low at a given period of time. Then it is multiplied along centuries. Stochastic interactions between facts and people enabled past discoveries, but trying to understand which one exactly made the body of the key appearing is like trying to identify which one of many low signals announcing changes was suddenly the enabler (signals announcing stock exchange growth, economic or political crises, thunderstorms, earthquakes).

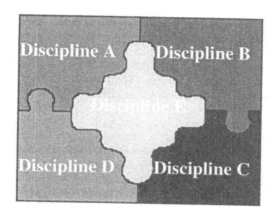

Figure 7.1. The multidisciplinary puzzle.

Enterprises are made of people whose individuality has a piece of the necessary knowledge, and altogether they constitute a new entity that is not only a juxtaposition of knowledge pieces but much more a puzzle where the symbiosis process helps to have pieces at the right place like a kind of sum. Figure 7.1. illustrates the multidisciplinary skill puzzle facing companies during the traditional partnership relations. Symbiosis is concurrency between natural elements that mutually bring something to the others in order to reach a situation that they can't reach alone. How symbiosis is demonstrable by the fractal theory is another interesting question where concurrent organization theory could be a good link between the two. Did you notice that water is for the earth like blood is for the body? Life exists on the earth due to the water flow, and all existing entities on the earth operate concurrently with the water flow exactly as cells in your body operate concurrently with the blood flow.

A concurrent organization is characterized by a system having a main conducting flow or stream where all existing entities belonging to that system are contributing to this flow in a complementary harmonized way (symbiosis). Exactly like the earth with the water flow, the body with the blood flow, or a tree with the sap flow, an enterprise should be organized around a specific flow. This is a knowledge flow, which starts by needing understanding and then continues by creating ideas that are transformed into solutions satisfying the needs. Concurrent organizations are multidimensional where different systems can contribute to another one, from infinitely small toward infinitely large or vice-versa. To understand how a concurrent organization operates it is necessary to know interdependencies between its constituting entities. Here it might be helpful to explain to deciders, such as politicians, and managers, that before undertaking any decision should try to simulate its impact in running a model made of interdependencies just to check whether it will be consistent or not.

7.2.2. The real enterprise richness

It's clear that employees constitute the real richness of any enterprise as only people can create and innovate. But it is also widely agreed that a group of people can learn and progress, even when some of them are leaving or entering the group, if they can model their knowledge in order to reuse and improve it. Just look at society to be convinced! What you will see is formal knowledge expressed as laws and regulations in term of rules, and informal knowledge as behavior in the presence of those laws and regulations. That means that any organization of living entities can learn how to be more efficient but that the type of organization, closed or open, is conditioning a slow or fast evolution. Within the enterprise evolution, people should find their own evolutionary way to contribute to an enterprise success.

7.2.3. The best enterprise asset

The best asset of any enterprise is its own capitalized knowledge that could be used by people for increasing the creativity potential and speeding up the innovation process. This knowledge is improved by the learning process, as there is always something new to learn (the humility rule). It's the best asset of any enterprise, as it will sustain the adaptation process for staying competitive.

Enterprises inherited the heavy hierarchical organization from the traditional army organization used for centuries. Organizations evolved very slowly due to barriers or boundaries that limited knowledge dissemination between different cultures. Consequently, people were willing to continue doing the same thing just because they knew it perfectly, they felt good with it, and they did not know there was something better elsewhere or just ignored it. A hierarchical organization is based on a kingdom principle where boundaries are the other kingdoms. They all are fighting against each other in order to have the larger kingdom or to protect what they already have. Knowledge is dispersed throughout the different kingdoms.

7. 3. Concurrent enterprise and electronic commerce

Enterprises have to learn how to be more efficient in operating concurrently, which means sharing part of their own knowledge with their trading partners to sustain a successful collaboration. Concurrent enterprises are organizations building up different business models that are accessible through a network where they are registered for business collaboration in specific domains with particular targets. Those models are continuously updated on the basis of the lessons learned, new means, and new technologies that benefit their next collaborative opportunities.

Concurrent enterprises register for a business network for trading and exchanging models. Concurrent enterprises tender through a request model and answer calls through available models.

This principle of using business is modeled on a network where enterprises are registered for business collaboration. This is illustrated in Figure 7.2. Each enterprise is building up business models by using their knowledge about the needed interactions for operating with eventual trading partners. Using those business models any enterprise is able to answer to every call for collaboration, issued in the business domains they are registered for, in a faster and efficient way. It further allows enterprises to look for collaborative partners, registered on the network for a specific domain having specific expertise, in trying their business models for checking their compatibility with the targeted objectives in terms of offered solutions, availability, computed prices and lead time, and so on.

Furthermore, the application of this principle will enable real access for SMEs (small and medium-size enterprises) to the global market because their business models will be available on the network where they are registered for their specific expertise or capabilities in specific domains.

Now, looking the Figure 7.2., let's imagine that an enterprise is willing to sell a new product or service and to launch a marketing campaign they need to design, produce, and distribute specific marketing documents. Now they have to select a marketing campaign consultant, a document designer, a printing, and a routing company, which all will have to join the multidisciplinary team already working on the new product or service to be sure that everything will be done in an efficient and coherent way. For that, they search on the network, directly or by using agents, for each specific expertise they are looking for in using their requirements in a call model. The call model is composed of needs and requirements.

Figure 7.2. Models interchange on a business network for business deal opportunities.

Then the network will provide a list of enterprises, responding to the needs of the appropriate domain having a business model matching the requirements provided in the call model. Different criteria could be used to elaborate a shorter list of possible solutions that will be further simulated in the global project perspective by changing parameters to select the most appropriate enterprises for the final global solution. In this way, enterprises that will be the trading partners that collaborate on specified projects are selected according to rational criteria that satisfy global needs and requirements rather than according to constantly moving criteria when discovering dramatic implications of choices.

After the enterprises selection, each partner will customized its models to the targeted solution and achieve a virtual prototype that covers the entire life-cycle parameters in order to design an optimized solution. This virtual prototype will support interactions for a tradeoff between the disciplines of the trading partners. On the Figure 7.2, color boxes circulate throughout the network to other enterprises. they simulate possible solutions by using models to eventually answer a specific call. The virtual prototype, representing the new product or service life cycle, is also composed of operating models provided by the trading partners. Part of the virtual prototype could also be used to check how the market will receive the new product or service and what could be done to better answer market demand.

Electronic commerce is not only a way of selling goods or services electronically to consumers but also a way of doing business electronically by enabling enterprises to operate concurrently with their market, between trading partners and even with users in order to better answer rapidly changing market demands. If not, it means it is necessary to create the electronic business domain for covering this need of wider, faster, and cheaper business collaboration offering real opportunities to SMEs to access the global market through the network. Concurrent enterprise is not only another Internet issue but rather a business issue in linking enterprises expertise and capacities to provide new business opportunities, which is related to the business integrator strategy for SMEs, and real access to the global market. It's also a way of linking trading partners' know-how for operating concurrently to better serve the customer demands. It is intended to systematically establish networked dynamic interactions for improving the global efficiency during all the project stages either bid preparation, marketing, design, manufacturing, assembly, test, support, maintenance, or even sales.

7.4. From traditional projects in partnership to concurrent enterprise

Projects are more and more realized by consortia (see Figure 7.3.) where each trading partner uses its own expertise to perform its dedicated tasks within the global business process. Differences between consortium members make the richness of a project in partnership but also bring difficulties that negatively impact quality, time to market and cost. First of all, a common understanding is difficult to achieve due to the differences between partners' cultures and languages, in the case of multinational cooperations. Second, each company uses its own regulations and procedures, which make project participants choosed between its mother company and the project objectives. Third, they all use their own sequential processes independently from the others while some of them may apply concurrent engineering. Then it is also necessary to consider that they are operating from geographically dispersed sites and encouraging people to organize more meetings for coordination and progress report purposes. Furthermore, their information systems are radically different even when they are using the same tools as they may have different requirements they have different applications. Figure 7.3. illustrates this situation.

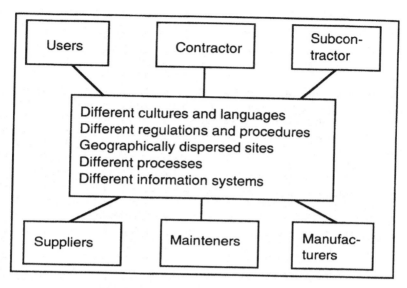

Figure 7.3. A project in partnership.

Traditional projects in partnership are always based on a cooperation strategy where trading partners are operating separately to achieve their part of the project and nothing more. The main contractor is operating like a buyer, and the other participants more or less like suppliers providing what has been ordered. They are, altogether, discussing the requirements for allocation and interfaces between parts but never quite about the global solution and how to envision it.

Consequently, the level of interaction between trading partners is very low due to the cooperation strategy and to a communication system based on contractual deliveries (see Figure 7.4.) rather than on dynamic interactions between partner disciplines.

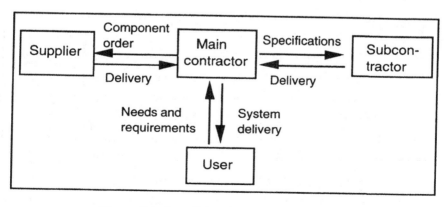

Figure 7.4. A traditional project cooperation.

As we see, during traditional project cooperation, the level of interaction between trading partners is very low due to a communication system based on formal exchanges.

This business cooperation strategy has been issued, at least, to minimize the level of risk and to provide a better access to new markets or to dramatically reduce national budget contribution in developing defense systems ordered by several Ministries of Defence. Otherwise, it has not been intended to improve operations for optimizing solutions. This way of operating is a kind of weak relationship where no one is willing to bring a part of his own knowledge due to confidentiality and other security purposes. So, it was generally admitted that this way of operating was not the more efficient, but it allowed a better confidentiality for each participant. Several program or project management guidelines have been issued at different levels, either national or international, but each company is finally using its own procedure more or less based on standardized guidelines. At the end, each trading partner separately applies those different guidelines, and the interoperability level is quite low.

There is always the famous homogeneous strategy that pushes enterprises to use the same tools to provide a good level of interoperability. In fact, tool rationalization reduces costs by reducing the support team and buying larger quantity of same tools. After that, there is a tools provider dominant position because there are no more competitors for comparison. Furthermore, if the tools provider disappears then it could be a dramatic situation as everything will have to be translated to another environment and that takes time and costs a lot. As it has been already demonstrated, using the same tool does not mean that the applications made for different requirements will be compatible or even interoperable. Instead of the idealistic homogeneous situation, it is much more interesting to develop a common architecture, in an heterogeneous situation, integrating different tools that could be easily replaced when necessary and respecting the requirements differences.

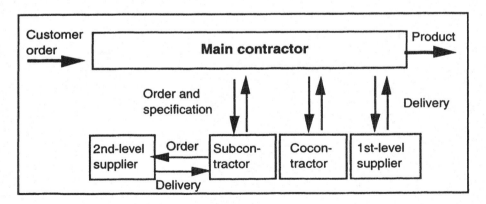

Figure 7.5. Mode of operation.

As illustrated in Figure 7.5., the main contractor or the business integrator plays the integration role. Contractual matters regulate all the relationships between the consortium members. Project management is based on the schedule of deliveries and responsibility level given to each partner by the nature of the consortium. Security, power, and confidentiality level have generated a black-box attitude where people don't want to explain how they do things. It is an important barrier to global efficiency either implementing concurrent engineering across disciplines or in reengineering a business process.

The major problems encountered are the following:

- Low level of interaction,
- Coordination based on formal deliveries,
- High level of overhead due to differences and geographically dispersed sites,
- Increased costs and lead time due to the increased level of complexity, postproduction iterations, and high level of overhead,
- Communication system based on formal document exchange and deliveries, and
- Collaboration blocked by a black-box attitude and lack of colocation.

Those problems are generating well-known weaknesses:

- Lack of clearly defined process that should be shared between trading partners,
- Operation mode (task sequences and decisions) too much based on regulations and procedures of individual company,
- Poor level of visibility of tasks progress,
- Communication mode mostly based on formal exchanges,
- Coordination mode limited to the formal deliveries,
- Collaboration mode restricted to person-to-person relationships and blocked by the exchange regulations, and
- Lack of common services and colocation of experts.

Within a company different disciplines are more or less interoperable, because the company forms a common entity that is absolutely not the case for a project in partnership. Here, there is a need to use the project as a common denominator between the partners where a common culture and language could be developed as well as common regulations and procedures, processes, information system, and people rewarding system. This idea of sharing something in common is very well supported by the virtual enterprise paradigm.

The ROCHADE (Reengineering of Complex Aircraft Development Process in a Distributed Environment) ESPRIT project, gathering together industrial companies of the aeronautic sector (such as Daimler-Benz Aerospace, British Aerospace, and CASA), recognizes that about 40 percent of the overall development costs are accounted by collaboration overhead, harmonization, and information exchange, which are in fact non-value-added activities. This project demonstrates that common operation architecture could be designed on the upper level to ensure a good interoperability level between project partners. This common architecture includes processes, information system, and team building, including collaborative attitude.

ROCHADE is addressing the need to have in a virtual enterprise all the necessary resources belonging to a same project.

7.5. Virtual enterprise and concurrent enterprise

We use this short definition for explaining virtual enterprise:
"A virtual enterprise (VE) is a temporary business organization set up between trading partners for the duration of a project" (more details in Chapter 3).

Otherwise, a has no wall around it and no legal constitution. Resources still belong to companies participating in the project, but they are delegated to the project tasks. Partners can decide together about the common language, regulations, procedures, processes, information system, and particularly reward system to be used during the project's lifetime. Human resources are not necessarily delegated to only one project but rather to several projects to optimize the use of expensive resources.

As illustrated in Figure 7.6., a virtual enterprise, relationships between trading partners operating in a common project should not be represented as connection lines between partners but much more as connection lines between mother companies (partners) and their delegated resources to the project. Without electronic colocation, a virtual enterprise is not easily realizable, as project participants will progressively lose contact with their project colleagues. A virtual enterprise implies using a collaboration strategy, as disciplines will be gathered together to support a more efficient way of operation.

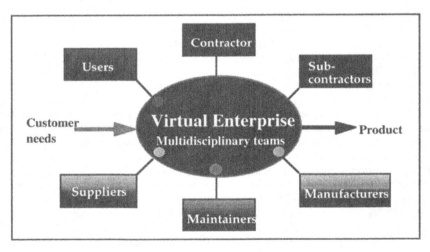

Figure 7.6. A virtual enterprise.

Re-engineering, write M. Hammer and J. Champy (1993), "is a fundamental rethinking and radical redesign of the business process to achieve dramatic improvements in critical, contemporary measures of performance, such as cost, quality, service, and speed". The definition contains four key words:

- *Fundamental.* This means to ask basic questions about the company. Reengineering first determines what a company must do and then how to do it. It concentrates on what should be.
- *Radical redesign.* This means disregarding all existing structures and procedures and inventing completely new ways of accomplishing work. It is business reinvention, not improvement.
- *Dramatic.* This means blowing out the old and replace it with something new.
- *Process.* This is the most important word in this definition. The authors define business process as a collection of activities that take one or more kinds of input and create an output that is of value to the customer. As an example, they give order fulfillment, which takes an order as its input and results in the delivery of the ordered goods. This delivery to the customer's hands is the value created by the process.

The authors explain that this is a key concept in this new revolution promised to business. The truth comes after two centuries dominated by Adam Smith's notion of breaking work into its simplest tasks (division of labor) and assigning each of these to a specialist. Under this concept managers in modern companies continue "to focus on the individual tasks in the process and so tend to lose sight of the larger objective, which is to get the goods into the hands of the customer who ordered them."

These basic concepts contributed to developing a movement for reengineering business process (BPR), which reached the developed countries. Many techniques were proposed during this time to accomplish a better reengineering of companies. Nevertheless, difficulties appear, and success stories were diminishing. Why is reengineering not always successful? Why can companies not reap the benefits promised by the manifesto?

Actually, most collaborations with suppliers or any trading partners still use a traditional working method, in which several organizations have different cultures and languages, geographically dispersed sites, different process and technologie, and different behaviors. Within this context, classical solutions such as BPR, by suppressing non-added-value activities or rationalizing the use of means, are quite limited. For example, BPR never can solve the problem of companies having, say, more than 50 percent of the product added value coming from providers. BPR does not consider business processes as an evolving system, and it does not involve, systematically, external project partners. The only acceptable solution should be to reengineer a process concerning all the companies involved in this business.

But BPR has other drawbacks. It concerns only the business process, but companies are working with many process and, in a particular case, a manufacturing company is working with a design process, a prototyping process, a manufacturing process, a testing process, and so on. Furthermore, as reengineering is a radical and dramatic change, it must take place once and not continuously. Companies performing one reengineering must wait for another one if it is not sufficient or even if success is follow by a new crisis. Figure 7.7. illustrates this case. The figure shows the adaptation versus reengineering on the plane formed by time (in years) and market needs and technology. We can see the radical changes of BPR below the curve of constant adaptation. This curve presents the evolving enterprise concept.

The business process reengineering approach (BPR) has been widely experimented with companies and demonstrated that just few of them were successful. BPR is a kind of revolution where you never know what will be the exact output. Unlike BPR, the learning organization is an evolving entity that permanently makes adaptations to stick with the evolution of its environment. A concurrent enterprise should be seen as a kind of learning organization where the knowledge is formalized through models that are updated in using a learning process. Figure 7.7. shows an application of BPR, compared to the evolving enterprise and the need for a concurrent enterprise approach, in order to better answer the market needs and technology dissemination during the time. Concurrent enterprise as was shown in Chapter 6 is then a challenge for all companies whatever the country or the sector of the economy in which they are operating. We take often the example, which is not an extreme one, represented by the evening television news show. This is a typical information product, and it is prepared in a concurrent manner but using many virtual steps to get out the best presentation and the best images - as for example, CNN does. And during this intermediary step we have virtual enterprise operating as an entity for producing the best results in order to satisfy millions of people.

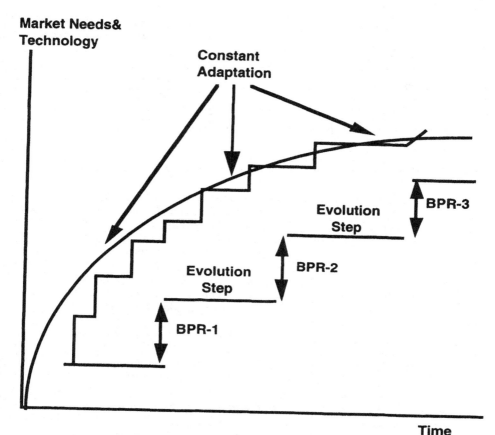

Figure 7.7. Adaptation versus reengineering.

The results of the COBRA project - launched by the European Commission for examining what is happening across Europe with the actual application of BPR, emerging technologies, and other means of corporate restructuring - have been published by Policy Publications as "The Responsive Organization: Re-engineering New Patterns of Work" (COBRA, 1995).

The COBRA team found that substantially greater involvement and participation could significantly improve the acceptability of BPR outcomes without necessarily increasing the implementation time. They are also many options for radically improving how we can access, develop, harness, and apply the commitment and talents of people.

There are new models of organization such as virtual corporations or network organizations that could be adopted and that are more flexible and responsive than the relatively bureaucratic forms we have inherited from the past. While they present new management challenges, they may be more fun for those who work within them and hence more conducive of innovation and learning. They can also enable smaller organizations to successfully compete against those that are much larger.

Rather than stop - as most BPR exercises do - at the boundaries of an organization, they could embrace the whole supply chain. Network reengineering - focused on the supply chain and with an emphasis on changing how organizations interact in the marketplace - has enabled radically new services to be introduced without necessarily turning the worlds of existing employees upside down. It can also create new opportunities for SMEs to cooperate and collaborate. Of course, processes can be reengineered. This is the territory of BPR. But most reengineering exercises fail to take account of new ways of working and learning.

7.6. Concurrent enterprise as a tactical approach

Collaboration is the business strategy that pushes to improve creativity potential and innovation capacity, but as we discovered that concurrent engineering is rather difficult to implement, it could be the same for transforming an enterprise into a concurrent one. Otherwise, concurrent enterprise is a tactical approach that should concretely support a collaboration strategy while permanently evolving with its business environment. To become concurrent an enterprise has to develop different business models that represent its knowledge about how they interact with the market, eventual trading partners, and users. This tactical approach is built on the concurrent organization theory applied to the knowledge flow that characterizes a concurrent enterprise.

The knowledge flow is constituted by the business models accessible on the network for identifying possible business partners, registered for a specific business domain, through the simulation of their models. If the models meet the needs and requirements specified in the call for partners, then after being selected enterprises will concurrently develop products or services in sharing part of their own knowledge for achieving the global solution. Trading partners work concurrently in sharing models and assessing solutions. They may operate on a twenty four hour basis due to complementary locations around the world if reduction of lead time is a major objective.

Implementing the concurrent enterprise tactical approach should support trading partner interactions by defining and using a common infrastructure. It will further give a strong reality to virtual enterprise that does not physically exist. To elaborate a common infrastructure based on global process efficiency and effectiveness, it is necessary to assess the models and support the interaction needs between partners' expertise according to the global process. This should be done in differentiating local company tasks and common activities and in defining the necessary shared information to support common activities. Enterprises will interact through the definition of interfaces with the common infrastructure. Within this implementation, the Internet technology plays a crucial role in providing the electronic colocation mean.

It is an organizational approach toward electronic commerce applications for collaborative work between trading partners. It consists of defining and implementing collaboration activities using a shared process, common services, and virtual spaces for electronic colocation. It is intended to provide a dynamic interaction support for people operating concurrently from geographically dispersed sites with the objective of increasing global creativity and innovation capacity and allowing interactive tradeoff, negotiation, and decision.

Improvements

- Rationalize the global process.
- Differentiate local company tasks and common activities.
- Interface local company process with the global process.
- Organize tasks concurrency on the basis of constraints and shared parameters.
- Adapt the organization for a maximum process efficiency.
- Create multidisciplinary project teams according to the process needs.
- Temporarily allocate company experts to the multidisciplinary teams.
- Delegate responsibility and decision to the multidisciplinary teams.
- Define common services for shared tasks and working spaces.
- Globalize and distribute the shared information (communication).
- Synchronize data exchange for cross-functional activities (coordination).
- Support interactions between complementary experts (collaboration).

Motivations

- Improve innovation and creativity potential.
- Optimize solutions.
- Reduce project overhead.
- Improve time to market.
- Reduce product life cycle cost.

Support VE reality

Members of multidisciplinary teams are electronically colocated

7.6.1. Communication and collaboration

Communication and collaboration are seen by Michael Schrage (1995) as very different, even if many managers think there is a close relationship between the two and if you fix one then you will automatically fix the other. Exactly as many people thought that product data management systems will allow developers to share product information and then they will be automatically applying concurrent engineering.

Communication is purely information exchange either by signs or any esoteric language. Communication flow is a vehicle of facts, ideas, or opinions between different interlocutors; it means that they are exchanging information - not that they are collaborating. Collaboration is much more about sharing common objectives and strategy to achieve the objectives in creating shared concepts and understanding.

According to Schrage collaboration is the process during which something is created that individuals realize they could not have done on their own. This is why collaboration is the best strategy for improving dramatically creativity potential and the innovation process. Then it is necessary to specify interaction needs between collaborating people and to support those interactions within a shared space. The shared space represents the shared concepts and understanding where each actor can operate simultaneously.

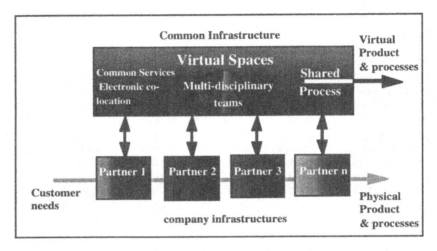

Figure 7.8. Concurrent Enterprises.

7.6.2. Evolution of the development process

Companies are more frequently developing new products in two phases (see Figure 7.8.) - (1) designing the product and its processes models and analyzing, simulating and experimenting with these models to check that everything is right before entering the second phase, and (2) the concrete realization of processes and products. This development approach is very closed to concurrent engineering concept implementation, but it further requests having trading partners provide models during the first phase and physical components during the second one.

Now we know how to implement concurrent engineering in designing and simulating product and processes models. Do people belonging to multidisciplinary teams remember each time everything they have to check? They have too many things to remember. Multidisciplinary teams are very useful for cultural changes, but team members strongly need concrete designs they can manipulate together to reach a common understanding and to undertake the best decision. Concurrent activities do not bring this concrete support to team members. Concurrent activities are there only for managing interactions between expertise during the maturation stage. So the only thing team members can manipulate are prototypes. Years ago it was physical prototypes, and nowadays it is much more virtual prototypes that are built up using virtual reality models (VRM), even if physical prototypes are still in use for the characterization of virtual ones.

New processes and team organizations are not sufficient for implementing new development approaches even if they are conditional entry points. It means that people should accept a new development approach, processes should be updated for the benefit of the new approach, and people organization updated on the basis of updated process requirements. But then it is necessary to support the new development approach by providing new methods, techniques and tools that will enable its concrete implementation. That was exactly the case with concurrent engineering before the emergence of VRM where the lack of specific methods, techniques, and tools for supporting interactions between different expertises made full-scale CE implementation far from reality. Nowadays, it is possible to integrate and test components belonging to a product or a process before manufacturing them by simply using VRM.

No one could have planned the impact of CE on management and support processes, even on the learning process. We were too much busy to making it a reality in the development process. Project management is going to radically change as models allow multidisciplinary teams to start their work by reusing the formalized knowledge for design tradeoff. Using models for managing interactions between different expertises also means it is mandatory to support real-time consistency checking when changes are going to be made.

Virtual reality models reflect the consolidated know-how and provide an opportunity for improving them in real time when people face problems. When a new participant joins a multidisciplinary team, he is not starting from scratch because he will make use of existing models. Furthermore, people from one project team can reuse models and enhance them along the project life cycle when they join other project teams.

7.7. Virtual Prototyping

This section presents a virtual prototyping approach using Internet technologies. This is a contribution authorized by two well-known Finish experts - Petri Pulli from VTT Electronics and the University of Oulu, and Similä Jouni from CCC Software Professionals and the University of Oulu, Department of Information Processing Science and Infotech Research. These authors have developed specific and vital questions concerning the virtual product models for the Internet-based virtual enterprise.

7.7.1. Internet virtual enterprise concept

Electronic commerce is expected to reduce coordination costs in the value chain of manufacturing and sales of products and thus holds promise for increasing trade volumes. This can already be seen to take place in Internet markets with relatively simple products. In this section the prerequisites for electronic commerce for nonbulk, value-added intelligent products, such as electronics and telecommunication products, are analyzed. When compared with bulk products, there are many challenges in electronic commerce for such intelligent products, as product search and evaluation, customer needs and product matching, product configuration, and agile manufacturing of differentiated products based on customer order.

Virtual reality technique in product marketing, customization, and selling might be used, for instance, in the following:

- Providing an Internet virtual salesroom where potential customers may experiment with various product features and ultimately also make product purchases;
- Providing interactive customization of products through the Internet before ordering and delivering (for example, the color and shape of products may be selected from a predefined set of alternatives; customer may also pick up options from the list of additional features or even propose new features);

- Collecting user preferences in customer clinics for guiding development toward products with higher customer appeal and satisfaction; and
- Presenting and launching leading-edge products prior to physical products being available through manufacturing and sales channels.

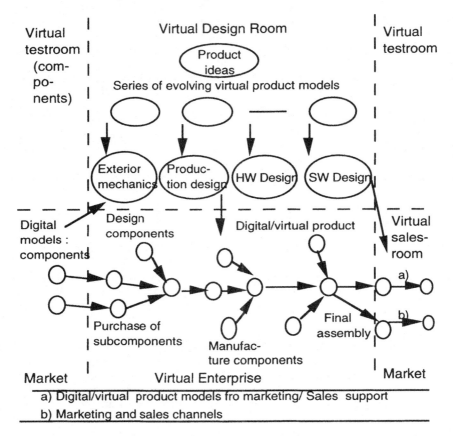

Figure 7.9. Virtual product models in the context of the value chains of a virtual.

A scenario of the different ways of utilizing virtual product models in the various phases of product development, manufacturing, marketing, and sales is described in Figure 7.9. in the context of the different value chains connected to the virtual enterprise (Wigand and Benjamin, 1995).

Virtual prototyping models offer an entirely new perspective for electronic commerce on the Internet since they provide a strong sense of reality and the means to test the model of a product through meaningful interaction. All-digital prototypes resemble their physical counterparts as closely as possible in terms of visual three-dimensional images, behavioral, haptic, and auditory characteristics. Online trial of the goods could also be offered, which means that customers browsing in an Internet salesroom can test operations of a virtual prototype, which is simulated, like its physical counterpart.

An Internet virtual salesroom concept is proposed to be based on a virtual three-dimensional photorealistic salesroom environment featuring a selection of virtual product models (Figure 7.10.). A particular enabling technology, virtual prototyping, in the context of consumer electronics and telecommunications industries is addressed. Virtual prototyping is the application of advanced modeling

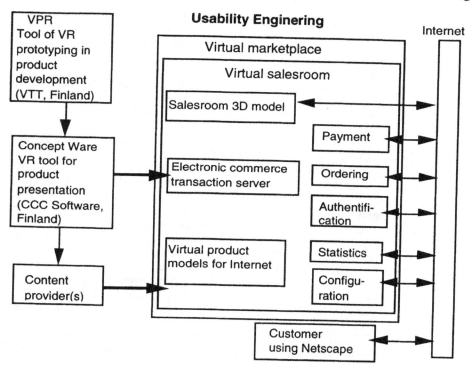

Figure 7.10. The proposed concept for Internet electronic commerce utilizing digital virtual product models in marketing and sales.

and simulation techniques, user interface techniques and virtual reality techniques to support electronic commerce for customers and also business-to-business electronic commerce in the value chain - that is product design, manufacturing, and sales (Sarker, Butler, and Steinfeld, 1995).

7.7.2 Virtual Product Models

A virtual world is a computer-generated, often three-dimensional environment in which a user has a sense of presence, where she or he is able to navigate around and can interact with the objects included in it. A virtual prototype is defined (Hang, Kuhl, and Tsain, 1993) as a computer-based simulation of a prototype system or subsystem with a degree of functional realism that is comparable to a physical prototype. Virtual prototyping means the process of using virtual prototypes instead of or in combination with physical prototypes, for innovating, testing and evaluating of specific characteristics of a candidate design. The following aspects are dominant:

- *Functionality.* The intended functionality of the prototype that is created virtually is clearly defined and realistically simulated (for example product functionality and dynamic behavior).
- *Human Interaction.* If human action is involved in the intended functionality of the prototype, the human functions involved must be realistically simulated, or the human must be included in the simulation (that is real-time operator-in-the-loop simulation).
- *Environment.* If no human action is involved in the intended functionality of the prototype, then either an offline (non-real-time) computer simulation of the functions can be carried out, or a combination of computer (non-real-time) and hardware-in-the-loop (real-time) simulation can be carried out.

In virtual prototyping, a virtual world comprises both the VR model of a product under development (that is virtual prototype), and the model of the product's target environment, called virtual target environment. Virtual worlds, the VR models, are highly advanced human-computer interfaces based on virtual reality techniques, providing a strong intuitive sense of reality and the means to change the world through meaningful interaction. Virtual worlds may include various levels of reality, thus enabling us to concentrate on any desired aspects of the product.

The interaction between the user and the virtual world can be based on different kinds of interaction interfaces (see Figure 7.11.). The most elementary interaction interfaces can be a keyboard and a mouse with a conventional window-based two-dimensional user interface. A more sophisticated virtual prototyping environment with a 3D user interface may include, for examplea head mounted display, a 3D position and orientation tracking device, and auditory and haptic feedback devices. The type of representation in a virtual prototyping environment may be spatial, *n*-dimensional with abstract information spaces, or various combinations of video, natural and computer-generated images. During the development process, a virtual world can be seen as a model that best matches reality.

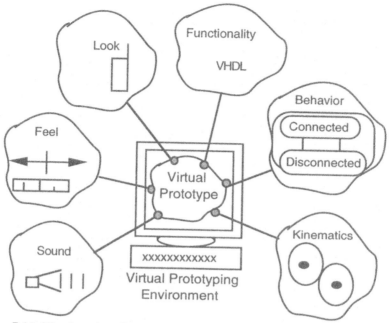

Figure 7.11. The functionality of typical virtual product models for intelligent consumer electronics and telecommunications products.

Virtual prototype worlds might be used, for instance, in the following:

- Universal combining of different models to improve communication in development projects,
- Prototyping the user-observable behavior and the look and feel aspects of the product that are difficult to specify explicitly,
- Collecting user preferences in customer clinics for guiding development toward products with high customer appeal and satisfaction,
- Providing early visibility of a new product in order to demonstrate its capabilities and features,
- Modeling systems that cannot be implemented using contemporary technology but that are expected to be feasible in the future if technology advances at a predicted rate of progress, and
- Providing a virtual salesroom where potential customers may experiment with various product features and ultimately also make product purchases.

A necessary aspect of the full exploitation of the results of virtual prototyping is the requirement for the communication of the results to the interested parties. These may include persons taking part in actual product development - digital signal processing designers, software and hardware designers, and mechanical designers - or people involved in the sales and marketing of the product - marketing and sales representatives, wholesale and retail representatives, and of course customers. Quite

166

often these persons may be quite widely geographically distributed, so solutions based on utilizing communication networks are needed.

7.7.3. Virtual models in product design

Industries in many high-volume global businesses, such as consumer electronics and telecommunications, are moving to a two-phased product development paradigm with a speculative all-digital frontend to develop the product concepts and an agile production capability to manufacture and market the product. Virtual prototyping is the application of advanced modeling and simulation techniques, user interface techniques, and virtual reality techniques to support speculative product design.

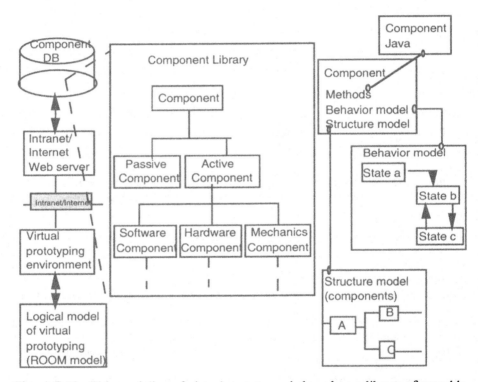

Figure 7.12. This modeling of virtual prototypes is based on a library of reusable components, each consisting of software, hardware and mechanical elements described in an object-oriented graphical notation and Java language.

An object-oriented, virtual-reality-based development environment for consumer electronics and telecommunication products is described. The aim is to develop all-digital prototypes resembling the physical products as close as possible in terms of visual 3D image, behavioral, functional, and haptic and auditory characteristics. The modeling approach is losely based on the Selic, Gullekson and Ward ROOM approach enhanced for software and hardware codesign. Implementation is based on Java (http://java.sun.com), VRML (http://www.sdsc.edu/vrml/), and Silicon Graphics OpenInventor platforms.

Currently, a research environment is being built to study the previously described virtual prototyping approach when applied to consumer electronics and telecommunication products and services. The environment runs on a Silicon Graphics Indigo2 workstation. A virtual prototype is built by converting the CAD-CAM model specifying the geometry and mechanics of the product into a VR model. Then, the simulation models of the software and hardware parts of the embedded control system are integrated with the VR model to give the virtual prototype the ability to have functionality and behavior. If necessary, the target environment of the product under development is modeled using VR modeling tools to produce a virtual environment model, which is also integrated with the virtual prototype. To achieve an efficient and rapid prototyping capability, a shared database will be used to store reusable VR model components, software components (object-oriented libraries), hardware models, and product data (Figure 7.12.).

In 1996, a national research project (VIRPI) in Finland was set up with three research institutes (VTT Electronics, University of Oulu, and University of Arts and Design, Helsinki) and five industrial companies (CCC Software Professionals, Nokia Mobile Phones, Polar Electro, Metsävainio Design, and C3 Suunnittelu). An evaluation of the approach has been done in three different cases: an existing product and its environment, product and service enhancement, and a totally new product concept development. In the first case, modeling a virtual cellular phone that has been demonstrated widely to the industry was studied. A limited version of the virtual cellular phone (http://www.ele.vtt.fi/projects /vrp/vrp.html) is also available as a VRML model on the Internet. This experiment has given us a much-improved position to explain the industry representatives what are the possibilities and limitations of virtual prototyping. For the second and third cases, the problems of developing totally new kinds of wearable cellular phones were tackled. Experience so far indicates that a good place to start introducing virtual prototyping inside industrial companies is to start with industrial designers responsible for product exterior and visual appearance. They seem to be lacking a way to communicate with the designers responsible for product interior.

The coexistence of virtual and physical prototypes and their relative merits and role in the development process will be studied. Because it is possible to develop virtual prototypes of future products and services that cannot be implemented using the technology available today, it is possible to start development projects and market analyses earlier.

7.7.4. *Virtual product models on the Internet*
The Internet is a viable medium for communicating of the results of virtual prototyping to parties in distributed concurrent product development. An even more interesting scenario is, however, the use of Internet as a commercial medium and market for the products utilizing virtual prototypes distributed on the network. The tremendous growth of the Internet, and particularly the World Wide Web, has led to a critical mass of consumers and firms participating in a global online marketplace. The Internet is rapidly expanding from a communication medium to a new market. The present popularity of the WWW as a commercial medium (in contrast to other networks on the Internet) is due to its ability to facilitate global sharing of information and resources, and its potential to provide an efficient channel for advertising, marketing, and even direct distribution of certain goods and information services.

As a commercial medium, the Web offers a number of important benefits, which can be examined at both the enterprise and customer levels (Hoffman, Novak, and Chatterjee, 1995). Enterprise benefits arise from the potential of the Web as a distribution channel, a medium for marketing communications, and a market in and of itself. Customer benefits arise primarily from the structural characteristics of the medium and include availability of information, provision of search mechanisms, and online product trial, all of which can lead to reduced uncertainty in the purchase decision. It is especially the last one - online product trial (cf. [MATHSOFT], [DEC]) - where virtual prototyping would seem a superior technology.

An interesting aspect of the Web is that it seems to offer opportunity for competition on the specialty axis instead of the price axis (Hoffman, Novak, and Chatterjee, 1995). From a marketing perspective, it is rarely desirable to compete solely on the basis of price. Instead, marketers attempt to satisfy needs on the basis of benefits sought, which means pricing is dependent on the value to the customer, not costs. Such an opportunity arises when the offering is differentiated by elements such as convenience through direct electronic distribution of software, or enjoyment through a visually appealing and exciting Web site. A visually appealing photorealistic operational virtual 3D prototype of a product would certainly fall in the same category. As evidence that this kind of behavior is already happening on the Web, consumers indicated that price was the least important product attribute when making online purchases (Gupta, 1995). The ability to compete on dimensions other than price will become especially critical in categories where brands are perceived as substitutes (for example most hand-held electronic devices), since it allows for more opportunities to differentiate along other dimensions. SRI's analysis (SRI) of the Web population gives further insight into the Web visitor and identifies two broad categories of Web audience (cf. also (Hoffman, Novak, and Chatterjee, 1995)). The first group is called the upstream audience and represents 50 percent of the current Web population. This group is estimated to represent 10 percent of the U.S. population, is 77 percent male, is educated (97 percent have at least some college education), and is upscale. Members of this group are what SRI terms *actualizers*, successful men and women with high self-esteem and active take-charge lifestyles. Upstream Web visitors typically receive institutional subsidies for Web usage and represent the pioneer Internet users. Because most upstream users are already online, future Web growth must come from the downstream segment.

If the SRI analysis is valid, then the rate of adoption of the downstream or other half of the Web will determine when and if the Web achieves critical mass as a commercial medium. The other half already online represents the lead users of the other 90 percent of U. S. society. This group is noticeably less gender-skewed than the upstream group (64 percent male and 36 percent female), younger (70 percent are under 30), and on its way to being just as educated (89 percent have at least some college education) as the group is comprised of students or recent college graduates. The other half are predominantly made up of what SRI refers to as *strivers* and *experiencers*. According to SRI, strivers are unsure of themselves and seek approval from the world around them. In contrast, experiencers are enthusiastic and impulsive, seeking for variety and excitement from life.

Without going into an extensive psychological analysis of the type of persons that would be thrilled at chance to experiment with virtual prototypes, it would seem that the current "leading-edge early adopter" Web users (SRI) would be likely candidates. They are also in the potential market segment for mobile telecommunication products and services. Already 3D images of products are accessible through the Internet. The approach taken here goes much further than that by providing simulation of close to real life experiences of actually experimenting with and using the products. For the first phase this experimentation would naturally be limited to visual effects and sounds with some simulation of functionality, behavior and kinematics. The virtual prototypes should be integrated into a commercial website comprising an online storefront and a company Internet presence (DEC).

There are barriers to the commercialization of the Web. Accumulated industry experience, anecdotal evidence, as well as personal experience strongly suggest that the main barrier is ease of access. In the context of the Web, ease of access is a multidimensional construct and includes high-speed access (the bandwidth problem), ease of finding a service provider, and the diffusion of the computer hardware/software/modem bundle into the home (Hoffman, Novak, and Chatterjee, 1995). At the moment the high-speed access barrier is a serious constraint for using virtual prototypes in the Web since they involve extensive calculations as well as extensive amounts of data to be sent through the network. As mentioned, a combination of VRML and Java is being investigated as a possible solution here. The secondary barriers are ease of use, price, and risk, including such factors as privacy and security (Hoffman, Novak, and Chatterjee, 1995). At present, the issue of the security of financial information transmitted over the Internet is affecting customer behavior on the Web. The majority of consumers use the Web to browse or search much more than to actually purchase something (Booker, 1995). However, as anyone who follows ordinary newspapers knows, the situation is changing rapidly. For example, a recent survey conducted in Finland indicated that companies expect electronic commerce to be a general phenomenon in a few years.

7.7.5. The virtual salesroom authoring tool Cybelius

In order to facilitate the immediate use of the research results gained already, CCC Software Professionals has begun the technology transfer of the results to one of the companies in the research consortium. The company has started its own development work based on the earlier described themes and sees the utilization of virtual product models in electronic commerce as the most promising area at present.

The research environment described earlier (see Chapter 3) is suitable mainly for heavy product design purposes requiring for example, the design and testing of haptic characteristics. However, in the electronic commerce area a lighter approach is seen as sufficient. CCC Software Professionals is at present developing a software product for 3D authoring. The aim is to create a commercial tool, that enables the easy design of functional, three-dimensional, portable, and photorealistic virtual models of different products. Note that the haptic characteristic as well as the stereo 3D visualization aspects are left out.

The tool's working title is Cybelius. The customers of the software tool being developed are seen to be the marketing, selling, and product development departments within companies as well as design offices offering services to these departments. The virtual product models are expected to be used by clients and cooperating partners interested in the existing products as well as partners participating in the product-development processes requiring a more minimal set of product characteristics. No corresponding tools have been found in the market, yet but the need for them is clearly seen, for example, in the rapidly growing interest in electronic commerce in general.

To find maximum audiences the virtual prototype must be distributed through the Internet and run on a PC-class computer. The creation of photorealistic VR models and the simulation of their functions have so far required special and generally quite expensive hardware and software. The situation has, however, changed dramatically in the last few years. The worldwideweb with its browsers and VRML2 with its browser plugging have made the use of low-end PCs possible in 3D VR since September 1996. Using Java programming language has made Cybelius itself. The models created with Cybelius are made from CAD and/or VRML 2.0 descriptions. Therefore, Cybelius supports thoroughly VRML 2.0 standard.

The main task to be achieved with the tool is to add functionality to existing CAD or VRML models. For modeling purposes there are several tools available and the idea is to support most of them through the use of the emerging VRML2/ISO standard. The approach is based extensively on the use of both generic as well as application area and company specific component libraries (see Figure 7.3).

There exist basically two kinds of functionality. The first is graphical functionality like a lid opening or a button going in when pressed. The second is inner functionality evidenced, for example, when a user presses a button on his or her watch and the display changes to show the date instead of the time. Graphical models are normally described with tool-specific files. At present, there are already some graphical modelers that support VRML2, and their number will clearly grow very fast. Fortunately, there are several good converters to put the native format into VRML2 format. A much bigger problem in producing virtual product models is that the photorealistic 3D models contain an enormous amount of graphical elements. To achieve a PC presentable prototype, which may be sent over the Internet in a realistic time frame, simplification of the model is needed without losing its reality-look. The Cybelius tool is basically used in the following way:

- Take the graphical model, simplify and convert it so that it is small enough to be sent over the network.
- Define the graphical functions of the active parts of the prototype and add these to the prototype.
- Define and add the logical parts to the prototype.

The tool contains a graphical user interface for each phase and libraries for both graphical and logical standard parts to be added. Examples of the first kind are buttons, lights and displays and of second kind state automatons, logical functions, and time counters.

7.8. Conclusion

Virtual reality product modeling technology can be seen as one enabling technology for electronic commerce. It is believed that it can improve customer satisfaction and time-to-market aspects of new products. The domain of consumer electronics and telecommunication has been studied here, and the attention has been limited to intelligent, relatively small products, such as hand-held cellular phones and their accessories. It is believed that the virtual reality technology can scale up also to larger products although not necessarily using the same kind of virtual reality environments. Business-related activities where virtual model are foreseen to be beneficial include the following:

- Collecting customer preferences,
- Balancing the product features with customer/market segment expectations;
- Integration framework in the business in the value chain,
- Product external design and visual appearance early demonstration,
- User interface design and validation,
- Product information dissemination, especially important for value-added intelligent products,
- Marketing,
- Purchase influence,
- Sales and launching platform for paying and delivery processing,;
- Interactive online product versioning and differentiation based on customer specification,
- Provision of customer information,
- User training, and
- After-sales services visualization and launching platform.

To improve the understanding of benefits and potential of virtual product modeling technology and electronic commerce, more research and controlled field experimentation needs to be carried out. But this is a matter of more discussions and, principally, the involvement of new research communities.

References
Booker, E. (1995)."Web Users Cruising for Info, Not Purchases." Computerworld (February).
CORBA Team. (1995)."The Responsive Organization: Re-engineering New Patterns of Work."
    Policy Publication.
Coulson-Thomas, Colin. (1996)."Re-engineering New Patterns of Work: A Holistics Approach." *I&T*
    Magazine (Appril).
Gupta, S. (1995)."HERMES: A Research PProject on the Commercial Uses of the Web."
Hammer, M, and J. Champy. (1993). *Reengineering the corporation*. New York:Harper Business.
Haug, E., J.Kuhl, and F. Tsai. (1993). "Virtual Prototyping for Mechanical System Concurrent
    Engineering." NATA ASI Series F: Computer and Systems Science, vol. 108.
    Berlin:Springer-   Verlag.
Hoffman, D., T. Novack, and P. Chatterjee. (1995). "Commercial Scenarios for the Web: Opportunities
    and Challenges." *Journal   of Computer-Mediated Communication* 1(3) (December).
Schrage, M. (1995). *No More Teams! Mastering the Dynamics of   Creative Collaboration*. New
    York:Doubleday.
Sarker, M., B.Butler, and C. Steinfeld. (1995)."Intermediaries and Cybermediairies: A Continuing Role
    for Mediating Players in the Electronic Marketplace." *Journal of Computer-Mediated
    Comunication* 1(3) (December).
Wigand, R., and R. Benjamin. 51995)."Electronic Commerce: Effects   on Electronic
    Markets."*Journal of Computer-Mediated   Comunication* 1(3) (December).

8 CONCURRENT ENTERPRISING

8.1. Introduction

Today, it is commonly said that the enterprise environment has become more complex, more uncertain, more turbulent. The emergence of underdeveloped countries (representing 80 percent of the world population) in the global market constitutes a supplementary competitive pressure for the enterprises of developed countries. Enterprises from these underdeveloped countries built business strategies targeted on decisive comparative advantages and on opportunistic alliances for penetrating and rapidly dominating specific global markets. Furthermore, those enterprises are more and more well implemented in developed countries and largely contribute to the local employment and economical growth.

Nevertheless, a second business environment transformation factor plays a more and more important role. This factor is technology. Since 1970, we have been experiencing a technology explosion. This trend affects all economic and human activities. New products, services, and processes appear each day and rapidly replace old ones. The creation and innovation rhythm of acceleration is clearly evident. In spite of this, it is quite difficult to keep a technological competitive advantage for a while because the imitation speed is accelerating in the same proportion. Technological explosion combined with users' and consumers' new requirements (demands for more and more customized products) contribute to reduce the life cycle of products, services and processes.

Based on these considerations, enterprises have to develop new aptitudes and strategies in order to maintain or improve their competitiveness. This necessity meets three requirements. First of all a "concurrency for competitiveness" strategy should be set up for transforming a traditional enterprise into a reactive and flexible one. Second, a collaborative attitude should be promoted inside and outside the enterprise. Third, creativeness and innovation should be used as a tactical weapon for any enterprise looking for lucrative sources and willing to satisfy both customers and shareholders.

The "concurrency for competitiveness" strategy is, in my mind, the only one able to, through organizational flexibility, provide any enterprise with the capability to precisely locate, in its traditional markets or elsewhere, new business opportunities as well as significant changes. Enterprises will develop a permanent adaptation aptitude to grasp business opportunities at an early stage. For this, it is necessary to set up a flat and distributed organization. After this necessary major structural change, it should be considered that people's attitudes are an important criterion in any successful change. Boundaryless and freedom as well as encouraging people initiatives and ideas are key issues conditioning people's acceptance of changes. Furthermore, the best possible promotion of having a systematic collaboration attitude is to update the employees' rewarding system toward team gratification rather than purely individual review. At the enterprise level the best reward system change would be a kind of profit-sharing system where any organizations participating in a consortium will receive a part of the success based on their demonstrable contributions to the success of a project. These changes are much more based on trusting people than regulations, policies, and procedures.

Operating concurrently with the market, trading partners, and users is a capability that generates reactiveness potential as well as increasing creativeness and innovation aptitudes. Enterprises have to be conducted by market demand; business deals opportunities with trading partners and by customers requirements and not any more by controlling its resources. Here is the crucial point of contradictory attitudes where people are looking for freedom in their initiatives and the enterprise is still thinking in term of control of decisions regarding opportunities, projects, and employees. The implicit solution is to have a boundaryless enterprise where top management is promoting transparency and where decisions are based more on team demonstration than on any form of control. There are some risks in this strategy, but we should consider carefully this golfing rule: "Never up, never in." It means that if you have never failed, then probably you have never won, as we always have to learn the playing field by making some mistakes before finding the right way to be successful.

A concurrent enterprise is an enterprise operating concurrently with the market, trading partners, and users in a reactive and flexible way for improving creativity aptitude and innovation potential. As shown in Figure 8.1., the creativity and innovation potential is higher when a collaboration strategy with trading partners provides a wider expertise in a specific domain. Furthermore, operating concurrently provides a strong opportunity for confronting ideas with market actors as well as looking for small signals and therefore precisely locate, in its traditional markets or elsewhere, new business opportunities as well as significant changes. Then the right question is how to transform an enterprise into a concurrent enterprise. Concurrent enterprising is the process that allows any enterprise to achieve this transformation.

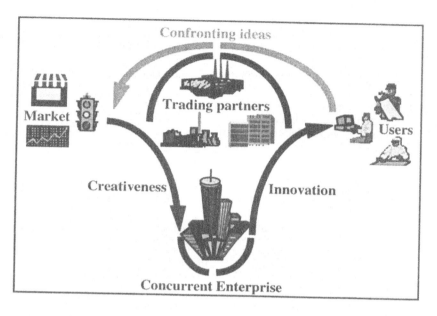

Figure 8.1. Operating concurrently with the market, trading partners, and users.

Concurrent enterprising is a transformation process that should provide the necessary capabilities to a traditional enterprise for operating concurrently in its business environment. From the concurrent organization theory point of view, it means that creativity and innovation activities should operate concurrently with the knowledge flow, which is the characteristic stream of this new enterprise organization. At the upper level, everything is organized around the value or money flow, which is the characteristic stream of the business environment. Therefore, concurrent enterprising starts on the basis of a generic model illustrating key factors and their relationships for operating concurrently. This transformation process is based on the combination (see Figure 8.2.) of a concurrency reference model and a capability assessment method that could be used to evaluate the actual concurrency and collaboration capabilities of an existing enterprise. Following the results of this evaluation, shared and concurrent processes will be created for answering every specific business case or project involving consortia. Then a distributed infrastructure, including shared processes, services, and virtual spaces will be set up in order to efficiently support the global business process. At the end a measurement technique will be used to evaluate the concurrency and collaboration performance that has been reached and its impact on the business process. If these evaluation results do not meet the objectives, then a new capability assessment and process modeling will be executed until the final performance will be compliant with the business objectives.

The concurrent enterprising process uses several components, such as the following:

- A concurrency reference model,
- A concurrency and collaboration capability assessment,
- A concurrent and shared process modeling technique based on interaction needs,
- A distributed infrastructure including shared processes, services and virtual spaces,
- Concurrent and shared processes,
- An interaction protocol, and
- A concurrency and collaboration performance measurement technique.

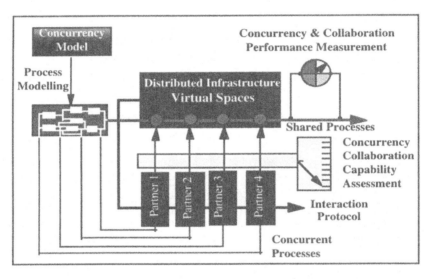

Figure 8.2. Concurrent enterprising synopsis.

8.2. Concurrency reference model.

Operating concurrently seems to purely be common sense, and we ask ourselves why we did not apply it before as it so obviously reduces lead time and cost. Today, with the considerable background on concurrent engineering implementation, we know that implementing concurrent activities is far from being trivial (see Chapter 4). The concurrency reference model is simply a generalization at trading partner level of what has already been done between disciplines in applying CE within a same enterprise. What is not trivial is to identify the interaction needs between different disciplines involved in a same project in order to reorganize the related processes. The following stage concerns the support of those concrete interactions, and here information and communication technologies play a crucial role.

Translating this CE implementation background to the concurrent enterprise implementation means that the identification of interaction needs between trading partners will allow concurrent processes to be established. And the support of the trading partner's interactions will have to be extended to dispersed geographical sites. Otherwise, it has already been the case, during CE implementation, that a single organization was operating from different geographical sites or even using teleworking practices for delegated employees such as support teams as well as sale teams.

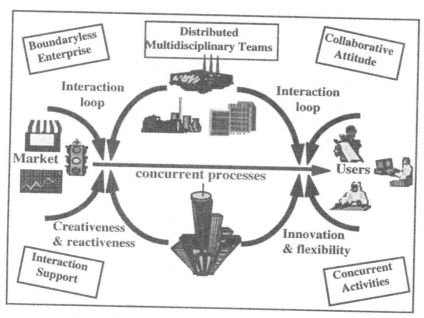

Figure 8.3. Concurrency reference model.

Reactiveness and flexibility are essential to survivability because they form the ground for the adaptability aptitude. A business model having deep boundaries, as is often the case today, could not provide good reactivity. Concurrency (see Figure 8.3.) means having the capability of operating in a boundaryless environment, sharing part of the trading partners' knowledge, enabling the identification of a symbiosis point where concurrent activities have to be implemented, as well as providing strong support for synchronous and asynchronous interactions involved in those activities. Concurrency also means having the ability to operate through a distributed infrastructure where trading partners are using shared processes and virtual spaces (via electronic collocation) to share a common understanding and development of concepts that should considerably improve the creativity and innovation potential. In a fast-changing business environment, creativity and innovation potential constitute the real enterprise assets that allow maintaining or improving competitiveness.

Concurrency theory has been widely develop in the computer science domain. According to Rocco De Nicola and Scott A. Smolka:

Abstraction in the description of concurrent systems can be obtained by devising a theory of observations. The semantics of concurrent processes heavily depends on their interaction with other processes and on their reaction to external stimuli. Thus, different formalisms and models can be used depending on the environments in which systems are going to operate and on the kind of properties we are interested in. We can resort to observations consisting of sequences of possible interactions if we are interested only in describing completely abstract behaviors or if we assume sequential users. We can, instead, make use of sequences of multiset of interactions if potential concurrency (performance considerations or multiple users) has to be taken into account. Finally, partial orderings of potential interactions are appropriate when one is interested in using systems descriptions as guidelines for concurrent implementations. Whenever the environment within which a (sub-)system is going to be used is known, and the system designer has a clear idea of the properties of interest, then sets of observations can be devised to fix its semantics.

Concurrency in the computer science domain seems also based on interaction purpose and concerning the application of the concurrency theory. As De Nicola and Smolka say:

The future of concurrency practice looks bright. Successful case studies - concerning practical problems such as communication protocols, hardware design and verification, process control systems, and traffic control systems - appear regularly in the literature. New and improved algorithms, upon which tools can be built, are being developed. Advances in system technology, such as larger memories, faster processors, and computing with networks of workstations, increase the range of concurrency practice. The question remains, though, whether concurrency practice can keep pace with the increasingly complex applications it is likely to be subjected to. The answer from this position is a cautious but optimistic yes, and we believe that such successes will be fueled by a continuation of the close interplay between theory and practice that we are currently witnessing. In the field of concurrency we often see application and experimentation going on in parallel with the development of new theories. This was not the case with the foundation theories of sequential programming, where significant advances in theory did not lead to comparable advances in software production.

Considering the practical application of concurrent organization theory in the business environment and enterprise organization domain (or what we like to call "concurrency for competitiveness"), we should take into account the lesson learnt in the recent past by the application of business process reengineering (see Chapter 7), which has been very successful for a few cases and an absolute nightmare for most cases. BPR is articulated around a simple concept: track and suppress non-value-added activities and automate low-value activities by using technology. It is very easy to understand that BPR could be the best or worst thing to do, as root problems are not really studied either at the interaction level between expertise or between people and technology or even between technologies. If by chance what has been done with BPR helps to solve the problem, then it could be a great success. If, unfortunately, what has been done with BPR doesn't help to solve the problem, then it could be a nightmare because the new situation will certainly be much more problematical and inextricable.

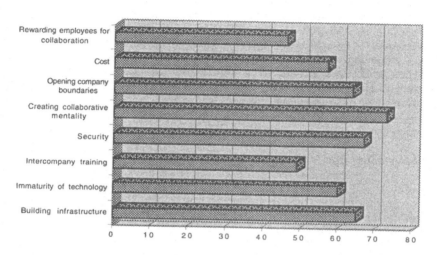

Challenges to implement collaboration between trading partners

Figure 8.4. Challenges in implementing collaboration between trading partners.

To stay realistic with the implementation objectives, the concurrency reference model should involve three interrelated layers. The first one, the process layer, allows the description of a more efficient way of operating between trading partners and complementary disciplines or expertises. The second one, the people and organization layer, provides an opportunity for eliminating any organizational boundary and for promoting a distributed form of organization where teams are directly negotiating and deciding. Otherwise, people like to change only when a benefit is clearly demonstrated. That is exactly why rewarding systems should evolve toward team performance rather than individual performance, or individual performance in the context of team performance. A recent study done by the European Society for Concurrent Engineering (ESoCE) shows that a collaborative attitude between disciplines was rated as being the most important challenge for a successful concurrent engineering implementation. Nevertheless, distributed negotiations and decisions are also key factors in getting people to accept changes. The third one, the technology layer, is absolutely necessary to set up the infrastructure supporting both processes and people. Clearly, without ICT, at least, it would be impossible to implement concurrency between dispersed geographical sites. I'm persuaded that interaction support and knowledge management without ICT would not be efficient at all. Using a physical prototype for demonstrating feasibility of ideas is costly and slow. There are three layers because processes should no longer be organized separately. Attitudes and organizations should fit with the process objectives, and finally technology should meet process and people requirements. That clearly means having no more boundaries between processes, between disciplines, and between applications.

A study on "Project in Partnership", realized by the ESoCE for the FREE (Fast and Reactive Extended Enterprise) ESPRIT project, shows that the greatest challenge in implementing collaboration (see Figure 8.4) between trading partners is to create a collaborative mentality. At the opposite situation, rewarding employees for collaboration is the lowest one. This is quite conterintuitive, except if interviewed people thought that opening company boundaries in building a distributed infrastructure, while guaranteeing security, is the real driver enabling collaborative work and therefore enabling people to change their attitudes. Nevertheless, to change attitude it is worthwhile to update the employee reviewing system to consider individual contributions to a team's success as a collaboration value.

8.3. Concurrency and collaboration capability assessment

Collaboration is a process conducting from the sharing of common objectives and strategy towards the creation of shared concepts and understanding. Collaboration is the process during which something is created that any enterprise realize it could not have be achieved with their own know-how (see Chapter 7).

Collaboration is clearly based on how different forms and sources of knowledge lead to shared concepts. Different authors have examined issues related to the knowledge-creating company, and they have defined it as a living organism with a collective sense of identity and fundamental purpose (Nonaka, 1991; Takeuchi, 1995; Argyris, 1993). There are, at least, two very well-known forms of knowledge - tacit and explicit. Tacit knowledge is the personal knowledge constituting mental models, lessons learned, and beliefs. Explicit knowledge is based on formal languages and can be described in books or electronic databases. The combination of or interaction between tacit and explicit knowledge allows new knowledge to be created.

In fact, the capability assessment method to be used for adapting a traditional enterprise into a concurrent one should be divided into two different targets. As illustrated in the figure 8.3, a concurrent enterprise is based on reorganizing things without any boundary, which is relevant to the concurrent organization theory (see Chapter 7) and concurrency reference model. Adapting processes and people organization is one thing, but having enterprises or people collaborating is another relies on strategy and attitude, which are relevant to the symbiosis world. It means that if you can provide something very useful for someone, then you will get something useful for yourself in return. It is based on share and mutual trust.

The capability assessment is twofold. First, evaluate concurrency implementation, and, second, evaluate the collaborative attitude and the practical environment for supporting collaborative activities. Nevertheless, as for a successful CE implementation, capability assessment should be evaluated on three complementary layers - process, people organization and attitude, and technology. Therefore, concurrency is relevant to the process, people organization and attitude, and technology layers in order to operate in an efficient way. Collaboration is relevant only to enterprise strategy and people attitude; otherwise technology should actively support it via interactions and knowledge management.

This three-layer assessment approach is very simple to understand. Imagine you have the best processes but your people organization does not fit with the processes or technology is not appropriate to answer to processes requirements. It means that expected capabilities are not really achieved. Or imagine you have implemented the best technology but you are still using the same processes and people organization. It means that the technology is not usable at the top of its normal capabilities and that return on investment will not be achieved. Otherwise, the people organization and attitude have two views - one about the role and responsibility and the other about behavior and trust, as it should not be forgotten that when people are reluctant to change, there is no possible progress. Implementing capabilities is quite more complex than is presented in most of the capability assessment methods we have studied where relationships between processes, people organization and attitude, and technology are not described and even, most of the time, simply not considered at all.

This concept of interrelated layers for capability assessment methods has been introduced, for the first time, in the RACENT (Readiness Assessment for Concurrent Engineering Needs and Technology) assessment approach developed during the CENT ESPRIT project. Within the RACENT assessment approach, only two interrelated layers were described due to budget limitation, but at the earlier stage of the study three interrelated layers were considered as indispensable for a successful implementation of capabilities. The two layers described in the RACENT assessment approach were processes and technology. Processes have to be restructured with concurrent activities to provide the capability of designing concurrently a product and its related processes while technology should be used to support those concurrent activities and interactions between complementary disciplines with new working methods and tools. The third possible layer that has been studied during the earlier stage of RACENT was people organization and attitude where a new organizational form was based on a multidisciplinary team in order to facilitate interactions and negotiations between disciplines and to undertake rational decisions rather than hierarchical decisions. It is quite easy to understand how, for example, the triptych concurrent activities on the process layer, multidisciplinary team and collaborative behavior on the people organization and attitude layer, and the virtual prototyping method and tools on the technology layer could fit together.

Within the CCCAM (concurrency and collaboration capability assessment method) approach, the critical elements of the concurrency reference model constitute the basis for the necessary capabilities. Concurrency and collaboration capabilities are expected to provide a better reactiveness and flexibility as well as improved creativity and innovation potential. The assessment method could be based on three overlapped layers, as it has been already illustrated, using maturity stages where for each stage a set of capabilities is expected for the three different layers.

A questionnaire could be used to check whether capabilities already exist and could be organized around main topics questions (see Figure 8.3):

- Does your enterprise operate as a boundaryless organization within a collaboration strategy?
- Do employees have a collaborative attitude?
- Are processes structured with concurrent activities?
- Are people organized into multidisciplinary teams?

- Does the implemented technology support interactions between trading partners' disciplines?

Then each main topic question should be subdivided in several sets of questions reflecting the different maturity levels in a top-down/bottom-up approach where each question in a set could be subdivided again, and so on until reaching the basic capabilities.

8.4. Assessment considerations and approaches

The particular technique of capability assessment, proposed here, is intended to be applicable by large enterprises as well as SMEs, which are participating to a project consortium. Traditional capability assessment techniques are tailored to the big firms, too heavy for SMEs, and most often focused on only one subject. In fact, both individual organization and project consortium have to be evaluated according to different criteria impacting the reactiveness, creativeness, innovation and operating rapidity of a composite organization. What follows is a discussion about the overall assessment approach and key areas that have to be further evaluated in regards of existing experiences.

8.4.1. Assessment consideration.
Any business enterprise, to provide its products or services, uses a hierarchy of management control systems to monitor the resources and materials needed. These systems are generally used in a strategic planning function, a tactical function, or an operational function needing a daily performance. To discover new performance opportunities, the enterprise can analyze for improvements in: activities or functions, components or structures and economies in material. An analogy that compares athletic performance to the performance of every enterprise may be helpful in discussing the activity, structure and sociologic perspectives.

The activity perspective. Considerable improvements of individual athlete performance have been made during the last decade and today's sport competitors run and swim faster, hit harder and generally display athletic excellence beyond the dreams of our predessors. Performance improvement opportunities have been identified by analyzing the external view of how the athlete performs his/her activities. Different technologies, more or less sophisticated, are employed to evaluate the activity perspective. Playback of an sport event is often used in order to observe the performance and to identify improvement opportunities. Most often, a trainer evaluates the execution of every athlete's activity by measuring his/her performance using a stopwatch, or other devices. On the basis of this evaluation, he then coaches the athlete on how to improve the execution of his activity by adopting specific techniques.

The structure perspective. The evolution of technologies in the domain of orthoscopic surgery has provided a new understanding of the internal structure of the human body. This knowledge is then used to refine the execution of the athletic activity. Training and dietary programs have been developed to build an athletic muscle structure. It has already been proved that superior body structure gives strong advantages for activity performance. Nowadays, trainers, coachers and medical specialists play a key role in improving the athlete's performances.

The sociologic perspective. Experiences have shown that individual athlete performances are deeply dependending on the mental ability to overcome any encountered difficulty during the preparation and to go beyond their own performances. It is certainly more critical for an individual athlete than for a sport team where only one team member should have mental ability predisposition to be the team leader. Most of those top-level athletes have a well protected life environment from all day-to-day problems. Furthermore, sociologic experts are more and more involved in conducting special training to strengthen an athlete's willingness and confidence to win and to make sure they are not at all afraid by losing a competition.

Improve performance by using several perspectives. Application of complementary perspectives is required to improve, and perhaps maximize, athletic performance. Technology is used to study the athlete's body structure, and this knowledge is then applied by a team of professionals working together over time to fine-tune the external activity effects of the athlete. Some other activities - such as relaxation and concentration disciplines - are used by sociology experts to develop mental control mechanisms abilities. The results have been proven by dramatic improvements in athletic performance.

Companies - looking for effective ways to improve performance - can apply the activity, structure and sociologic perspectives to their businesses as they are to the athlete. Additionally, professionals - with their team of business professionals - are needed to analyze several perspectives within the enterprise. But a business enterprise is not a static environment. Activities, processes and sociologic environment are constantly and dynamically changing. If only the activity perspective is analyzed, it then becomes extremely difficult and costly to adapt systems to the dynamic needs of this environment. To improve its performance, the enterprise must also analyze the structure of its working environment, climate, or conditions.

8.4.2. Different approaches to assessment.

Traditional capability assessment methods. A study of the present capability assessment methods has been carried out in a special review document (Existing capability maturity models - SEI CMM, PCMM, SE CMM). Most of existing methods are process and level oriented, as it is easier to identify the current and expected situations, and the way to progress along the following maturity stages. Structure of these is :

- Maturity levels. They indicate process capability and contain key process areas,

- Key process areas. They achieve goals and are organized by common features,

- Common features. Tthey address implementation and contain key practices that describe infrastructure or activities.

This should be understood as a requirement list on the processes (what and how) aiming at the homogenization of practices in order to improve the global quality level for a better performance.

Innovative climate. However, the effectiveness of those practices is strongly conditioned by the psychological climate. The organizational psychologist Göran Ekvall has made extensive research on which factors are linked to an innovative climate in an organization (Göran Ekvall, 1993). Among these factors, there are the challenge, conflicts, dynamism, freedom, idea-time (time to new ideas), idea-support (way to meet new), playfulnes, risk-taking (ability to handle uncertainty), and trust.

All the other factors are positively correlated to the psychological climate. One question is to determine if an organization is innovative or stagnant. One way for doing it is to compare the scores the organization gets in an assessment - based on a list of questions. The problem is to compare one organization with other organizations, and to get a picture of where the organization is situated between an innovative and a stagnant organization (Lars Bergman and Sten-Erik Öhlund, 1995).

Organizational values. Another factor that influences an organization's ability to develop products and services is the level of development orientation existing in that organization. Göran Ekvall (1993) has divided organizational values in three different orientations.

- Structural orientation. The influence of people must therefore be minimized and subordinated to structural elements.For example, routines structure an organization.

- People orientation. The organization is viewed first of all as consisting of people. People are seen as fundamentally active, rational, social and constructive. The organization is there to take care of the creativity and the initiatives, which exist in the people.

- Development orientation. The central value here is that the organization must continuously be able to change itself and adapt quickly to the change in demand and other external changes. Status quo is seen as a step backwards. The focus is to continuously create new products and services.

A real organization is of course always a combination of these different orientations. If the focus in the organization is to develop new products and services in a more competitive market, it is no longer possible to live on achievements, particularly in a situation where the product lifetime is getting shorter and shorter. In this case a development orientation becomes crucial in order to survive on the market.

8.5. Capability assessment

Large enterprises and SMEs can use the capability assessment technique, more or less insisting on collaboration effectiveness and efficiency. This result in a simple and self comprehensive method based on the most possible reduced assessment scope to avoid the traditional long and confused questionnaire associated with any capability assessment approach. Furthermore, to avoid any possible confusion during the assessment it is recommended to structure the capability assessment along three complementary layers. This layered approach has been created during the CENT ESPRIT project in developing the RACENT capability assessment method for CE readiness assessment (ESPRIT CENT Project, 1996).

8.5.1 A multilayer capability assessment

Traditional capability assessment techniques use maturity stages, or levels. Within the SEI (Software Engineering Institute, Carnegie Mellon University), CMM (Capability Maturity Level), maturity levels indicate process capability and contain key process areas; then key process areas achieve goals and are organized by common features; Common features address implementation and contain key practices that describe infrastructure or activities. For example, level 3 gives a defined characteristic to the process where several key process areas and common features have to be implemented: requirement allocation have to be done by a multidisciplinary team while it was only requested to be done by the system team at the level 2, or requirement tracking is requested by the level 3 while it was not for the level 2.

Within the same maturity level both activities and structure perspectives can be addressed, and only a few perspective points concerning people are addressed such as training program. There are separate existing specific capability assessment techniques for project management processes or human resource management (4).

RACENT considers that activities have to be implemented by concrete methods and techniques, or key practices to guide people, and then have to be coherently supported by tools used by people. Thus, activities belong to one layer while structure belongs to another layer, each layer interacting on the other one enabling or not a global capability. The mapping of the two layers allows to demonstrate inconsistencies between activity implementation and support offered by tools, showing that a certain capability was not really there. A third layer, regarding people organization and behavior was also planned but the limited time do not permit to experiment it. One of the RACENT conclusion is that a global capability is only there when processes or activities are planned for, technology is fully supporting them, and people are prepared, organized, as well as motivated to apply these new processes and technologies. This is illustrated by the figure 8.5. where project objectives and performance are ensured by well optimized processes. This explains why it is proposed to use a three layers assessment approach to bring consistence and coherence to global capability assessment, an approach which is particularly helpful when trading partners have to collaborate.

Partners self assessment or project consortium assessment. The next very important point to be discussed is related to the assessment application. Let's take a look at two different case studies:

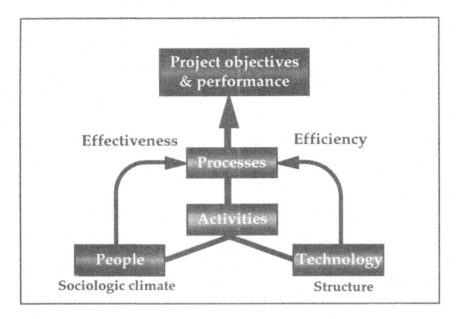

Figure 8.5. A multilayered capability assessment approach.

1. The majority of trading partners, constituted by large enterprises, have a configuration and change management practice while the minority, constituted by SMEs, not When the present configuration and change management practices are not compatible between them, it becomes quite clear to understand why the project overhead is so heavy during project in partnership.

2. The project consortium has selected a common configuration and change management practice meaning that large enterprises have to interface their own configuration and change management practice to the common one. SMEs can choose to adopt the common one in a kind of technology transfer or even to go for a specific one they will also have to interface. In this case, experimented by different industrial consortia, adopting a common configuration and change management practice, the interoperability level between partners has been more effective and contributed to dramatically reduce project overcost.

In conclusion, the global capability is unfortunately not the sum of the local capabilities. Behind this simple statement there is another interesting question: Do local capabilities have to be assessed for a global effectiveness and efficiency?

8.5.2. Needed key areas.

There are two complementary needs for this particular capability assessment.
Partners self assessment. A self-assessment to assess the ability of the individual organization to operate efficiently within a project consortium. It must considers:

- *Adaptation.* It is the capability of integrating or interfacing company practices into any project consortium aiming at global effectiveness and efficiency. Activities are prepared to deal rapidly, simultaneously and concurrently with different consortium. Processes are well-defined, characterized and potential interaction points already identified. A specialized business adaptation team exists, named enterprise engineering, for optimizing processes of every new project consortium.

- *Collaboration.* A common virtual spaces are in place between disciplines for enabling shared concepts and common understanding. The management promotes a collaborative attitude, and a system to reward collaboration is in place. Education of personnel for global performance and symbiotic system is continuously performed.

This kind of assessment could be represented by a single pertinent question such as: Is your organization oriented in a boundaryless fashion?

Project consortium assessment for assessing the consortium capacity to be effective and efficient. It must considers points as follows:

- Coordination. Sequential, parallel and concurrent activities are distributed to multidisciplinary teams according to the work breakdown structure (WBS) and organization breakdown structure (OBS) description as well as interaction needs. Consistency of requirements and constraints enable coordination requests between disciplined experts and subsystem teams.

- Communication. A distributed information environment is selected and designed to promote technology. Electronic means for virtual collocation are in place and a personnel training program is planned. Interfaces for interoperability between partners applications are specified, developed and applied.

- Collaboration. The common virtual spaces are in place between trading partners for enabling shared concepts and common understanding. A collaborative rewarding program for trading partners is in place.

- Process focus. A common platform for global shared processes is selected. A program to train process practitioners is planned. Global objectives and yardsticks are already well defined. Interaction needs between trading partners experts are identified and concurrent activities specified.

- Product life cycle. Distributed multidisciplinary multipartner teams are constituted according to the WBS and training program that is planned. A platform for global requirements and constraints consistency is selected. The consortium business adaptation team prepares customization according to interaction needs.

- Flexibility. Distributed multidisciplinary multipartner teams are constituted of required and justified experts temporarily assigned to specific tasks. Team members are not necessarily employed full time by a project. Distributed teams are sufficiently empowered for directly negotiating and making decisions without having to refer to higher management rank to their own organization.

- Interoperability. Every decision is immediately understandable and applicable by concerned project participants whatever their own organization, culture or language. Every action is immediately executable independently of the different infrastructures.

Challenge, Conflicts, Debates, Dynamism, Freedom, Idea-time, Idea-support, Playfulness, Risk-taking and Trust could be used as they are or combined in a more subtle classification for defining Key Areas corresponding to the sociologic part of the people involved (assess the collaborative attitude, creativity and innovation potential).

8.5.3. Capabilities coherence and consistence.
It must considers the following three layers:

1. Process layer. According to the ESPRIT COBRA team (1995), consortium can consider complementary processes underlying project performances - business, management, support and learning processes. The recommended maturity levels (See Table 8.1.) represent capabilities for different processes. The second maturity level corresponds to the management and support processes. The third maturity level corresponds to the business process and the fourth one to the learning process.

2. People layer. This layer addresses the related people organizational and sociological aspects. The main point is the project participants adhesion to activities and technology deployment, ensuring a good level of potential success.

3. Technology layer. Technology could be considered as an enabler for different capabilities such as virtual collocation (electronic collocation) between people working from geographically dispersed site.

Maturity levels	Business objectives	Business strategies
Traditional cooperation	Shared cost and risk	Access a market
Project management collaboration	Reduce project overhead	Satisfy shareholders
Development collaboration	Reduce lead-time and costs	Satisfy customers

Table 8.1. Maturity levels and business strategies and objectives relationships

Each maturity level (see Table 8.1.) must study the best practices (at the three different layers and their interdependencies) to be sure that a capability is truly implemented.

8.5.4. Maturity levels.

Capability or maturity levels can be defined in various ways. According to the layered assessment approach, it is necessary to select generic level names applicable to the three assessment layers. Capability or maturity levels can also be described in terms of business objectives and strategies, and then declined as a generic status applicable to the process, people and technology layers. The maturity levels of the capability assessment should be in direct relationships with business strategies and objectives (Table 8.1.). The following levels are important:

• Traditional cooperation. The first maturity level of trading partners objectives, participating in a common work program, is to share project cost and risk by individual contributions according to their expertise. Only the main contractor is responsible for the project, each partner being responsible for its contribution. Partners work separately, and the main contractor is responsible for the final integration,

• Project management collaboration. The main objective is to reduce drastically the project overhead, and overcost (see Section 4.3). A global interoperability between trading partners should be achieved,

• Development collaboration. The objectives are to reduce lead time and product cost while improving product quality in implementing concurrent activities to satisfy the partners interaction needs. Shared process capability, shared multidisciplinary teams, and shared spaces are mandatory,

• Business collaboration. The main objective is to improve creativity and innovation potential for answering to the market demand changes. Capabilities to build, use and share virtual models in a distributed business environment are in place. When trading partners are dealing together they have capabilities to operate with distributed processes, expertises and working spaces.

Table 8.2 illustrates the relationships between maturity levels and process, people, and technology layers. A same qualifier is used for the three different layers. Traditional cooperation maturity level is related to the qualifier separated. Project management collaboration maturity level is related to the qualifier interoperable. Development collaboration maturity level is related to the qualifier shared. Business collaboration maturity level is related to the qualifier distributed.

Objectives and strategies maturity levels	Process layer	People layer	Technology layer
Traditional cooperation	Separated processes	Separated teams	Separated infrastructure
Project management collaboration	Interoperable processes	Interoperable teams	Interoperable infrastructure
Development collaboration	Shared processes	Shared teams	Shared infrastructure
Business collaboration	Distributed processes	Distributed teams	Distributed infrastructure

Table 8.2. Maturity levels and assessment on interrelated layers.

8.5.6. Case studies.

Several existing cases - such as construction, large scale engineering and shipbuilding - could be used to study key areas related to a significant collaboration improvement. Other existing business cases are available in the automotive and aerospace industry, but they are more oriented toward the extended enterprise. In this case, one dominant organization disseminates its practices and technologies among a selected trading partner group.

A list of existing consortia will be experimentally assessed to check the validity of the proposed layered approach as well as its simplicity, effectiveness and usability by SMEs. Furthermore, the assessment results will be used to define some organization profiles in the objective of benchmarking existing or new organizations. One example of this is concurrent engineering European network of excellence (CE-NET), which involves several industrial organizations from different sectors and countries, and offers a suitable platform for case studies and validation. At the end, CE-NET is designed for shaping the concurrent enterprise paradigm in Europe.

In addition to that, it is quite clear that the assessment questionnaire - for organizations entering a consortium, and a consortium assessment -should be simultaneously accessible by each one. Each section of the questionnaire should correspond to a specific key area where an interactive score will be displayed. An explanation will be associated to each question and section as well as for the overall assessment method. To have the easier and cheapest interactive assessment, it is proposed to use a shared questionnaire based on HTTP protocol for simultaneous access, HTML (hypertext) for text navigation, and JAVA for animated objects such as displayed scores and graphic figures. Several research organizations involved in CE-NET are already operating in this area of capability assessment implementation, and made significant progress for simplifying the usage of such techniques.

8.6. Virtual shared spaces

The most significant deficiency of collaboration is the failure to capture the knowledge that is generated during the collaborative process. It could be further explained by the fact that most collaboration are essentially ad-hoc processes looking for solutions matching with encountered problems but without any infrastructure to support this process. As a result, the valuable knowledge deriving from collaborations is used only once and probably lost forever. This is exactly why simple models should be built to capture this knowledge and avoid dissipating the expertise created by collaboration. Collaboration is essentially based on knowledge interaction between complementary expertise, but for that there should be a common understanding allowing creating new concepts. The distributed and shared infrastructure is composed of virtual spaces constituted of virtual reality models that could be manipulated by complementary expertises of trading partners. Those virtual creations and manipulations by multidisciplinary teams enable people to reach a common understanding and to elaborate shared concepts in a better and faster way than any long discussion during meetings. Furthermore, creating and updating models provide a pragmatic way toward knowledge management for reusing existing solutions or part of them. There is no doubt about the benefit. Even more, virtual spaces shared by disciplines provide a collective sense of identity and fundamental purpose as requested by the knowledge-creating company. Here, the practical problems are much more to identify the rationale of any interaction need and interdependencies between entities manipulated by complementary disciplines and, to be able to manage the consistency of generated constraints.

There are different examples of possible applications of the virtual shared space, such as virtual project office, virtual design room, virtual salesroom, virtual trial room, virtual maintenance room, and virtual assembly room. This is not something futuristic. Existing enterprises are already using part of this concept such as NASA (National Agency for Space and Aeronautics) with its virtual research center.

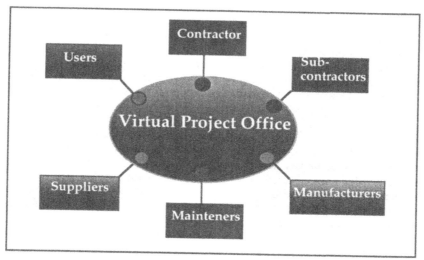

Figure 8.6. Example of virtual shared space: the virtual project office.

The virtual project office example of virtual shared space will be demonstrated in the EPICE ESPRIT project, where several industrial trading partners forming a consortium will use the virtual project office as a distributed infrastructure (see Figure 8.6).

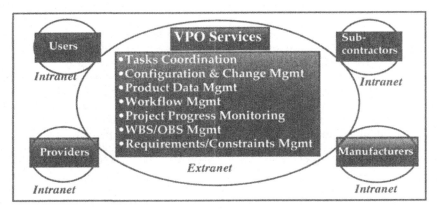

Figure 8.7. Example of a virtual shared space implementation.

On the implementation side (see Figure 8.7), the Internet and Web-related technologies are used through Intranet (Internet tools used on an enterprise private network) and Extranet (Internet tools used on a trading partners private network). Otherwise, encryption systems and large bandwidth on the Internet should allow trading partners to avoid the use of a costly private network. The security aspect should not be underestimated as it was rated as the second greatest challenge in implementing collaboration between trading partners (see Figure 8.3). Expected virtual project office services to be distributed to the trading partners include the following:

- Work breakdown structure (WBS) and organization breakdown structure (OBS) management on the Web,
- Workflow management and tasks coordination,
- Requirements and constraints consistency management;
- Project progress monitoring, and
- Configuration and data management.

This kind of virtual shared space applied to project management between trading partners should dramatically reduce project overhead. Other applications of virtual shared spaces such as virtual design room and virtual test room are widely using virtual prototyping (see Chapter 7) on the Internet to support concrete interactions between complementary expertises. Virtual marketing or salesroom is an example of virtual space shared between the enterprise and prospects or customers for testing potential user reactions to a new product with new fonctions. It could also be used by prospects for understanding the benefit of some fonctionalities and better specifying their product or service configuration as a function of their real needs. Even the product or service reference and user's guides could be directly accessed through the Internet as well as customer support.

As soon as there is an identified need for interaction between expertises or disciplines, there will be a need to exchange information and not necessarily the complete set of data as recommended in data interchange standard. Applying the concurrent activities principle and technique, it can identify what makes the interaction indispensable, what needs to be shared in terms of information, and when it needs to be done in terms of events. This is exactly why this interaction protocol is based on the fact that interacting parties have to be registered to the interaction network as a supplier or as a user or both and should specify what objects they are supplying on the network and what objects they would like to use (see Figure 8.8). Events are there for coordinating object supply or for use by a registered interactor. This kind of interactive information bus is intended to support both synchronous and asynchronous interactions. The implementation of the interaction protocol is planned to be developed with the Internet and Web-related technologies as an optional layer and should enable faster, cheaper interaction between trading partners. An implementation prototype is expected during 1999 within the EPICE (Electronic Commerce for Program Information sharing between trading partners in the Concurrent Enterprise) ESPRIT project.

Every object supplied on the interaction network comes from registered expertises or disciplines, called interactors, and then flows to the expertises or disciplines that have declared their willingness to use those objects or part of them.

Figure 8.8. Example of registered interactors supplying and-or using information.

194

8.7. Conclusions.

The perspective of economical growth in the United States will largely depend of its capability to develop and successfully apply new technologies declared Alan Greenspan, president of the Federal Reserve, during a speech at Syracuse University (New York). This further demonstrates that an implementation process such as concurrent enterprising is indispensable for successfully applying the new technologies requested by this new business model in adapting processes, organizations, and attitudes.

Technology for electronic collocation, such as the Internet and the Web-related technologies, declined as Intranet or even Extranet is a driver toward the virtual enterprise. But efficiency and impact on business depends on how this technology will be implemented. A pragmatic consulting expert would recommend using the technology and checking at the end to determine whether it conforms with the business objectives. If it does not, then the business should try another way or another technology. A Cartesian consulting expert would recommend identifying how the technology should improve the business and therefore define how to implement it. If at the end, it is not in line with the business objectives, then it is necessary to identify what was wrong with the change process. It means that when a problem occurs, it is not only a question of fixing what was wrong, but it is also necessary to fix the process that generated the error.

While concurrent enterprise is the business vision, concurrent enterprising is both a pragmatic and Cartesian implementation process toward successful application.

References

Argyris, C. (1993).*Knowledge for Action*. San Francisco: Josse-Bass.

Association for Computing Machinery (ACM). (1995).*Computing Surveys* 28a(4)   (December).

Bergman, Lars, and Öhlund, Sten-Erik (1995). »Development of an Assessment Tool to assist in the implementation of Concurrent Engineering ». Paper presented at CE95 Conference.

CENT (1995)."Concurrent Engineering Needs and Technology." Esprit Project 9810. Brussels.

COBRA. (1995). »Project Team. Brussels ». COBRA Esprit, Brussels.

Ekvall, Göran (1993). »Creativity in Project Work: a longitudinal study of a product development project ». Creativity and innovation Management.

Nonaka, I. (1991). 'The Knowledge Creating Company.'' Harvard Business Review.

EPICE. (1998). "Electronic Commerce for Programme Management Information Sharing in the Concurrent Enterprise." Esprit Project 27089. Brussels.

ESPRIT CENT (1996). »Readiness Assessment Guidelines ». Esprit Cent Project 9810. Brussels

FREE (1997). "Fast Reactive Extended Enterprise (FREE)." Esprit Project 23286. Brussels.

De Nicola, Rocco, and Scott A. Smolka. (19   )."Concurrency: Theory and Practice." Universita degli Studi di Firenze, Dipartimento   di Sistemi e Informatica; State University of New York at Stony Brook, Department of Computer Science.

Nonaka, I., and H. Takeuchi. (1995).*The Knowledge-Creating Company*. Oxford: Oxford University Press.

Pallot, Marc. (1997). *From Concurrent Engineering Toward Concurrent Enterprising*. Tutorial of CALS Europe '97. Frankfurt.

Pallot, Marc (1997). *From Concurrent Engineering towards Concurrent Enterprising*. Tutorial of CALS Europe'97. Frankfurt: MP Consultants.

CONCLUSIONS

The universe seems to be organized into interrelated layers, from the small world to the infinite world, where each layer is built around a main flow or stream. No one will live long enough to say whether it is really an efficient organizational mode or not, but from our perspective it seems to be very effective in its 100 percent recycling and regenerating system where each next step is more adapted to the new environment. In the universe everything die, at least once but may be several times, and will be born again and again in a more performant form.

This is an appropriate metaphor for demonstrating that enterprises should not remain, as they are but exist for a specific duration with a specific target and then generate new enterprises more adapted to the new business environment. Enterprises should be built around a main flow or stream, and every element should operate concurrently with this main flow. As it has already been said in Chapter 7, this concurrent enterprise is built around the knowledge flow. Within the concurrent enterprise, the knowledge flow provides the means to deal with every change, to learn faster, and to improve creativity and innovation potential as it is a boundaryless organization where all expertise forms a symbiotic system.

According to Petra K. Schruth (Shell International), Change is the only constant and the only certainty; in business, change is happening more rapidly today than even before. We have seen organizations change shape dramatically and repeatedly. Companies downsize and out-source; corporations give way to networks, alliances, and partnering deals. Change is a dangerous opportunity and in the information age, more than ever, we must learn faster than the rate of change if we are to survive. However, we believe that "the ability to learn faster than your competitors may be the only sustainable competitive advantage" (Arie de Geus, Head of Shell Group Planning).

Stressed by market changes, the value chains have to be more flexible and responsive in a very short timescale. Working concurrently at a early stage of every project provides the best opportunity to decrease global product costs and to shorten time. Then concurrency becomes a key factor for competitiveness because it integrates the new ways of working, managing, and learning in business restructuring.

Within this context the new concurrency approach must then be thought of in terms of strategy, tactical, and operational solutions to be undertaken, according to the local conditions in which every company integrating the business network is evolving. But this needs a rethinking of the overall enterprise activities and its position to extract the real benefits. It is necessary to consider any trading partner as a part of a virtual enterprise where partners' enterprises have the capability to operate concurrently.

The existing networking technologies should assist the construction of the concurrent enterprise. Internet, Intranet, or Extranet provide the cheapest solution, easily accessible by SMEs, for supporting interactions between trading partners operating from geographically dispersed sites. Both large enterprises and SMEs can share knowledge and related information to create new ideas and improve their innovation potential by having concurrent activities through such networks. Customer demand is expressed in terms of value based on needs and requirements. The feasibility, costs, lead time, and quality are expressed in terms of constraints. At the end, values are studied through design alternatives, assessed in terms of constraints satisfaction. For each design alternative it is possible to simulate interactions between both the virtual product and virtual processes to evaluate, how it will satisfy the requirements and how it will conform to the project and processes constraints.

There are already many tools operating on the Web, and others need further developments such as virtual prototyping, based on VRML, for remote testing of a future or existing product; co-analysis, co-simulation, co-design or any other groupware tools that allow the exploration of and assessment of alternatives across different disciplines; and, more generally, all shared knowledge-based methods and tools providing opportunities for reusing capitalized expertise from previous projects.

In virtual rooms, people from different disciplines will be able to interact in a very similar manner as in the virtual salesroom, which is emerging from the actual development of electronic commerce.

This is an exiting world. On the one hand, there are a lot of organizational theories and approaches to confront in the new business environment, and on the other hand, technologies are evolving faster than customer demand. New technologies are funded by new business perspectives and opportunities. Is business overseeing a social evolution? Or is the information society creating new business perspectives? Or does technology drive both the information society and new business perspectives?

The concurrent organization, defined as a boundaryless structure, is not only a business purpose but a society purpose too. It should provide the ability for everyone, and especially children, around the world to share knowledge for the good of humanity.

INDEX

CPSIA information can be obtained
at www.ICGtesting.com
Printed in the USA
LVOW13s2328130418
573480LV00007B/124/P

9 781461 368236